Paola Ramos

FINDING LATINX

Paola Ramos is a host and correspondent for VICE and VICE News, as well as a contributor to Telemundo News and MSNBC. Ramos was the deputy director of Hispanic media for Hillary Clinton's 2016 presidential campaign and a political appointee during the Barack Obama administration, and she also served in President Obama's 2012 reelection campaign. She's a former fellow at Emerson Collective. Ramos received her MA in public policy from the Harvard Kennedy School and her BA from Barnard College, Columbia University. She lives in Brooklyn.

www.paolaramos.com

FINDING LATINX

FINDING LATINX

In Search of the Voices Redefining Latino Identity

Paola Ramos

VINTAGE BOOKS
A Division of Penguin Random House LLC
New York

A VINTAGE BOOKS ORIGINAL, OCTOBER 2020

Copyright © 2020 by Paola Ramos

All rights reserved. Published in the United States by Vintage Books,
a division of Penguin Random House LLC, New York, and distributed
in Canada by Penguin Random House Canada Limited, Toronto.

Vintage and colophon are registered trademarks of
Penguin Random House LLC.

The Cataloging-in-Publication Data is on file at the Library of Congress.

Vintage Books Trade Paperback ISBN: 978-1-9848-9909-5
eBook ISBN: 978-1-9848-9910-1

Map by Steve Walker
Book design by Steve Walker

www.vintagebooks.com

Printed in the United States of America
10 9 8 7 6 5 4 3 2 1

To my mother, Gina, and my father, Jorge,
whose love carries me everywhere I go

Contents

FINDING LATINX

Introduction: Coming Out as Latinx

I never really came out.

Until recently.

Even after my loving parents sat me down a couple of times in high school, with open minds yet suspicions of my sexual orientation, I refused to use the word "gay" to describe the way my heart chose to love. Then, when I moved to Washington, D.C., to work in politics, I caught myself cringing when I entered "Hispanic Group Meetings" for networking and idea exchange—not because they weren't welcoming but because I often felt that I didn't quite fit in. From afar, when I watched my father's newscast on Univision, staring at a screen full of women who appeared to have just finished a Latin American beauty pageant, I questioned my own identity as a "Latina." And even when I gave speeches throughout grad school, my Mexican Cuban heritage was overshadowed by an aggressive Spanish accent I unintentionally picked up during my childhood in Spain. Growing up between Madrid's progressive environment and Miami's conservative Cuban community muddled my own political views at a young age. Where, exactly, did I fit in?

Yes, I am queer; I am Latina; I am Cuban, Mexican, and first-generation American. These are words I was not ashamed of saying out loud—but there's a difference between passive recognition and really owning one's identity. I openly had girlfriends, checked the "Hispanic" box on school applications, carried three passports, and admired the way my parents' immigrant journey was central to our being. Yet the truth is that for years I had either blindly danced around these identities or felt I had to choose one over the others. Almost as though I had to wear different hats depending on the rooms I entered or the prejudices I encountered. Safe here, but not so much there. Of course, tiptoeing around these spaces was nothing but a reflection of the immense privilege my citizenship status and light skin granted me in life. Had I been undocumented, or simply a shade darker, I'd carry a target on my back.

Looking back, I realize now that I never really "came out" as my whole self—as fully *me*. All of this changed the moment the word "Latinx" started rolling off my tongue.

Even though this mysterious term had been tossed around the Web since the early 2000s, I started using it shortly after Donald Trump won the 2016 presidential election. At the time, I didn't fully understand exactly *where* that word came from or *what* it meant—all I knew was that it felt *right*. It felt more like me. It was a word I couldn't recognize but one that seemed to know exactly who I was. That addendum, the "x," set free the parts of myself that had deviated from the norms and traditions of the Latino culture I grew up in in a way that, interestingly, made me closer to, not further from, my own community. A word that wasn't familiar but one that seemed to tout the uniqueness and diversity that had defined the sixty million Latinos living in the United States. One that felt it aimed to awaken not just a few of us, or half of us, or 90 percent of us—but *every single* one of us. Even those who had never been seen as "Latino" to begin with. And I wasn't alone in feeling this.

With Trump's unforeseen win came a desire for belonging. His victory mobilized millions of people—women, youth, students, black communities, Latinos, immigrants, Dreamers, victims of sexual assault—to take to the streets and fill a void with their voices. People marched with furor, organized their communities, and spoke up in boardrooms and town halls, louder than they had before. Fear induced courage, and the undercurrent of racism that was now fully exposed pushed many of us to embrace inclusion. It was sometime amid this resurged movement that I noticed the word "Latinx" had started to become part of the daily vocabulary of the resistance. Latinx quickly became normalized in my circles, appearing everywhere—protest signs, conference calls, press releases, Twitter feeds, chants, and headlines. "What does Latinx even mean?" some colleagues and I would often ask one another. "Where did it even come from?" We didn't know, but we kept using it.

There are different answers to that question. But language inevitably evolves with time. A changing vocabulary reflects how a community's demographics transform the struggles a community faces during different periods in history. Language tells stories, and stories change.

Harvard University fellow Dr. Nicole Guidotti-Hernández points out that the use of the "x" is actually *not* a new phenomenon. As she writes in one of her articles: "Earliest uses of the 'x' come on the front end of Nahuatl-inspired writing of the word Chicano/Chicana as Xicano or Xicana." In the 1960s and 1970s, the "x" was inserted to "indigenize" Mexican Americans. It was used as a tool to counter Latin America's colonial history and ensure that indigenous peoples were not erased. Dr. Guidotti-Hernández also provides several historical examples of other ways in which the Latino community pushed back against linguistics in efforts to correct for misrepresentations, gender inequities, or exclusions of nationalities. That's why, as she underscores, baby boomers fought so hard to institutionalize "ethnic studies" like Cuban American studies and Chicano studies programs on college campuses across America. The boomer generation prioritized nationalities over generalizations. *That was the story then:* in being able to say "Mexican" or "Guatemalan" over "Latino." At some point, the word "Latino" was also controversial. Even though it is technically meant to include *two* genders, the word itself is still masculine. That's why in the 1990s, people saw feminists rallying to demasculinize the gendered Spanish language, inserting symbols like @ or the neutralized *o/a* into their daily vocabulary. *That was the story then:* achieving gender equality and being able to explicitly say, "I am Latina." Like human beings, language is meant to *adapt,* not to remain *stagnant.*

There's been a long debate centered around the appropriate way to address our community: Do we say "Hispanics" or "Latinos"? Which one do *we* use? Which one should *others* use? For decades, the term "Hispanic" was mainstreamed. It was a term coined by a Mexican American staffer in the Richard Nixon administration, Grace Flores-Hughes. As has been reported, one of the reasons Grace advocated for the term "Hispanic" was that it explicitly stemmed from "Hispania," the Spanish Empire. The word was able to more closely associate the community with its white European colonial past than with its Latin American roots. By embracing the term "Hispanic," the community's historic ties to indigenous people, enslaved Africans, and mestizos (the offspring of colonizers and indigenous and/or enslaved Africans) were erased from the picture, washed away as conquistadores swept over the Americas in the fifteenth century. *That was the story then:* to whiten the community as much as possible. Eventually, however, using the term "Latino/ Latina" became more popular over time, as it more deliberately embraced our Latin American ancestors. (By the way, Grace Flores-Hughes ended up becoming a member of the National Hispanic Advisory Council for Trump.)

Around 2004, coinciding with the Internet's explosion, Latinx started popping up in online communities of queer Latinos. They were inserting the "x" as a way to express their breaks with gender binaries and welcome gender-nonconforming folks into the conversation. *There,* the initial story was about giving voice to the silenced and often discriminated-against LGBTQ Latinos, a point that was later strengthened by the 2016 Pulse massacre of forty-nine people, most of whom were queer Latinos. By 2018, as Latinx became more colloquial, *Merriam-Webster's Collegiate Dictionary,* Eleventh Edition, officially added it to its pages, defining Latinx as "of, relating to, or marked by Latin American heritage—a gender-neutral alternative to *Latino* or *Latina*." And if you go into Google Trends, you'll notice a steady rise in searches for the term.

Yet a few years later, people are *still* wondering what the hell Latinx really means. If Latinx were used just to be more inclusive of queer folks, then perhaps the term wouldn't cause such controversy and confusion. If the word were used simply to check the "queer" box, then perhaps people would be more okay with it, less afraid of it, more at peace with it. But Latinx is transcending all imaginable borders. All the borders that separated us by race, age, gender, issue, nationality, sexual orientation, and identity. All the ones that divided "us" from "them," liberals and conservatives. Latinx is not constrained by the explanation given to us on paper by dictionaries, pollsters, and scholars. And that's why, over the years, people from all different backgrounds kept resurfacing the term, signaling the beginning of the change we were all aching for.

The reality is that for decades that ache for change was inside many of us. It was an ache that craved more unity, acceptance, and inclusion—an ache that simply wanted us to be seen. This ache wasn't felt just inside the bubbles of activism, D.C. politics, and media—it was a sentiment that lay mostly in the *fringes* of those very elite spaces: inside homes and out of the public eye. It was in these places that I started recognizing that a lot more people than I thought were not only coming out as Latinx but giving life to that word in a way no dictionary could.

Queer and gender-nonconfirming Latinos who had faced discrimination in their own households could relate to that ache. So could Afro-Latinos who had once been told they didn't "look Latino enough." And transgender Latinas who were continuously reminded they weren't "really Latinas," Asian Latinos who had *never* been asked about their background, Cuban Americans who wanted to part ways with their family's long history of conservatism, young Latino men who never found a voice in the criminal justice system, *mamis* and *abuelas* who wanted to pave a different path for themselves, Gen Zers who had once been ridiculed for "not speaking Spanish," midwestern Latinos who felt completely "neglected," Latinos in the Deep South who said they were "forgotten" by all of us, indigenous migrants whose history had been erased, and millennials in border towns and rural communities who wanted a greater platform than those typically given to those residing in the far edges of the country.

For almost a year, as I prepared to write this book, I hit the road in search of these Latinx voices. I did this before the COVID-19 pandemic swept through the nation and the murders of George Floyd, Ahmaud Arbery, Breonna Taylor, and Tony McDade, among others, erupted a massive social movement for justice from coast to coast. But what both of these crises have exposed is *exactly* what I witnessed on the road months before our nation felt like it was burning: our American system, as it currently stands, is *not* built for us. And the only way to change it, so that it actually counts for black and brown people, is by first recognizing who *we* are.

I crisscrossed the country from west to east, driving through small towns, big cities, urban and rural areas. As I did this, my intention was to rediscover the places I thought I knew, to hear the voices that are often neglected in the back of the room, and to see the hidden faces that lay before our eyes all this time. I met people along the way who identified with many different labels. Some wanted to be called Latinos, others Hispanics. Some wanted to be seen as indigenous peoples, others as white. Some wanted their nationalities to define them, while others wanted their skin color to be the first thing people thought of when they introduced themselves, and many had no idea how to refer to themselves at all. I met people who wanted to be labeled through the eyes of Allah and others through the legacy of the ancient Mayans. And through it all, I understood for the first time that all these seemingly unrelated people—divided by gender, racial, religious, regional, political, and sexual orientation—had more in common than I had ever imagined. While the purpose of this book is to capture a more holistic picture of who we are as a community, one person and a mere 325 pages cannot do justice to our entirety and our richness. My hope, however, is that this book marks the beginning of that portrait.

Unfortunately, if you fast-forward to where we are now, many of the people I interviewed for this book ended up becoming COVID-19's victims. From undocumented folks to transgender asylum seekers, Afro-Latinos, and essential workers, Latinos are testing positive for COVID-19 at disproportionate rates in almost every state, and in cities like New York, they are dying at higher rates than any other demographic. As I type these words, Latinos are redefining what it means to survive in this country. But this unprecedented pandemic offers the perfect example of why it's so crucial to look at our community through a Latinx lens. Through it, you comprehend how interconnected our lives and issues are. This crisis is not the wrongdoing of the virus, but the culmination of an intersection of preexisting conditions and fractures, many of which are explored in this book, that have led us to this point.

I approached each interaction I had throughout this project juggling multiple hats at once: a journalistic one that would allow me to capture the facts on the ground, but also the hat of an activist that would allow me to read between the lines in a way that pure objectivity, at times, doesn't always allow one to. I understand that these two approaches don't necessarily go hand in hand—in fact, it could invite criticism—but if I've learned anything in the last couple of years, it's that journalists, too, have to take a stand at certain times, particularly in the face of abuse and injustice. In my eyes, the only way to tell the Latinx story was by using both of these hats at once. The pages you're about to read are therefore filled with my own field research, with some of the reporting I did through VICE Media and Telemundo, and with my own insight that derived from conversations. You'll hear from people who wanted to use their full names and from others who preferred pseudonyms. I will note those cases when an alias is used. And to be clear, the views in this book are my own.

Even though some of the people I spoke with throughout this journey were not using the word "Latinx" to identify themselves, and even though some would outright reject it, I noticed that Latinx was able to capture what other terms had not in the past—it captured the stories of all these people under one umbrella, spanning so many separate identities. *All* their stories, their struggles, and their aspirations had a home under *one* roof. It invited voices that had gone unnoticed to step in, speak out, and start claiming their own presence.

I'm not necessarily claiming that the word "Latinx" is what prompted people to share their stories, but I am saying it created a type of collective solidarity I hadn't experienced in my lifetime, at least not around my own community. "Latinx" became a validation of feelings I didn't even know were lingering among my peers, family, and strangers. It incited an unconscious call on *everyone* to step into the spotlight, to see one another face-to-face, and to expand our very own understanding of what it really meant to be "us" in America. I believe that Latinx could lead people to see the power they carry inside them. In fact, the noticeable rise in the use of the word coincided with unprecedented levels of Latino voter turnout in the 2018 midterm elections. It would be a stretch for me to say that there was a direct correlation there, but I have no doubt that the grassroots movement that impacted those high numbers was based on the same premise Latinx stems from: to make *everyone* count. To help *everyone* be seen. That's what Latinx comes down to.

Despite attempts by various scholars, wordsmiths, and right-wingers, to this day there is no clear definition of the word. And that's precisely its hidden power: this fluidity has allowed us—regardless of our backgrounds—to embrace a single community. Unlike Black Lives Matter or the Women's March, two movements that have clear definitions, platforms, and mission statements, Latinx is still transforming from a word into a movement. And that's because many of us are still in the process of coming out as a community of sixty million strong.

While my parents' generation was easily persuaded with a *sí se puede* in broken Spanish—a promise to pass "comprehensive immigration reform" and appearances on Univision—young Latinos across this country are creating a movement that is redefining what it means to be Latino in America.

This book aims to take Latinos—including me—on a journey of self-discovery and empowerment, shedding light on the voices that have been overlooked and giving life to the cryptic term "Latinx." I immersed myself in the subcultures and hybrids that carry this movement, so that this book could unearth and point to the voices that are not being captured by political polls, statistics, and stump speeches.

Media organizations and political campaigns attribute the power of Latinos to statistics. For one, they start with the fact that Latinos are the *youngest* demographic in the country, with an estimated 32.5 million millennials and Gen Zers across the country. Ten out of six Latinos are millennials or younger, and every single year, one million Latinos turn eighteen years old. Not only do Latino millennials have incredible political power, making up half of all eligible Latino voters, but we are also one of the country's most valuable consumers. In the eyes of marketers, our youthfulness means we fit the "perfect shoppers" description. According to a Nielsen report, our buying power rose from $213 billion in 1990 to $1.5 trillion in 2018. By 2023, that number is projected to increase to $1.9 trillion. As the report notes: "Latinx consumers represent one of the most sure bets for future growth." Additionally, we are more active online than non-Latino millennials and are also the most religious TV watchers among the millennial generation. All these numbers are certainly incredible measures, but unless we *tell* the stories of people's lives, they remain nothing but digits on papers and screens.

These numbers point to a future that is being written by us, but we haven't yet shown the full power of our numbers at the ballot box. The 2016 elections, which I saw from up close in my role as deputy director of Hispanic press in the Hillary Clinton campaign, perfectly reflected this. On Election Day, our community proved to be more asleep than awake—and it's important to understand it wasn't our fault. It's the fault of the system's inability to fully understand who we are. At a time when the majority of pollsters pointed to one of the most unprecedented turnouts in the "Latino vote," millions of young Latinos chose to stay home—even in the face of Trump's anti-immigrant narrative. When I look back at my time in the campaign, I have no recollections of ever publicly mentioning the words "Afro-Latinos" or "trans-Latinos"; no recollections of seeking the stories of the millennial activists on the U.S.-Mexican border or of the growing Asian Latino community; no memories of embracing the English-speaking Latinos or even paying attention to the lost Latino voices in the Midwest—red political territories we've at times given up on trying to win over. Words matter, and we simply didn't have the vocabulary then to articulate how the community we thought we knew was changing in front of our eyes. So if we didn't see them or call them by their name, why should we have expected them to vote for us?

Similarly, as I traveled the country to register young Latinos to vote ahead of the 2018 midterms, I noticed a trend that may become the Democratic Party's worst nightmare: young Latinos are increasingly registering as Independent and nonpartisan. There were already signs of this trend as early as 2013. That year, Gallup did a survey that found that more than 50 percent of Latinos younger than thirty initially identified as "Independent." Young Latinos were more likely to be Independent than older Latinos. From what I witnessed during the 2018 midterms, that trend is solidifying today. Whereas our parents have historically represented a solid voting bloc for Democrats, young Latinos are unknowingly creating a new sociopolitical force that is subtly breaking schemes. Today, it's not enough for Democratic candidates to take the Latino vote for granted; they have to work hard to understand what is making the younger generation stray from beaten paths and from the Democratic Party. That's why telling this story is so important, because our inability to leverage the movement thus far lies in our incapacity to verbalize the meaning of Latinx—and we must learn how to do this before it's too late.

So far, we've heard only half the story. For decades, the dominant narrative has focused on the immigrant journey. What no one has been able to capture thus far is what we've chosen to do with the freedoms our parents and grandparents fought for; *how* we've chosen to live freely in between hybrids and mold into America while still holding on to our roots. It's as if we're waiting for someone to hand us a mirror so we can finally see our *full* reflection—and that's exactly what this book intends to do.

When I came out as Latinx, stepping into my identity under the umbrella of that word, it was over the phone at my *abuelo* Carlos's prodding. After listening to me mention the word several times and reading some of my articles, he finally said:

"*¿Pao, qué carajo es Latinx?*" Pao, what the hell is Latinx?

I briefly paused. I attempted to give him a scholarly definition that would satisfy him intellectually, because I knew that's what his brain would register. But I ended up pausing again. This time longer.

I simply said: *"Latinx soy yo, Abuelo."* I'm Latinx, Grandfather.

I felt nervous but liberated when I said this. I felt as if I were coming out for the first time to him. I followed up: "I believe Latinx stands for all the people in the Latino community who have *ever* felt left out, *Abuelo*. That 'x' is simply an invitation for every one of those people that can't fit into one identity, for people that want to challenge norms, or for those that simply want to reimagine themselves. And guess what?" I said. "You're Latinx, too!"

He laughed and then stayed silent. I wish I could have seen my grandfather's face on the other side of the line—him in Miami, me in New York City. But I'm pretty sure that in that moment, my grandpa understood exactly what the term entailed, because my *abuelo* embodies the *very* sentiment of the term: he is a Cuban exile who reinvented himself after he escaped from Fidel Castro's oppressive regime. When my mother and grandparents arrived in the United States after fleeing Havana, leaving behind the only land and language they knew, they had to start all over again. Once labeled as a "terrorist" by Fidel Castro, my grandfather had to build a name for himself from afar. Not only did he become an avid activist against injustices but he also founded his own publishing company and became a prominent journalist, novelist, and loving dad and grandfather. Every step of the way, my grandpa Carlos was reimagining himself—defying the odds that had been stacked against him and constantly discovering the lengths freedom had to offer him. Through the years, my grandpa opened his house as a safe space for other Cuban exiles—gay men, Afro-Cubans, dissidents, single moms, sick people. People who had once been told they

weren't worthy enough by Castro had a place to be themselves under my grandpa's roof. To me, my *abuelo* exempli-
fied the term "Latinx" even before it became a word.

People may want to write the narrative of the Latinx
community using terms we already know, like "Latino" or
"Hispanic." They may say that "Latinx" is insulting, unpopu-
lar, and unusable. "A butchering of the Spanish language,"
they might claim. "Just liberal propaganda," they might yell,
dismissing it as a "millennial thing." And in *all* of this, they
may not be able to even see the beautiful complexity we hold
and the understanding that *this* is a story about *them, too*—
about claiming our collective belonging in this country. It
is a manifestation of the rights our community has been
working toward for decades.

Given that the country unearthed its white supremacist,
anti-immigrant, and anti-Latino tendencies after the 2016
presidential election, the question may be asked, "*Why* call
on the community to unite under a controversial banner?
Why come out *now* as Latinx?" The answer: That election
will be remembered in American history as a moment
that made a lot of us lean into our Latin identity. Language
evolves, and it evolves as an expression of the political time
we're in—and I believe the Latinx movement is the next step
in this evolution.

Through writing this book, I've started to see what this
evolution looks like. Let me tell you, it's incredible. It's full of
potential. It's full of power. But it's also full of pain, fear, and
wounds that deserve to be healed. Through these pages, my
only intention is to hold up a mirror, so *you*—the reader—
can finally see a full reflection of what this community looks
like.

While I was writing this book, I visited my father's family in Mexico City. One morning while we were having breakfast together, my *tía* Carolina looked at me and said: "You know, you've always been different. You were different as a kid. And you still are now." She said this with so much pride in her eyes that it caught me off guard. It felt as if she were trying to subtly acknowledge my sexual orientation without explicitly mentioning it. But I somehow gathered that her words meant much more than that. She was alluding to the unconventional journey my life had taken, to the deviations I had made time and time again, and to the complexity of a character that cannot be defined in one word.

I looked at her and said: *"Tú también, Tía."* You too, Aunt.

"You've always been different," I said to her.

She simply smiled.

The next few pages of this book are filled with the portrait of a community that has always been uniquely different and one that maybe, just maybe, is ready to tell its story in its own voice.

I know I am.

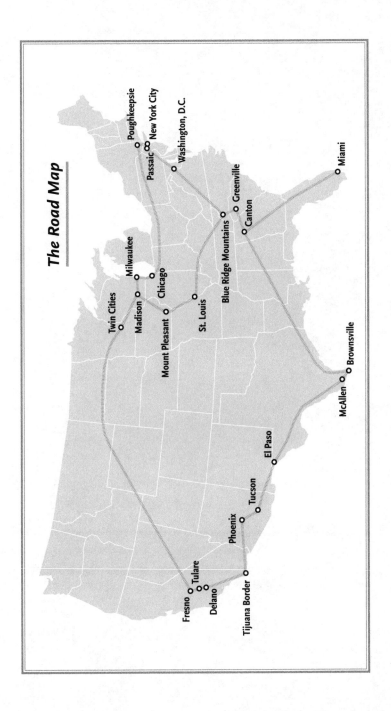

The Road Map

A Journey from the West to the Southwest

Part Two: Out of the Southwest

1

The Heartland

I begin this journey as far west as I can. Contrary to what you may think, the heartland lies at the edges of the United States, not the center. Along California's Central Valley, the endless acres of land are responsible for growing more than half of the country's nuts, fruits, and vegetables. This region of America is home to the voices that nourish our soul and fuel our wallets every single day. Many of those voices are undocumented, which reflects a national reality. There are approximately 2.5 million farmworkers across the country. More than half of them are undocumented, and more than 70 percent identify as Latino. For decades, Americans have grown accustomed to looking at these rural areas through a one-dimensional lens of immigration because of stats like these. Yet the Latinx frame forces one to look beyond that narrative and see the lives that lie inside these regions and communities.

The day starts in the Central Valley. Two hours north from bustling Los Angeles, where the mountains that follow you into this drive are majestic and lush, lies labor leader Cesar Chavez's memorial, nestled in the former headquarters of the United Farm Workers Union in the city of Keene. It's been more than five decades since Chavez led the 1965 Delano grape strike, when Mexican and Filipino farmworkers around this area walked out on grape growers to demand better working conditions. But in these hills, you can still feel the roar of the 1960s and 1970s throughout the valley. The echoes of marches, protests, fasts, and boycotts that laid the foundation for La Causa, a cry to protect the most basic rights of all farmworkers.

Like countless children of farmworkers in this area, Byanka Santoyo, a young local environmental justice activist from the Central Valley, grew up in Kern County watching the abuse her parents endured in the fields. But when injustice is no longer defined just by physical abuse, it takes longer for the eye to detect right from wrong.

When Byanka was eight years old, both of her parents were directly exposed to a pesticide drift while working in the fields alongside their *cuadrilla*, their crew. As I learned, these "drifts" refer to the unintended movement of pesticide residue through the air. Imagine standing in a clean area and suddenly feeling pesticide dust that has been sprayed on a neighboring crop. Well, as Byanka recalls, after her parents' *cuadrilla* was drifted on, some of the farmworkers felt small but immediate side effects such as vomiting and nausea. Today, more than a decade later, three women from the *cuadrilla* have died of breast cancer and Byanka's mom suffers from an autoimmune disease. Coincidence or not, the pain and abuse that were once normalized by Byanka's

Byanka, in front of fields in the Central Valley. (Courtesy of Dayana Morales)

parents for the sake of better wages and opportunities are now the battle Byanka is taking on. It's no longer just a fight for better rights but a fight to *live*.

"Are you still dealing with the same fight Cesar Chavez led?" I ask Byanka in the car.

She pauses.

"Now you're talking about the day you're here, and the day you're not here," she tells me. "I don't want my grandkids to suffer problems with cancer or autism . . . I want it to be different for them."

It almost feels as if every small victory gained in the farmworkers labor movement has come at the expense of life itself. As if for every major legal turning point won, years of life were taken away from people and these lands. The bureaucratic agricultural system is partly to blame. Family dynasties, big corporations, and corrupt money that measure farmworkers' lives by the number of pounds picked instead of the number of breaths taken.

"When you roll down the window and smell something different," Byanka instructs me, "you've *gotta* roll up the window." I leave the window down for just a second longer, and here's what I see:

From afar in the passenger's seat, I continue to see endless rows of beautiful crops around me, and occasionally I spot farmworkers hidden among them.

Byanka reminds me that all this beauty is likely coated by an invisible toxic cloud that goes by the name of chlorpyrifos, a potent pesticide known to stunt children's brain development. In fact, according to the Sierra Club, chlorpyrifos is a derivative of chemical substances the Nazis used as sarin nerve gas during World War II. In other words, it was used to kill. And even though President Barack Obama attempted to ban this pesticide from food crops, building on prior initiatives that withdrew chlorpyrifos from all residential use, Donald Trump reversed Obama's efforts as soon as he landed the presidency. Reports indicate that today chlorpyrifos is one of the most widely used insecticides in the country. California accounts for more than 20 percent of its use, and most of it is concentrated in the Central Valley.

Rows and rows of the picturesque oranges, walnuts, almonds, and cotton that I'm seeing on this drive contain pounds of chlorpyrifos to deter insects. And even if you completely roll up your car window, Byanka reminds me, this poison can silently creep in through the cracks.

Byanka now parks her car in front of her daughter's day care, a school that looks so small compared with the immense landscape that surrounds it. We walk up to the thin metal fence that separates the playground from the fields, a barrier that's meant not only to contain kids' toys but also to draw a redline between the school and the orchards, the kids and the farmers. Overstepping that line could mean a predestined death sentence.

"There's times my daughter plays outside and smells something weird. But *¿qué puedo hacer?* What can I do? I can't keep her inside all the time," Byanka says.

In the state of California, there's a school buffer that prohibits growers from spraying pesticides on fields within a quarter mile of schools between the hours of six A.M. and six P.M. Yet, as Byanka notes with frustration, many farming-community parents who can't afford to abide by these schedules are forced to drop off their kids by five A.M. or pick them up after school hours, exposing their little ones to potential drifts.

With or without regulations, with or without metal fences or laws in place—it's clear that we're standing in a battlefield where reality and agriculture go hand in hand. Where there's no real way to separate the two worlds: they follow each other through sunrise and sunset. The pesticides become the love and affection, the sweat and tears, and the pride and curse of families. Because even though you want to protect your kids from this toxicity, the natural instinct of parents is to hug their children after work. Their clothes—still carrying the aroma of sulfur—tightly embracing their *bebés;* their cars—still carrying dust from the field—tightly squeezing families together on the drive back home.

There's no escaping this. It's almost like a spell that follows generations.

"I say I was born into it, because the day I was born my

mom was picking oranges," twenty-one-year-old Lety Lopez tells me in Visalia, another small town in the Central Valley. "So that goes into why I ended up being born prematurely."

Lety, now a fierce activist in her community, believes that exposure to pesticides and the heavy crates of fruit her mom had to carry contributed to her preterm birth. "I thought it was normal that they sprayed in the fields . . . but we never took into consideration how much it affects our health."

To be born into this, as she says to me, means to be a product of systemic racism: to be deemed unworthy enough to breathe and live freely. Multiple reports have found that babies with chlorpyrifos in their blood have lower IQs, higher rates of attention deficit hyperactivity disorder (ADHD), and higher risks of developing autism. But you don't really need statistics or long reports in order to confirm the malaise you see around you, because a short visit to rural California is as real as it gets.

"It's awful to say that we're not worth anything."

Byanka's words stick with me. Because that's not the only way these farmers have been told their lives don't hold value. In many ways, farmworkers, particularly undocumented female farmworkers, have traditionally been the *perfect* victims for sexual predators. For one, they perform a lot of their labor in isolation—either in private residences or in large rural fields like the ones I saw in the Central Valley. Working away from the public eye makes them uniquely vulnerable to harassment and violence. The "innocent" grabbing. The unsolicited comments. The inappropriate touching and groping. And, in some cases, rape.

In November 2017, leveraging the momentum garnered by the allegations against Harvey Weinstein, Mónica Ramírez submitted a letter to *Time* magazine titled "Dear Sisters." Mónica Ramírez is a third-generation Mexican American who grew up in rural America. In that letter, Ramírez, who is a cofounder of Alianza Nacional de Campesinas and the founder of Justice for Migrant Women, wrote on behalf of seven hundred thousand female farmworkers—most of whom were Latinas—spotlighting the pervasive, widespread sexual harassment and assault culture ingrained in their industry. To give you a sense, campesinas are ten times more vulnerable than others to sexual assault and harassment at work. Most of these women are migrants—the unsung heroes of the country—who likely pick the food that sits on your dining table each morning. Most of them have been suffering in silence not just because of this toxic culture but also because of their lack of papers and legal immigration status. As Mónica said, many farmworkers were "living in the shadows and were paralyzed by the shadows."

Countless reports point to the fact that the majority of female workers have experienced sexual harassment and violence at some point. But it's not just their physical workplace that makes them targets; it's also their legal status. As the Southern Poverty Law Center (SPLC) has pointed out through qualitative research, abusers—whether supervisors or male farmworkers—deliberately take advantage of their victims' undocumented status, knowing that they are unlikely to report the abuse for fear of deportation or losing their job. Some activists have called this an "epidemic"; others have even compared the conditions in the fields with "modern slavery."

As it stands today, the rights of female farmworkers are not *fully* protected under federal law. Even though basic legal

protections are in place and several states have made progress, major loopholes still exist. For example, Title VII of the
Civil Rights Act of 1964, which is considered the foundation
of antidiscrimination legislation, exempts certain employers
from liability. Under this provision, companies that employ
fewer than fifteen people aren't held accountable if they fail
to prevent or address sexual harassment in their workplace.
In other words, if you are a female farmworker who works
with a team of fourteen in the fields, you are not protected
by our government.

For decades, so many Latina farmworkers have endured
this reality. So many felt they had no option *but* to accept the
status quo—fear and repression—as the norm. No option
but to remain silent. Until a new generation of Latinas like
Mónica Ramírez, a daughter and granddaughter of migrant
farmworkers herself, helped many break that silence. That
newfound courage and solidarity is characteristically part of
the Latinx movement—that strength to find a voice you didn't
even know you could use. One that tells you you deserve
the same protection as any American. That was always this
country's promise, no?

During my conversation with Mónica, I ask her why she
didn't write this letter sooner, because the letter went viral
immediately. Just after it was posted online, Hollywood
celebrities like Reese Witherspoon started sharing it. It was
so powerful that it helped spark the larger TIME'S UP movement, which officially launched on January 1, 2018. On January 7, Mónica was walking down the red carpet as actress
Laura Dern's guest at the Golden Globes. As they walked,
Dern told Ryan Seacrest on E!'s live coverage, "I reached out
to [Mónica] to say that she stood with all the seven hundred

Byanka and me, staring at a large oil field in Central Valley's Kern County. (Courtesy of Dayana Morales)

thousand women farmworkers in solidarity for the women in our industry who were brave enough to speak out about sexual harassment and assault."

Even though the letter ignited such momentum, surely this was not a new reality for women.

"That letter had been done before. But no one paid attention," Mónica says.

No one paid attention, until now. The farmworkers' voices may have once been lost in the fields and the far edges of the country, but they started finding a choir among us.

And even when you drive away from these Central Valley fields, you're never *really* able to leave them. Soon, rows of almond trees, blueberries, and peaches quickly unfold into boundless rows of oil wells. Soon, digging up dirt for food becomes digging up dirt for petroleum. All at the expense of whom?

As I continue my drive through this valley, it hits me: Latinos at these edges of the country are entrenched in a never-ending chain of exploitation. The mayor of the city of Arvin, twenty-three-year-old Jose Gurrola, who is one of the youngest elected officials in the Central Valley, tells me point-blank that the agriculture and oil industries keep people stuck in cyclical poverty here. I saw it around me, where many of the people were not only too poor to take care of their own health but also too poor to buy the food they cropped with their own hands.

Jose reiterates, "Immigration is not the number one topic of my constituents . . . it's whether the tap water will make you sick or not, whether my kids will have an asthma attack."

But there are many ways to cope with pain and reality in the Central Valley. There are many ways to define life in the heartland. For some, it's easier to be numb. Especially in the city of Fresno. A quick detour from the scenic route of fields and wells, continuing north up Interstate 5, leads you into Fresno, the second-largest city of the valley and also one of the poorest in America.

One of my really good friends from grad school is from Fresno, whose population is more than 50 percent Latino, and setting foot in this city immediately helps me understand Maria so much more. Maria is her pseudonym. In the classroom, Maria always appeared to have unbreakable thick skin, the type that could take anything and anyone that lay in front of her. Nothing, it seemed, was ever too painful, too scary, or too hard for her. She typically sat in the back of the room, remained silent, observant, and always vigilant. You really needed to win Maria's trust in order to call her a friend. It took me a while, but I got there. I remember admiring how grounded and true to her core Maria was, unwaveringly principled. Now I thought I could understand why: if you're from the Central Valley, I don't think there's any such thing as letting go of your roots, not even for a second. Because in that classroom, I realize now, Maria was carrying the same determination that must have helped her beat the odds while growing up in Fresno. The same drive that must have kept her away from being numbed by methamphetamine.

During one of my conversations with Maria more than a year ago, she casually mentioned that several members of her extended family were meth addicts or had previously suffered from meth addiction. I assumed this was a one-off story, but Maria corrected me and said, "No, so many Latinos are addicted to meth around there. There's an epidemic." Fresno is considered the "meth capital of the United States" by various experts. And it's mostly affecting Latinos.

This realization is what eventually led a crew of us from VICE Media to dig into this crisis and shoot an episode that was later titled "The Crystal Meth Epidemic Plaguing Fresno." Lara Fernandez, James Burns, Alex Rosen, and I spent almost a week in this city trying to understand the role of this drug. Why meth? Why here? Why were so many Latinos turning to this drug? And more than anything, at a time when all eyes were focused on how opioids were devastating white communities, why weren't we also paying attention to brown communities?

In many ways, our reporting in Fresno confirmed the *same* reality I witnessed in the fields of Kern County or on the roads of Tulare County: many Latinos here in Fresno are sucked into a vicious cycle of oppression. The stigma, the scarcity of opportunities and resources, the absence of upward mobility, the normalization of abuse, the lack of papers, and the *literal* toxicity of the environment all seem to contribute to a domino effect that is leading many toward meth. Fresno's deputy sheriff, Leticia Baylon, put it best for me: "It's so many different factors compounded into each other that make it the perfect, perfect storm. And all you need is that one opportunity . . . to take the pain away. . . . If that works the first time, you're going to keep on chasing it."

For many in Fresno, that pain relief is meth. Just a few blocks from the hotel in downtown Fresno where I am staying with my crew from VICE, we stumbled upon a homeless encampment. Rows and rows of abandoned lives crammed into an empty lot. As we walked across the field, a dealer randomly approached us with his bike to find out what we were doing there. It didn't take us long, not even a couple of hours in this city, to meet someone who had been touched by meth in some way. The dealer, who had just sold almost two ounces of meth that morning, told me that many of the tents that were camped out in front of us were inhabited by people he once knew, like the former head chef of IHOP.

"Every one of those people are on heroin or meth, or both," he said to me.

"Why is this happening?" I asked.

His response crystallized the underlying cause of this storm: "The proximity to Mexico, as well as the rural areas that surround the San Joaquin Valley, means that we're inside the 'umbilical cord' to meth. It means we're on the 'mainland vein' to meth," he said.

As we found out during our VICE report, methamphet-

Meth dealer in downtown Fresno.

amine is the *number one* threat for the Central Valley High Intensity Drug Trafficking Areas. According to the U.S. Department of Justice and the California Department of Public Health, Fresno has some of the highest rates of injection drug use in the nation, and it's also associated with most of the drug-related violent crime and property crimes in the Central Valley. During the 1990s and early 2000s, the valley—with its mountainous curves, endless farmlands, and dispersed population—was the ideal location for meth manufacturing. Department of Justice reports indicate that in 2009 a total of 119 meth labs were removed from the valley. But today, most of the meth found in the region is manufactured in Mexico. As Robert Pennal, a retired commander of the Fresno Methamphetamine Task Force, told our crew, the cartels make the crystal meth in Mexico, dissolve it with a solution that camouflages it into diesel fuel, cross the border checkpoints, and eventually transport the meth up I-5 straight to hidden Central Valley labs to package and distribute the drug. And because meth is so cheap to make and to buy, this drug coats the city just as pesticides blanket the fields—looming reminders of how much is broken amid all this beauty.

"What led you to meth?" I asked a farmworker who was a former meth addict.

"There's times that one's self-esteem drives you to that," he responded in Spanish. I asked the same question of mothers, pastors, grandparents, the old and the young, and in their answers, I started noticing a pattern among these stories of addiction: they got hooked on meth to work faster in the fields; they felt lonely; their parents did it; they missed their loved ones in other countries; it was a way to cover feelings.

Some may look at these addicts and see "druggies" or "losers." Some may not even bother to see them at all. But what I saw around me were victims, not criminals. And similar to the ways in which thousands of farmworkers are forced to normalize the abuse in the fields, countless Latinos normalize the pain that comes with mental illness and the trauma that comes with life itself.

"Do you think this meth crisis will ever end?" I ask Dr. Marc Lasher of the Fresno Free Medical Clinic. He responds with a stare that tells me he sees no end in sight. By the time we left his mobile clinic in north Fresno that morning, Dr. Lasher had already collected twenty-one thousand dirty syringes. Meth is not just smoked; you can also inject the drug intravenously.

As I get ready to leave the Central Valley, I tell everyone I've met along the way: *"Regresaré."* I mean it sincerely: I'll be back. But almost each time I say this, they look at me with a deep skepticism and suspicion that's accustomed to abandonment. Faces used to never being seen and hopes used to never being fulfilled. Their words echo across the valley as I drive farther away from them.

"It's like the Wild West out here, no one is doing anything about it."

"Out here, nobody cares if something happens to you. There are people that die in the fields and they simply send you flowers. That's it."

I keep thinking of what Byanka Santoyo told me. "Almond trees are beautiful. But if people *really* knew what was going on, you wouldn't see them as beautiful."

Welcome to the heartland of your country.

2

Shining Light

If you continue following the curves of the country's edges southward, you end up at the U.S.-Mexican border, a ribbon of land that extends 1,954 miles from the Pacific Ocean to the very tip of South Texas.

On the San Diego–Tijuana divide, the most western side of the border, I pass by Friendship Park, a federally allotted space that allows families on both sides of the border to meet every Saturday and Sunday from ten A.M. to two P.M. There's a wall and barbed wire between them, border agents among them. Yet a peek through the fence is all the affirmation these families need. *Hang on. We're still here. We got this,* they whisper. When this park was inaugurated in 1971 by First Lady Pat Nixon as a gesture of friendship, she said: "I hope there won't be a fence here too long." More than three decades later, as you know, the fence is still here.

Fences and walls are created with one intention in mind: to divide. But when I reach the state of Arizona, I'm reminded that not everyone succumbs to the obstacles that lie in front of them. Especially not people like Karolina. Karolina is a transgender woman from Mexico who's currently living in Tucson. Even with Arizona's dry heat, she always manages to keep her long, dark brown hair perfectly curled. Her eyes are the same color as her hair, but Karolina accentuates them with intense black mascara and eyeliner. This brings out her eyes, deepening her look. She often greets strangers with great excitement but quickly reverts to a more somber tone. Almost as if she doesn't want to be looked at. It may be because Karolina doesn't want to bring too much attention to herself. Attention is something that has caused her a lot of pain throughout her life.

Karolina is someone who has always felt different.

"Different" is a word that is casually tossed around all the time, but it takes on a whole other meaning when a person feels as though they were born with genitals and a body that simply don't match their being, their soul, and their presence.

"When I was a kid, they would ask me what my name was, and I *always* said my name was Karolina. Karolina with a 'K' not a 'C' because it was different."

Karolina chose that because she wanted to be renamed after her mother, who never accepted her for who she was: not a boy but a young girl.

Some kids tend to unconsciously shy away from following tendencies that go against socially constructed norms, but Karolina proudly tells me she "never spent a single day in the closet." Not even in her hometown of Mexico City, which may now be gaining the label of "progressive" but has long been anchored in patriarchal family structures, transphobia, homophobia, and sexism, especially during the 1980s and before.

Yet blind bravery comes with a cost if your name is Karolina. Karolina was not only sexually abused by her older brother and often beaten by her father, she was also constantly reminded by her mother that she'd never be accepted in their family. "In Mexico, to be dressed as a woman meant to be incarcerated," she tells me. So at the age of thirteen, Karolina fled to the United States by herself. Persuaded by an empty promise of "liberty," she took the leap of faith many immigrants embark on but not everyone survives: she migrated in her *own* transgender skin.

According to UN data, as much as 80 percent of transgender murders in the world take place in Latin America. In fact, chances are that if Karolina had remained in Latin America, she'd be dead today. It's rare for transgender women to make it past the age of thirty-five. It's easier to become a statistic than to live freely. But it's also easier to morph into a conventional life—to abide by what's expected—than to brave a future that can barely define your existence. Yet after negotiating with *coyotes* and crossing the U.S.-Mexican border, Karolina eventually made it to Arizona.

Talking to Karolina, you think you're looking into the glare of a woman who has been in this world for centuries. Eyes of wisdom, scars of experience, and a stare that reaches unending depths. But she's thirty-five, of the millennial generation. Just a couple of years older than me. "I soon realized that it didn't matter where I was, that I'd find homophobia and transphobia everywhere," she tells me.

Imagination led Karolina to picture a life in the United States where she had a shot at an education. More than fifteen years since her arrival in this country, she's still holding

Karolina and me in Tucson, Arizona. (Courtesy of Daniel Brothers)

on to that dream: she has never once had the chance to step into a classroom. The first job she had was as a housekeeper in a Phoenix Motel 6. Throughout the years, she's had count-less doors closed in her face and was later forced to accept a harsh reality: there would be no opportunities to embrace her dreams; her world was about survival. Eventually, Karolina ended up on the streets, becoming homeless and turning to prostitution. She became yet another statistic—one whose life span now seemed more promising than it did in Mexico but with a prognosis that still pointed toward struggle for the foreseeable future.

"At that point, I didn't have any more dreams. I didn't have a clear vision of who I was and what my life was about," Karolina recalls.

The reality is that for many transgender Latinas like Karolina, dreams can quickly transform into nightmares. Optimistic visions can become blurred by predestined fates. By glaring statistics that tell you what your bleak future will look like. And, by the books, to be a transgender Latina in the United States means that you'll likely fall into a population that is 21 percent unemployed, 43 percent living in poverty, 31 percent homeless, and almost 50 percent psychologically distressed. As Karolina remembers, arriving in the United States almost felt like walking into a dark hole that was sinking deeper and deeper and farther away from the light.

As Karolina looks back at this point of her life, her voice starts to shake. She begins the sentence with, "In that moment, I basically wanted to be deported. . . ." But she concludes the sentence in an unexpected way: "But unconsciously, I found strength to keep going. I don't even know from where, but I did it." Stripped of every ounce of dignity, Karolina kept pushing through.

In 2012, Karolina's expired driver's license prompted Phoenix police to arrest her. Eventually, a minor misdemeanor and her undocumented status turned into a U.S. Immigration and Customs Enforcement (ICE) detention that sent Karolina to Arizona's Eloy Detention Center, a privately run immigration prison that is a couple of hours away from the border. Eloy didn't have a specific unit for transgender immigrants (as of now, there's only one detention center in the nation that does), so they placed Karolina in an all-male unit.

Upon setting foot in Eloy, Karolina was allegedly forced by officials to strip off her clothes in order to confirm her sex assignment. "It's a man!" they slurred. Misgendered, bare naked, and humiliated: that was the beginning of a series of verbal, emotional, and physical abuses that would continue for more than three years of her life. Inside those halls—

tucked away from scrutiny and any form of accountability—Karolina was allegedly repeatedly raped, assaulted, and mistreated. She spent months in solitary confinement, at times bathed with chains around her body, and slept every single night with the fear of not waking up the next day.

"I thought I would die inside there," Karolina tells me.

Anyone would rightly assume that part of your soul *must* die there. Under those circumstances—numbed by neglect, bruised by pain, and ripped of pride—bodies venture to a side of darkness that appeals to surrender. It's easier to cave in than it is to keep going. But *those* are the degrees that separate people like Karolina from the rest of us. A choice to either build up resilience or let it go. A choice to either walk through total darkness or turn around. Karolina had the strength to keep fighting. She was able to wander into the depths of resilience and hold on tight to an imagination that projected a human that was worthy of living.

"I imagined a better life for me, and I knew I had to keep fighting," she says.

Three years and six months after she entered the Eloy Detention Center, Karolina was finally released. But when she was able to leave jail, there was *no one* waiting outside to greet her and welcome her back into the world.

Karolina, like countless transgender Latinas in this country, is still in the process of finding her destiny. As she puts it, she's able to see a light at the end of the tunnel, but it's still a very faint one. Karolina transitioned back into society completely alone.

As we talk, I can sense she continues to feel deep pain and resentment every time she's reminded of that solitary exit. The fact that no one was waiting for her upon her release.

Karolina and a group of people after writing letters of encourage-
ment to queer detainees inside the Eloy Detention Center. (Courtesy of Daniel Brothers)

Karolina was so scarred by that experience that it prompted
her to spearhead a letter-writing program for queer and
transgender detainees inside Eloy. A couple of times a month
she organizes people to write encouraging letters to the
detainees—that way they never feel they're alone. In a way,
Karolina is now becoming that voice she never had while
she was overcoming all these struggles herself. Thanks to
her, many transgender migrants now have letters to read,
advice to take, and steps to follow. Thanks to her, it's a little
bit easier to reach the end of the tunnel.

While she talks, she keeps sliding her hands through her
hair, looking at the mirror, and fidgeting with her makeup.
So I ask Karolina if she feels beautiful. It's a simple question.
To my surprise, she responds with a resounding *no*.

"I want to get breast implants. It's something I need in

order to be at peace with myself," Karolina tells me. "I've seen my friends go through it, and it's like a shield for them because they feel secure."

I remind Karolina one more time of how beautiful she is. Every single transgender Latina has her own journey with resilience. But often, all points end up converging in a shared search for beauty. A feeling that's far removed from vanity but instead grounded in the most basic form of survival: self-love. In a world that barely recognizes your existence, what do you hold on to if not yourself? And what if resilience takes another turn, leading you to reject beauty instead of seeking it? What if that's the only way you can survive? Unfortunately, for other transgender Latinas, making it in this country can mean shying away from truth, assimilating as much as possible, and giving up a part of themselves for a shot at American success.

One day, someone transmitted that message to me through a stare. I was in California's Central Valley visiting a religious rehab house for former meth addicts, all of whom were Latinos and immigrants. The second I stepped onto that property, I made eye contact with a young—self-identifying—man. It immediately felt as if Ricardo and I had known each other for a long time. (Ricardo is his pseudonym.) It almost felt as if we were both gesturing an "I see you" to each other. After we quickly nodded in silence, I toured the rest of the house and made my way back to the entrance once I'd finished.

Before I left, Ricardo stopped me and said: "Look at this picture. *This* is what I used to look like when I was sinning."

Ricardo stretched out his arms and showed me a photo he had pulled out on his phone. I paused and looked twice at the image I was holding: it was the photo of a beautiful young transgender woman smiling radiantly from ear to ear.

"That was my past, but now I've found God, and I'm back on track," he said to me, almost like a robot. In that moment, I inferred that Ricardo, at some point in his life, had been a trans woman, something he was clearly now deeply ashamed of.

As that sentence came out of his mouth, the various Latino men who were surrounding Ricardo, men who were also staying at the house with him, started clapping. They seemed to be proud of hearing Ricardo say, "I'm back on track." It felt as though they were all applauding his new-found masculinity. I zoned out everyone else around us, ignoring their cheers, and directed all my attention to Ricardo instead.

"Well, *I* see a beautiful person in that picture. There's *nothing* wrong with that woman. Can you see that?"

As Ricardo told me, for him, the image of that transgender woman was a reflection of a past consumed by drugs and sin. And the *only* way to escape that reality, he assured me, was by escaping the woman in that photo. That's why he ended up in that rehab house. As Ricardo said all this to me, more claps and affirmative nods ensued from the other men.

But Ricardo's words didn't match his stare, a soul aching to be unleashed again. His words didn't match his gestures of groomed machismo. And Ricardo's words didn't even match his own voice: shame masked in virility. Yet his resilience was *so* extraordinary that painfully concealing his true identity was Ricardo's form of survival at the moment.

Once I understood, I stopped asking questions.

At that moment, I understood there are two types of people in this world: those who need light to build resilience and those who can do so in utter darkness. Most of us are the former: we need some form of light to get us through the end of the tunnel. But then there are people like Karolina and Ricardo, who can push through to the end almost blindly. They are able to confront reality not with mere acceptance but with unparalleled imagination. They can imagine the dreams that belong to them, the rights that were promised to them, and a life that's yet to be fully lived. So, they keep going.

But there are other transgender Latinas, like Roxsana Hernandez, who have died attempting this very journey. Roxsana was from Honduras, and in May 2018, she presented herself at the U.S.-Mexican border to seek asylum in the United States. A couple of weeks later, Roxsana, who was HIV positive, passed away in ICE custody because she wasn't given the necessary medical attention to keep her heart beating. An independent autopsy report found that Roxsana had deep bruises on her body, was dehydrated, and had been medically neglected until it was too late. Our government's negligence killed her. And sometimes there's no form of resilience that can counter that type of injustice.

Roxsana's spirit carries on, though. It's stronger than ever. Because people like Karolina and Ricardo, the young man in the rehab house, continue to redefine the parameters of resilience. They continue to push boundaries, transcend borders, and grasp uncharted power. It's not textbook power. It's a type of power that can literally save people's lives through pure strength rather than through policies, politics, or money.

By the 2020 election, Karolina will have become a U.S. citizen, able to vote for the first time in her life. That power is invaluable. I've seen Karolina walk into a detention center's visiting room to greet transgender asylum seekers, and I've seen the way she turns their dismay into hope:

"When you leave this jail, what would you want your name to be? What are your pronouns?" she asks detainees. They've never been asked this question in their *entire* lives. And Karolina gives them the strength to keep fighting inside those walls. That's radiancy.

I've seen Jennicet Gutiérrez, a transgender activist, give purpose to the community by fearlessly chanting, "My exis-

Artwork commemorating Roxsana Hernandez.
[Art by Gran Varones]

tence is resistance!" She always chants as loudly as she can. And masses of people look up to Jennicet—seeing the reflection of their own dignity. That's radiancy.

And I've seen Nakai Flotte, a transgender organizer, assuage the fears of the LGBTQ refugees as she leads them through Central America and toward the U.S.-Mexican border to seek asylum. And, suddenly, migrants have a reason to keep moving forward. That's radiancy.

These trans women may have never had light to guide their journeys, but that, in return, has transformed them into an unstoppable shining light that can illuminate almost everything that stands in their way.

Even darkness.

3

American

Have you ever stopped for a second and wondered *what,* exactly, makes you feel "American"? I found myself confronted with this question south of Tucson, just miles away from the Mexico-Arizona border.

I was there to meet Blake Gentry, an advocate for indigenous rights. He immediately took me to Casa Alitas, a shelter that takes in migrant families who have been recently released from ICE detention and provides them with temporary housing and assists with their needs. This wasn't my first time visiting one of these humanitarian shelters, so I thought I had a pretty clear idea of what I was walking into. Left to right, the majority of the refugees I saw were from Central America. Some were waiting in line to pick up new clothes from the donation pantry, others were having their first hot meal in weeks by the kitchen table, and many were working with volunteers to arrange travel logistics to their next destination.

But as I was getting ready to walk out the door, I noticed a group of people sitting by the entrance. They were asylum

Outside the Casa Alitas hospitality center (close to the Mexico-Arizona border), which takes in migrant families that have been released by ICE.

seekers who had just arrived at Casa Alitas and were about to go through their first medical exam, a routine checkup to ensure they had not suffered any major injuries or illnesses on their journey to the United States.

"*¿Cómo te sientes?*" doctors and volunteers asked. How do you feel? What are your symptoms? Nods ensued and conversations started flowing.

Yet amid the group, there was *one* particular silence that struck me. It came from an observant woman, still and quiet. Blake immediately noticed her and took her and her son to the side of the room. This mother and son were sporting the same clothes they'd worn when they crossed the border just two days earlier: dirty jeans, stained shirts, and dusty shoes without shoelaces—a hallmark ICE stamp (when U.S. Border Patrol agents detain migrants, they force them to remove their shoelaces owing to safety precautions, mostly out of fear that they might attempt suicide). But Blake knew exactly what that woman's silence inferred and broke it in the simplest of ways: by speaking to her. In *her* language.

Blake quickly deciphered that this woman came from the highlands of western Guatemala and that she spoke Q'anjob'al, an indigenous Mayan language spoken primarily in Guatemala. He immediately opened a book and dialed one of the fluent Q'anjob'al interpreters he had on call. This interpreter was all the way in the state of Indiana.

"Ask her what her symptoms are," Blake said on the phone to the interpreter.

The woman noted, in Q'anjob'al, that she had a stomachache and a headache and that at times she felt like fainting, all signs of severe dehydration. Days of walking through the desert will do that to you.

"Ask her if she has stains on her feet," Blake continued on the phone, wanting to know how the woman's feet were holding up after that treacherous trek over the border.

"Is she pregnant?"

She was not, she affirmed.

"And where is she going after the shelter? Does she have family in the U.S. to look out for her?"

After forty-five minutes of this back-and-forth, the mother and son were cleared. They walked out of the waiting area very differently from how they'd initially entered, now welcomed. And that's the appalling effect of the American illusion we live in: our instinct is to discard the dark skinned as intruders, the unknown languages as foreign, and the immigrants as visitors. To conflate indigenous with "the other" instead of "the firsts."

Long before Christopher Columbus's arrival, the Americas were inhabited by indigenous groups that were spread throughout the north and south continents. Adam Rutherford, a British geneticist and author, states in *The Atlantic*: "These founding peoples . . . formed the pool from which all Americans would be drawn until 1492." So when we say "American," just remember that the intrinsic bravery the word carries in it dates back not to those white revolutionary men who declared independence in the eighteenth century but to those brown revolutionary people who fought to preserve their stolen freedom. And though it was taken from them, that American spirit never truly dies. That's the spirit that was present in Casa Alitas that afternoon.

Behind the silence the indigenous mother and son demonstrated that afternoon, there was a solemn bravery surrounding their presence. It was in the way they held their heads up high while volunteers at the shelter talked to them in languages they did not comprehend, such as Spanish and English. It was in the way they clung to their dignity, without any assurance of what their future would look like in the United States. It was in the way the mother distracted her son with playful gestures and toys, putting his joy first instead of succumbing to a grim reality.

Mayans have a history of perseverance. Not just through their legacy as mighty warriors but through the power of their minds. While Spanish conquistadores stormed through the New World, there was one thing they could not bury: Mayan spirituality. Spirituality is something that could never be fully slaughtered and oppressed. For the ancient Mayan civilization, that power lay in their belief that sacredness and spirituality live within *everything* that surrounds us. Not just in humans but in objects, animals, and nature. Many believed that time was cyclical, not linear; that gods could take on many different forms, not just one; and that death was followed by an afterlife, not an end. And when you view the world through that lens, nothing is insurmountable.

Americans are so used to the image of migrants and asylum seekers at the U.S.-Mexican border as Spanish-speaking immigrants that when another reality hits, it can be startling and unrecognizable. It should not be a surprise, though. As of 2019, according to *The New York Times*, more than 90 percent of the "most recent migrants" are actually coming from Guatemala. It's important to keep in mind that at least 50 percent of the population in Guatemala is indigenous, the majority of whom are of Mayan descent. This also means that they are likely to speak one of the more than twenty-two indigenous languages that are present in the country. From Q'anjob'al and Mam to K'iche' and Q'eqchi', many Mayans speak languages that have been around for thousands of years. And studies show that most of the Guatemalans we're seeing at the border right now are migrating from the western, poorest, and most rural areas of their country, which is typically where the indigenous communities live.

That's why the encounter I witnessed at the shelter with the indigenous mom and her son should never have been a surprise to begin with. In fact, Blake Gentry noted that the Arizona border generally sees more indigenous migrants than *any* other part of the U.S.-Mexican border and approximately 20 percent of the migrants they welcome in the Casa Alitas shelter are indigenous. A lot of these trends are explained by the unique routes Guatemalans take when they flee. The majority of Guatemalans coming to the United States migrate from the region of Huehuetenango, a majority-Mayan area that lies in the western highlands of the country. This means that the treacherous trek is done by bordering the west of Mexico until the migrants reach the U.S. Southwest, making Arizona one of their likely entry points into the country.

When visiting the border, I was accustomed to encountering faces and tongues that spoke like me, in that bustling Spanish we all shared. But that isn't an accurate picture of what is really happening on the ground anymore. To take a step back and reverse preconceived assumptions of what crossing the border looks and feels like, Blake put me in the skin of the Mayan woman and son I had met at the shelter earlier that afternoon. In great detail, he attempted to explain their reality:

First, the silence I'd witnessed earlier that shadowed the woman in the waiting room. As Blake explained, that was for a reason. It was a consequence of the internalized trauma the Mayan woman carried inside her. Blake clarified that indigenous people are constantly stigmatized—seen by others as a community that is backward, uneducated, and poor. And no matter how strong you are, these biases can get under your skin.

"This stigma of identifying as an indigenous person is also part of what we see as a behavior of quietness or silence," Blake noted. A quietness that can easily camouflage you as a Spanish-speaking Latino migrant. "Because the *hardest* problem we have here is not technically identifying persons of indigenous languages, it's having them tell us that they actually speak an indigenous language." Many times, "coming out" as an indigenous migrant is not a voluntary act. It's either forced upon them or it's accidentally exposed.

And what happens when they have to expose their indigenous language? What happens the moment they open their mouths?

Before arriving at a shelter on the U.S. side of the border, migrants have to endure several other arduous steps. Many of them will be apprehended by Border Patrol agents or other law enforcement officials along the way, and many will ultimately end up in detention centers. Typically, as part of the process to seek asylum, migrants have to go through screening interviews where they must prove "credible fear" in order to make the case that they qualify for protection in the United States. But what are those interactions like if U.S. government officials *don't understand* indigenous languages? How can they derive an appropriate legal assessment? Actually, forget legal assessments for a second: What if indigenous migrants cannot convey even their most basic, simplest needs? Like their health conditions or their children's asthma? Even though all humans have a right to speak in their primary language, the U.S. immigration system simply isn't built that way. It doesn't really account for those scenarios. In effect, things get lost in translation.

Which means that if you're indigenous, you're very likely to be misunderstood, ignored, and neglected. You're likely to face utter confusion. You're likely to recoil into silence and get by however you can. This really struck me: Blake recounted that a while ago he had asked former Border Patrol agents in his network if they had *ever* used an interpreter of indigenous languages during their time in the BP force.

"Never," the BP agents told Blake. The thing is, that word—"never"—can be a matter of life and death for indigenous migrants.

"You can get by, but sometimes getting by means very critical mistakes are going to be made and it can cost people dearly," Blake underscored.

At this point in my conversation with Blake—at least three hours in—I could gather that his soul seemed almost broken. Broken from the number of injustices he had witnessed during his decades of advocating for indigenous communities. For almost every other word that came out of Blake's mouth, a tear dropped from his eye. And that's because he'd seen how close these communities are to the verge of death.

"Remember the story of seven-year-old Jakelin Caal Maquin and of eight-year-old Felipe Gómez Alonzo?" Blake asked me.

Blake Gentry at Sentinel Peak, Tucson Mountains, Arizona.

"Of course," I said.

As the national media reported, both Jakelin and Felipe were young children who died in Border Patrol custody owing to the Trump administration's utter negligence. Jakelin allegedly died from dehydration and Felipe because of untreated influenza. However, it's safe to argue that the real cause was negligence. Yet there's one thing that the mainstream media failed to report. As Blake noted, *both* Jakelin and Felipe were not only Guatemalan but coming from indigenous Mayan language–speaking families.

They were identified as "Latinos" by the media but never as indigenous peoples. And that means we failed them. So we have to ask ourselves: Did language and cultural barriers cost Jakelin and Felipe their lives? Was their silence a death sentence? Were their lives lost in translation?

As I posed these questions to myself, my visit to Casa Alitas gained a whole new perspective. I understood that Blake's *life's* work was in fact to ensure that indigenous life does *not* get lost in translation. That it never surrenders to silence.

After our conversation, Blake gave me another tour of the shelter. This time I started noticing things I had completely missed the first time around. For example, the unintelligible words I'd seen earlier in the day on the whiteboard were translations of basic English words into Mayan languages. Those posters I'd seen of the human body weren't just odd anatomy drawings; they were a tool for indigenous migrants to point to their medical symptoms, using sketches instead of words. Those massive binders I saw weren't just bureaucratic paperwork; they were medical questionnaires that had been translated into several indigenous languages.

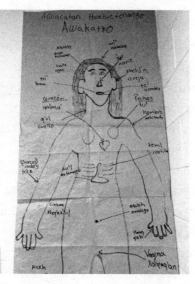

Drawing of the human body by Mayan
children at Casa Alitas in Arizona.

"Do you have a fever?" read *La k'o o q'aq'chawech?* in
K'iche'.

"Can you describe your pain?" was *La kakowinik kabij jas
le q'oxom.*

"Heart" was *qalma'* in Awakateko.

"Head" was *vi'* in Ixil.

"One of the magical things that happens in this office is
the connections," Blake said to me as I was looking around
his office in awe. It turns out that all the scribbles, drawings,
and notes I was seeing had been penned by young migrant
indigenous children at the shelter who helped Blake translate forms into indigenous languages. From medical-intake
questionnaires to transportation forms, the kids helped craft
materials from Spanish into Q'eqchi', Ixil, K'iche', Mam,
or Q'anjob'al, among others. In many cases, the kids were

more literate in Spanish than their indigenous parents and served as incredible assets at the shelter. These were, after all, the resources that would help people like the mother and the son I met earlier that afternoon get back on their feet and plan their next steps in the United States.

As for them, I later found out that their final destination in the country was Los Angeles, where they'd reunite with other family members and try to make a life for themselves. In just a couple of days—after crossing the border, being held in detention, and staying at the shelter—the mother and son would embark on this next chapter of their journey.

Many Americans have been face-to-face with Mayans or other members of the indigenous community who live across the United States. Even if they aren't immediately recognizable, they are there. In the classroom, it could be a student who's been dismissed as shy because he doesn't speak up. In line at the grocery store, it may be that older man who appeared "Latino" and tolerated people talking to him in Spanish, only to simply nod and smile. At the Laundromat, it may be that woman in the corner, the one who's always sitting in silence. These are the individuals many believe do not belong in this country. The ones the state is trying to mute, the ones the laws are trying to deport and the institutions are failing to see. They are the ones unconsciously viewed as the antithesis of America. But these are people who stood on this land *first*, who saw it morph through the centuries, and who will remain standing on this soil until the very end.

As I'm leaving Arizona and getting ready to keep heading east, I turn on the radio. The Brett Kavanaugh hearings are playing in the background, and I increase the volume,

Walking past Donald Trump supporters in Arizona defending then Supreme Court justice nominee Brett Kavanaugh.

listening like millions of women across the country who are waiting on a verdict that would do justice to Dr. Christine Blasey Ford, Kavanaugh's accuser. Dr. Ford's emotional testimony, where she painfully recounted how she was sexually abused by Kavanaugh in the summer of 1982, when they were both teenagers, captured the attention of millions of women, giving many more strength to speak out against the history of misogyny and sexual abuse American society has normalized for far too long. While the Senate didn't believe Dr. Ford's allegation, millions of women did. And that was telling.

I wanted to get a sense of how young Latinas around Arizona felt about the hearing, so I stopped to chat with several of them at a Phoenix community center, asking them to share their thoughts on Brett Kavanaugh. What struck me the most wasn't their firm responses—vehemently infuriated by the Republicans' attempts to discredit Dr. Ford's testimony—but the way in which the younger generation of Latinas organically brought their *mamis* into the conversation. As I posed questions, some young Latinas would look away from me, quickly search for their mothers in the back, and ask *them* to speak up and voice *their* opinion.

"*¿Qué piensas tú, Mami?*" Jalyna Ramos-Martinez asked her mom. What do you think, Mom?

Her mom timidly came closer to us.

"Sometimes we hold it in," Jalyna's mom said. "Not only that type of sexual abuse but other types of abuse, too. We don't speak up because we are embarrassed or because of fear. So, it's good people are speaking up."

That simple exchange in Phoenix between Jalyna and her mother signals not just that change is transcending generations of Latinas but that it's being encouraged *across* generations of Latinas, who are *pushing* each other to change.

As I hear Jalyna and her mother speak, I think back to what Mónica Ramírez told me: "What we have seen over the past year is that now there is this kind of collective courage that has been developed." That collective courage isn't visible just in the way younger Latinas are stepping up for their elders. It's also present in the way the younger generation of Mayans are acting as translators for their parents, helping them navigate daunting new languages but also new systems and environments. When Ramírez was speaking of collective courage, she was referring to the bravery women from all corners of the country are exhibiting, with campesinas, Hollywood actresses, CEOs, caregivers, and celebrities linking arms with one another in the face of sexual violence. But if you see the Latino community through a Latinx lens, then you understand how intertwined all these fights are: a win for women is a win for Mayans, for trans-Latinas, for the LGBTQ community, for Afro-Latinas, for undocumented families, and for all our *abuelas*. In the Latinx movement, people's rights are seen not separately but as *one*.

Toward the end of my conversation with Ramírez, she told me that our older Latina grandmothers and mothers lived during a time where rights existed but weren't actually enforced.

She's right. The difference now is that our *abuelas* and *mamis* have other voices to speak up for them—not just us, *but an entire community that sees their struggles as theirs.* That's the Latinx effect.

4

The Other Wall

Once I arrive in South Texas's Rio Grande Valley, I try to deviate my attention from Trump's wall. It's almost impossible, though. By the U.S.-Mexican border, the radio, the local TV stations, and the small protests outside my window continue pointing to the same growing humanitarian crisis. There's perhaps no better exemplification of the Trump administration's agenda than this state. North of here, in Collin County, ICE arrested 280 employees at a technology company in April 2019, marking one of the largest work-site raids in the country in the last decade. Along the Texas border, thousands of refugees are stranded in some of the most dangerous Mexican cities. As part of the Trump administration's "Remain in Mexico" policy, asylum seekers are now stuck waiting in violent border cities like Ciudad Juárez as they wait for their cases to be processed in U.S. immigration courts. From Brownsville, Texas, across the banks of the Rio Grande, you can see some of these migrants living in an inhumane makeshift tent city in Matamoros. Some of them will even wave at you with a smile, no matter how desperate they are. Meanwhile, in South Texas construction workers continue to deliver on Trump's campaign pledge to build miles of his new "big, beautiful wall" by 2021, here to remind us of Trump's vision for America: a country devoid of its color and diversity.

When I look at that wall, the first memory that comes to mind is one of the administration's most controversial orders, the "zero tolerance" policy enacted in April 2018. This cruel policy criminally prosecuted parents who were caught crossing the border unlawfully with their children and subsequently separated them from their daughters and sons. It was a way to deter other migrants from crossing the southern border. For months, families were being ripped apart; more than three thousand children were separated from their parents until the administration reluctantly reversed its own policy in June. The Rio Grande Valley region in Texas became ground zero for that policy. The *Houston Chronicle* reported that "more than half of all migrant families and children apprehended at the southern border" were coming through the McAllen, Texas, sector. Meanwhile, Stephen Miller, the architect of Trump's immigration agenda, unapologetically defended zero tolerance, stating, "It was a simple decision by the administration to have a zero tolerance policy for illegal entry, period. The message is that no one is exempt from immigration law." However, the policy produced a national outcry, with activists and officials invoking Nazi Germany when discussing its effects. CIA director Michael Hayden told CNN, "I know we're not Nazi Germany, alright. But there is a commonality there, and a fear on my part. . . . We have standards we have to live up to."

In the late spring of 2018, as the administration was being

pressured into ending zero tolerance, I traveled to the valley because, like hundreds of other activists and journalists, I wanted to see the damage that had been done with my own eyes. The trauma was clearly still lingering. At that point, Border Patrol was releasing countless immigrants—some of whom had been separated from their families, others who were lucky enough to be released in units. Once released, many migrants had nowhere to go and sought temporary refuge at the Catholic Charities Humanitarian Respite Center, a shelter in downtown McAllen run by Sister Norma Pimentel. In June 2018, it was reported that the shelter was seeing about one hundred immigrants per day. That's how undeterred migrants and asylum seekers were by Trump's zero tolerance policy: desperation is powerful. And one hot afternoon, I walked inside this small charity center, and I don't think I've been able to forget it since.

Once inside, for a couple of hours, I volunteered to hand clean towels to migrant women who were waiting in line for their turn to shower. Many hadn't been able to do so in days, even weeks. One by one, they'd rid their bodies of the dirt, the clothes, and the distress that had followed their treks to the United States. But I noticed that many of them started asking me for scissors. What do they need this for? I asked myself. And I soon realized it was to tear their jeans apart in order to allow their ankle bracelets to slip through their pants. Looking down at their weathered feet, I noticed all the women wearing thick, black ankle bracelets that allowed ICE to track and monitor their every movement, as if they were owner-tagged cattle.

"What was it like inside the detention facility?" I asked one woman standing next to me.

Women migrants wearing ICE ankle-monitoring bracelets inside the Catholic Charities Humanitarian Respite Center in McAllen, Texas.

Migrant baby at the Catholic Charities Humanitarian Respite Center in McAllen, Texas.

"They placed us in freezers and hit us," she recounted. *"En hieleras,"* she said. Iceboxes.

After seeing these women, I found it hard *not* to remain focused on Trump's wall and the humanitarian crisis that surrounds it. It was hard *not* to continue thinking about the border through an immigration lens. But while most reporters and officials remained focused on these developments, I started driving slightly north and away from the wall. As I took a deeper look inside our country, other pressing issues at the border became visible—not just immigration but HIV and women's rights, all realities that have been overlooked and obscured for years.

No matter how far inland you go, the reflection of the eighteen-foot-high steel bars is ingrained in your rearview mirror. And although *el muro* prevents you from seeing the entirety of the landscape, the deeper you go in, the more you understand that this wall represents one of the *many* hurdles that come with making it in this state. Especially if you're a Latina, like Rosie Jimenez. Rosie's name has been mentioned over and over again during my time in the Rio Grande Valley. She represents a silent truth.

In 1979, Rosie Jimenez was a college student living in the Rio Grande Valley, where she was studying to pursue a career in teaching. Rosie was a young working-class woman, the single mother of a five-year-old, and the daughter of migrant farmworkers. As the *Texas Observer* has chronicled, at the time, Rosie unintentionally became pregnant and was hoping her Texas Medicaid would cover an abortion. Enshrined in *Roe v. Wade,* women in America have had a constitutional right to safe and legal abortions since 1973. Yet rights in this country often come with a cost. Immediately after the *Roe v. Wade* ruling, an antiabortion movement, which included Democrats, began pushing back. In 1976, a Republican congressman from Illinois, Henry Hyde, introduced an amendment in Congress to prohibit the use of Medicaid to fund abortions. The amendment passed and has since continuously banned federal funding for abortions except in extreme cases like rape or incest. In practice, what this really means is that low-income women who do not have enough resources to pay for abortions out of pocket or through private insurance must bear the brunt of the cost of an abortion. According to the American Civil Liberties Union, once the Hyde Amendment came into effect, abortions that were handled through Medicaid funds "dropped from about 300,000 per year to a few thousand."

Rosie, like millions of others across the country, was one of the women impacted by the Hyde Amendment. Even though this country promised her a constitutional right, there was a wall blocking her from that freedom. Without having the means to pay for care at a local OB-GYN, Rosie was forced to resort to a cheap, unsafe, and illegal abortion. A couple of days afterward, Rosie contracted a bacterial infection in her uterus. Eventually, the infection spread throughout her body, and Rosie died from organ failure. Rosie was twenty-seven years old.

It's been years since this happened, but Rosie's legacy is stronger than ever around here. A story that continues to awaken a feeling among women that is as real now as it was back then: entrapment.

One after the other, stacked up against one another, a series of barriers confine women's integrity in the Rio Grande Valley. Many Latinas—constrained to rural grounds,

pinned against a wall, and tied to the law—push against barriers that slowly attempt to chip away at their dignity. From
this land, everything seems too costly to buy, too far to reach,
too criminalized to speak out against. Miles and miles away
from the Central Valley, the struggle at the border mirrors
the one in the fields: a battle to prove one's life is worthy of
living.

As I write this, there are almost forty anti-abortion bills
in session in Texas's legislature. One bill would assign an
attorney to an unborn fetus; another would ban abortion
after a fetal heartbeat is detected (this takes approximately
six weeks, and many women don't even know they are pregnant at that time); another would further cut access to health
care by barring local governments from partnering with
abortion providers; and, of course, several bills are seeking
to ban abortion altogether. All of this builds on decades of
right-wing efforts that have attempted to roll back the gains
made since *Roe v. Wade*. Like the enactment of House Bill
2 in 2013, which led to the closure of twenty-four of Texas's
forty-one abortion providers. Today, there's only *one* abortion
care clinic in the entire Rio Grande Valley, an area with more
than one million inhabitants.

"We can't say abortion isn't legal. But they make it as hard
as possible," says Ofelia Alonso, a young activist from the
Texas Freedom Network who's in her early twenties. "Here,
health care is in Mexico. . . . A lot of us rely on Matamoros [a
dangerous border town on the Mexican side], even for abortions. It's easier to get the pill there than here. In the Rio
Grande Valley almost no one has health insurance."

According to the *Texas Tribune*, in 2017 Texas had the highest uninsured rate of any state, and in the Rio Grande Val-

Trailer park, or *parquera,* inside one of the Rio Grande Valley's *colonias.*

ley, the uninsured rate is double that of any other region in the state. And the *colonias* are the valley's biggest testament to this reality. *Colonia* means "neighborhood" in Spanish, but what defines these small communities on this side of the border is precisely their lack of definition: their unpaved roads, unbuilt homes, and unfinished blocks. Inhabited mostly by low-income Latino and immigrant families, *colonias* are unaccounted-for lots of land that typically get overlooked on the map. If you've never been there, it's because you've never been able to see them.

In the Rio Grande Valley's Hidalgo County alone there are about nine hundred *colonias.* As I continue to leave the border wall behind me, I drive straight into one of them to visit Mayra's house in San Carlos. More than three thousand people live in this area, and the median household income is about $21,000. The drive to San Carlos isn't that long, but it seems eternal. Streets transform into muddy lanes, houses into dilapidated structures, and commercial stores into makeshift shacks. At times, miles can go by without much to notice around you—just rows of crops, occasional *elote* stands, taco trucks, stray dogs, and overflowing floods from the night before.

I park the car in a trailer park and walk up to Mayra's house.

"What's this neighborhood called?" I ask her.

"*¡La pequeña parquera!*" she says with pride. They call it "the small parking lot."

I enter Mayra's small and attractive trailer home, one that is decorated with so much love that it makes me forget the outside world. The smell of warm tortillas, the soft cushions, the family portraits. Inside her house lies everything you need. Because if you look beyond this humble home, what *else* would you find? The answer is glaring at you: nothing.

I immediately begin to smell the suffocation in the air—a feeling of entrapment that's silently encroaching on our surroundings. If Mayra wants to buy fresh produce, the closest supermarket to her house is fifteen minutes away by car. If she needs to schedule a mammogram, the closest women's health clinic is at least thirty minutes away. In the case of an emergency, it would take the ambulance approximately forty minutes to reach her house. In fact, Mayra recalls how her little niece was involved in a car accident not too far from *la parquera*. She died before the ambulance was even able to get there. Call it a health desert, food desert, or economic desert—the only thing that appears to be visible around this *colonia* is negligence.

There are barely roads around, no public transportation

around here or schools to be seen in the vicinity. But what you *do* see around here is *la migra*. Border Patrol agents vigilantly roam around these communities, monitoring the inhabitants' every move.

When you feel so far removed from civilization—living between food deserts and isolated lands—it's easy to forget what rights look like. When you're living in such dire conditions, injustice becomes normalized, and right from wrong can be a concept that's hard to discern. But sometimes, all it takes for one to realize what's at stake is to pose the question that is most dreaded:

"What if Rosie Jimenez were you?"

"Rosie Jimenez was from your community. In fact, she was from your county," Paula Saldaña, a field coordinator for the National Latina Institute of Reproductive Health,

Latinas of all ages, crammed inside a trailer home in the *colonias*, listening to Paula Saldaña talk about their reproductive health and rights. (Courtesy of Dayana Morales)

addresses a group of Latinas who are now crammed into Mayra's trailer. "Here, we break all the taboos that exist around reproductive health, and that means we have conversations about issues that, maybe, some of us feel uncomfortable with because they were never talked about in our families."

Paula is an activist who has dedicated the past twenty years of her career to educating Latinas about their health and their reproductive rights. Around here, though, they call her and her fellow army of organizers "las Poderosas," the Powerful. Once a month, las Poderosas go into corners of the valley that no one else is going to, breaking a silence about an issue many are afraid to discuss: abortion.

What once started with a small group of women in a truck has now become a movement. Through years of building trust with the community, las Poderosas are now able to fill spaces—like Mayra's house—with Latinas who are eager to discover their freedom, timidly curious to debunk their own myths. Around Mayra's little salon, I see more than a dozen young and old Latinas—mothers and grandmothers, babies and grandchildren. All of them gathered on couches, listening carefully to Paula's words: "We want to see you in rallies. I visualize you in front of a crowd full of people, in front of a podium, talking about your testimony and your story," Paula tells them. "Each and every one of you is a winner."

I visualize you.

The fight for Latinas' reproductive justice in the Rio Grande Valley is often seen among them as a fight for dignity. To have control over your body is synonymous not just with the ability to access abortions but with the ability to preserve one's own life. In these *colonias,* to control your body means to not be forced to eat processed food, to not be too poor to afford insurance, to not be too far away to reach the hospital, too scared to leave the *parquera,* too embarrassed to speak up, too tired to move. It's a fight about breaking a wall—not just the one at the U.S.-Mexican border but also the one that's barricading Latinas in these *colonias.* And more than anything, it's a fight to keep Rosie's story alive by finishing it with a different ending.

As she closes the meeting in Mayra's house, Paula looks at the small crowd and asks: "Who are we?"

"*¡Poderosas!*" the ladies respond in sync.

I ask Paula to describe for me the faces of the Latinas who come to these meetings. "Who are they?" She tells me that they are people who already have the seeds to be free. Ludi, a breast cancer survivor, comes here not only to take charge of her health but also to escape her husband's violence. Mary,

Las Poderosas. (Courtesy of Dayana Morales)

who once felt trapped in her own home, now uses these spaces as therapy sessions. "I'm diabetic . . . for me, this is like injecting insulin," she tells me with a smile. Kayla sees this as an opportunity to break with the silence her mom carried for so many years. At the end, all these women need is for someone to remind them that they are, in fact, free.

Once I say my good-byes to las Poderosas (after they feed me tons of roast chicken, rice, tacos, quesadillas, and more tortillas), I continue my drive through the border towns of the Rio Grande. I can't help thinking that these ladies have figured out the million-dollar question most progressive elected officials haven't: *how* to talk to Latinas about abortions. During the 2016 election, I remember we always shied away from using that term in the community, always tiptoed around an issue everyone deemed "taboo." For decades, we've been taught to think that our community's deep ties with religion—*con la Virgen*—have prejudiced our very own values of tolerance. But after meeting las Poderosas and driving around this region, I'm not so sure about that anymore. Because when you root this issue in a simple matter of dignity, it abides by the principles enshrined in faith. The same faith that drives Sister Norma to take in asylum seekers just miles down this road is the faith that ought to embrace these Latinas fighting for abortion. Delma Catalina, a former employee of the Whole Women's Health Clinic, the Rio Grande Valley's *only* abortion clinic, put it this way: "We have to reclaim what it means to be a person of faith. The people of color churches have *always* been about refuge."

After this trip, I'm more convinced than ever that every D.C. pollster and political consultant should come to the valley to craft their messaging. I keep hearing one of las Poderosas' comments ringing in my ear: "Politicians don't know our communities . . . they don't know how people live here."

The last time I was in the Rio Grande Valley was in 2018 with the VICE Media crew, when Adri Murguia, Luisa Conlon, Lara Heintz, Jaime Chew, and I traveled down here to do a story that was later titled "HIV Crisis on the Texas-Mexico Border." We were drawn to this because even though HIV infections and new diagnoses had declined throughout the country, they were increasing among Latinos. As the U.S. Centers for Disease Control and Prevention (CDC) found, between 2010 and 2016, new HIV diagnoses among men who have sex with men were stable. However, in 2016 they increased among adolescent and adult Latino men who have sex with men, with new infections across the nation rising by almost 30 percent. And, shockingly, this was something *particularly* felt in the Rio Grande Valley. As we noted in our documentary, one out of every four young Latino males in the valley will become HIV positive in their lifetime. It's a crisis, and it's one that no one is really talking about.

During the shoot, I asked a Mexican taxi driver, who was wearing his botas and sombrero in downtown Brownsville: "Do people know there's a crisis [HIV] here?"

"They know about the problem . . . but they look the other way," he responded.

As we came to find out, to no one's surprise, many queer Latino men, too, feel as though they are suffocating. From the entrenched culture of machismo to the lack of sex education and the scarce resources that exist, it often feels that the easiest way to "make it" is by putting your head down. By staying in the darkness to avoid the stigma and the backlash. And that's why HIV rates are continuing to increase significantly around here: there's not enough light to know even how to define the problem to begin with, let alone how to deal with it.

That was Ayden Castellanos's story before he learned he was HIV positive. After not feeling well for months, losing an enormous amount of weight, collapsing at home, and losing the ability to walk, his doctor finally hit him with the news: he was HIV positive. For months, he was completely unaware of his status.

When asked why it took him so long to know about his status, he responded, "The health literacy level in the area and in the state in general is very low. These conversations aren't happening. On top of that, this is a very poverty-stricken area, and so I couldn't afford to take time off from work to get tested." Now Ayden is the one who's fighting to break down the very barriers that led him here in the first place, with the same grit and bravery displayed by las Poderosas. All of them, trying to break the other wall.

5

Unbroken

To be a young Latinx in America right now is to understand that there are two stories to tell. One of them is about where we currently are. The other one is about where we come from.

On the morning of August 3, 2019, at 10:39 A.M., the El Paso police received a phone call about an active shooter at the local Walmart. When they arrived at the scene, they walked into a hate crime: twenty people had been brutally murdered during a shooting rampage undertaken by twenty-one-year-old Patrick Crusius, a white supremacist. Crusius had driven more than ten hours from his hometown of Dallas all the way to El Paso with one intention: to kill brown people. Among the souls lost that day were people who carried last names like Anchondo, Benavides, Velazquez, Mendoza, Manzano, and Sanchez. People like fifteen-year-old Javier Amir Rodriguez, who was described by many as a "passionate soccer player." Just a kid.

After the tragic 2019 massacre in El Paso's Walmart, marking the largest attack against the Latino community in modern U.S. history, a hashtag emerged, #ElPasoStrong. In the face of hate, the Latinx community wanted to show the world that they were strong, that they wouldn't succumb to fear, and that their resilience would carry them through. El Paso native and former presidential candidate Beto O'Rourke captured the sentiment in his remarks in the aftermath of the attack: "That means refusing to let hate win," he said.

But what effect did the massacre have on the youngest members of the Latinx community?

There's an ugly truth that's been staring us in the face for far too long: young Latinos in this country are suffering. They are in a lot more pain than they may have dared to realize. For years, studies have shown that Latino kids and teenagers are at greater risk of suffering from mental health problems than other demographics, a fact that is exacerbated by the disproportionate barriers the community faces to access help. As the Anxiety and Depression Association of America points out, only one in five Latinos with symptoms of a mental disorder will approach a doctor. Part of this is due to a general lower socioeconomic status that prevents them from affording basic care. But another part—a *big* part—is driven by the taboos that remain present in the households. Mental health isn't traditionally a topic that Latinx families openly discuss. A taboo within Latino communities, when it *is* discussed, may often be dismissed as a phony or frivolous excuse.

Just because the community doesn't traditionally speak on this topic doesn't mean that mental health hasn't taken a toll on the youngest generation of Latinos. In 2010, the National Center for Biotechnology Information found that first-generation Latino immigrant youths who were directly impacted by the effects of migration, such as dealing with citizenship status, facing discrimination, or living through a traumatic event, "were associated with depressive symptoms and anxiety." In 2015, the CDC found that Latino high school students were *more* likely to consider suicide than white and black students. Their studies found that almost 20 percent of Latino students displayed a "prevalence of having seriously considered attempting suicide" and that 11 percent had "attempted suicide." Then, in 2017, the CDC exposed just how grave the issue was among young Latinas in a new report. Referencing the CDC's findings, Ludmila Leiva wrote an article on Refinery29 titled "Latina Suicide Rates Are Out of Control—Here's Why," stating: "10.5% of Latina adolescents aged 10–24 years in the U.S. attempted suicide in the past year, compared to 7.3% of white females, 5.8% of Latino, and 4.6% white male teens."

What may be even more striking about that survey is often left unnoticed: the sadness that runs alongside those suicide rates. Sadness can be so subtle. It can be so easily camouflaged and normalized. It can weigh down a person, overshadowing their lives. According to the CDC, in 2017 approximately 50 percent of all young Latinas "were persistently sad or hopeless nationwide."

By 2018, a clearer picture emerged regarding the factors that could have been propelling all these feelings of sadness. The American Psychological Association (APA) conducted a study that found "perceived racial/ethnic discrimination was consistently linked to poorer mental health, lower academic achievement and more engagement in risky or negative behaviors." They also noted that young Latinos were more likely to show higher levels of depression in response to this type of discrimination than their black and white colleagues. So, *why* were Latinos *feeling* it more than, say, their black counterparts? What was unique about their experience? Researchers at the APA discerned the following: "Latinos experience a type of discrimination in which they are viewed as 'perpetual foreigners.'" Viewed as perpetual foreigners. As foreigners.

This contradicts the fact that most young Latinos are U.S. born. In fact, more than 80 percent of Latinos under the age of thirty-five were born in this nation. However, that doesn't make their perpetual feelings of foreignness any less real. Because there *is* something menacing about feeling like a stranger in silence versus diagnosing that feeling. There *is* something threatening about internalizing these emotions versus having them named and called out.

Then, when you hear that there are people in this country who actually want to kill you because of your background and the color of your skin, it all suddenly becomes real. That feeling of being a "perpetual foreigner" is no longer a feeling; it's a moving target, as we saw manifested in the El Paso shooting. And there is no escaping that. Latinx youth learned this on August 3, 2019.

But hate doesn't discriminate against age; it latches on to last names, skin colors, and stories it refuses to legitimize. Before the massacre, Crusius had allegedly posted a white supremacist manifesto online where he explicitly stated: "This attack is a response to the Hispanic invasion of Texas." The borderland city of El Paso, where more than 80 percent of the population is Latino, became his perfect battlefield: full of perceived foreigners.

A couple of months after the atrocious attack, I went to the site where it took place. Although the Walmart remained closed at that point, a beautiful memorial had been built around its perimeter. Hundreds of flowers everywhere, American and Mexican flags tied to the fence, and countless notes that read, "Hate will not divide the borderland," or, *"Ya no más actos de racismo!"* and many "El Paso Strong" signs and banners. But what I really noticed was the complete silence that surrounded me. It was so calm and quiet. You could have heard the drop of a pin. No longer any cameras on-site, no longer any frantic reporters covering the story, and, certainly, no longer any customers around. It felt for

Drawings, posters, and flowers outside the Walmart to honor the victims of the mass shooting that left twenty-three people dead in El Paso.

a second as if the country had moved on and all that was left on-site was not the urgency we once felt but lingering memories of immortalized pain.

In front of that Walmart, time stood still, and stories of the fallen lived on in those notes and in the survivors' memories, like the story of Jordan and Andre Anchondo, two of the young victims who also happened to be a couple and parents to a newborn baby. As was reported, when gunshots were fired inside the Walmart, Jordan covered her baby with her body. When they found the two-month-old at the crime scene, the little boy had his mom's blood all over him. They found him with broken fingers but breathing. Alive. He had miraculously survived.

As I walk around El Paso and into the main campus of the University of Texas at El Paso (UTEP), lines and lines of Latino students getting out of class walk by me—all of them with stories, backgrounds, and last names that can culminate in deadly hate at any second. Because no matter how bright the sun is shining today on this campus, there's still a silent understanding that *any* one of these students could have been victims of the Walmart massacre. And just because it didn't happen then doesn't mean they don't know it could still happen *today*.

What must that feel like?

I stop a couple of students to ask them directly, surprised that *they're* surprised I'm approaching them with these questions: "How are you feeling after the shooting? What's going on? Are you holding up? Are you okay?"

Slowly, answers begin to trickle through:

"I was really scared to go back to school," one student tells me. "More than half of the students are Latinos and I felt like, How will I feel safe in the place I study? What if something happens? What would we do? How would we react?"

Another student tells me that he's scared something similar could happen "in any moment."

"It makes me scared to be in the United States because someone could be inspired by him and come and do the same thing in this school," he states.

Then, I also hear anger. "I'm angry because he is pleading *not guilty* knowing what he did," one of the students tells me. "That's not fair."

Across campus, I overhear a student as she gives testimony before a government hearing that's being held at UTEP: "I want you to think about a loved one you know that is going to school," she addresses the government panelists. "And think about their heart pounding to their chest when they hear a loud noise across the hall, when they spend hours upon hours studying for an exam and they can no longer focus on it because of the real and paralyzing fear that they have of being shot."

But *this* comment is perhaps most worrisome of all, because it's the simplest: "As a Latina after the shooting, I feel scared to go out places. . . . But I'm kind of getting used to it."

This statement is terrifying, because it points not only to the normalization of trauma but also to that of inaction, which go hand in hand. In the aftermath of one of the largest attacks against Latinos in our history, the Texas state government passed absolutely no legislation to prevent another mass shooting from happening in its own backyard. Instead, adolescents and kids are being forced to accept living in a

Young Latina student at the University of Texas at El Paso.

state of fear. And in *that* reality, the reality of mental health concerns becomes not an exception but a norm. A way of life. An ordinary struggle, a daily activity.

The truth is that the pain around the Latinx community can become almost unbearable. It can become increasingly easier to give up, as statistics on the younger generations' mental health demonstrate. Every single day, the members of these communities are handed different opportunities to do that—to walk out their front door and remain in silence or to simply succumb to fear. But the younger generations of Latinos are choosing to not let statistics define them and opting to create a future that is brighter than the bleak picture painted by stats, the news, and the growing racism in the United States. Why? Because remembering where they've come from can help them keep pushing through.

And that can be an unstoppable force. Before I left El Paso, one of the students mentioned the university's library. He told me that in one of the corners on the top floor of the library there was a window that had a unique view. The view is almost like staring into two stories. On your right, you see the United States. On your left, right across the U.S.-Mexican border, you can see the city of Anapra, one of the poorest and most dangerous regions inside Ciudad Juárez.

The student then looked at me and said: "It's the ultimate check of your privilege. It makes you say, 'Holy shit, here I am. In this position, I have an opportunity.' I always think of that."

And while his words ring so true, it's still only half of the story. The El Paso shooting, in many ways, was the culmination of *all* the stereotypes society has *otherized* us with, all the barriers society has pushed the Latinx down with, and all the stigmas society has taught its members to internalize. It was a wound that exposed not just the pain that's inflicted by piercing bullets but all the different manifestations and facets of that pain: the pain of longtime discrimination. Perhaps older Latino generations have been able to shy away from it—to shake it off as normal—but the youngest Latinos are choosing to acknowledge it. To understand that real "fighters" get stronger only by recognizing they've been broken.

Sometimes, all you need to do is ask a question that's often forgotten. And it's the simplest one: "How are you feeling?" If you do, it's possible to trace back several sources of pain that were long forgotten:

BEING SILENT

There's a saying in our community: *"Calladita te vas más bonita,"* which translates into "You look cuter when your mouth is shut."

The term can be used in a variety of ways, mostly as offensive forms of sexism or misogyny. But it can also be used as a way to avoid taboos and conversations that make Latinos feel uncomfortable. For example, many times the elephant in the room is mental health. In that scenario, it'd sound something like this:

"*Mami,* I think I should see a therapist to deal with my anxiety."

The response? *"Eh . . . calladita te vas más bonita, mija."*

End of conversation. End of story. But sometimes that unspoken conversation can knock on death's door. When Esperanza was only eight years old, she contemplated taking her own life.

Esperanza means "Hope" in Spanish, and in many ways, she embodies exactly that. It's hope that carried Esperanza through some of the most difficult times in her young life.

"My dad passed away when I was five years old in a car crash when we were coming home from Mexico," she tells me at the very beginning of our conversation. "Since I was so young, I didn't really understand the concept of death and grieving. I went through elementary school being bullied for not having a father figure. My brother had to convince my mom to take me to therapy, since I was too young to handle those emotions. I went to therapy, and Mom abruptly put a stop to it because she thought there was no use to it. You know, obviously, the stigma we have as Mexicans with mental health. It's like: 'Ohhh, you don't have anything [wrong with you]; move on.'

"I kind of just pushed everything away. . . . I kept that to myself and kept it hidden," Esperanza adds. She points out that one of the biggest misconceptions about depression is that people expect you to be sad all the time. "That's not really what it is," she says. "Every person is different." During that time of her life, Esperanza recalls disguising her sadness by trying to make others happy: "I didn't want them to feel the way I felt."

Even though it was initially easier to retreat into the shadows, Esperanza eventually realized that life had something better in store for her. It wasn't until she reached her sophomore year in high school, years after she went to that first therapy appointment, that Esperanza understood that what she was feeling inside wasn't normal. It took meeting other students who were also suffering from stress, depression, and anxiety for her to realize that she wasn't alone in this fight, to understand that having the urge to commit suicide at the age of eight was a symptom of the silence that was forced on her. Shortly after that realization, Esperanza started a conversation about mental health with her mom.

Esperanza says that she sat down with her mom and said, "Mom, I've been feeling sad for so long, and I don't think it's okay. I don't feel comfortable talking about my problems to you because I feel like you're going to judge me. I need to go see someone."

There was no *Calladita te vas más bonita* in response because that silence had already been broken. After that hard conversation with her mom, their relationship became stronger than ever. "I finally went to therapy, and I feel so much better."

BEING A FIRST

Kimberly is a first.

She's a nineteen-year-old community college student and the first person in her family to go to college. "I don't really have anyone in my family or in my circles that has gone to a good school, or that has gotten a degree," she tells me over the phone a couple of minutes into our conversation. So I ask Kimberly to tell me a little bit more about her journey: "How did you get to where you are?"

As Kimberly explains, having seen the way the school system had failed her cousins, her parents decided to move to a new neighborhood so Kimberly could have a better shot at an education. She tells me that when she got to her new school district, it felt like a "culture shock." Even though many students were also Latino, they were fourth or fifth generation and seemed way more anglicized than she was. "I was in an immigrant community where all of us spoke Spanish, not because we wanted to but because it's our first language," she says. "We are translators to our parents, so when I moved there and people didn't speak Spanish, it was so weird and so different." She didn't really feel comfortable in this new school environment. "I didn't see myself."

Yet regardless of these difficulties, Kimberly was determined to succeed. "It was hard to transition, but I always knew I wanted a future," she recalls. This drive was what prompted her to enroll in AP classes and even become vice president of the student government.

"But, in all seriousness," I say, "this seems like it must have felt like a lot of pressure on you. How did you feel?"

"Being a first in something is always hard. I can't call my cousin and ask him: 'How did you do this? How did you get through college?' I don't really have that," Kimberly responds. "And even when you go to school, I can't really tell my mom about the SATs. She'd be like *'¿Qué es eso?'* I felt so much like my parents didn't really understand what was going on, so it's hard for them to even comprehend what I'm going through at that time."

Kimberly is the only one in her immediate community who truly knew what it was like. Despite all the extracurriculars she took and all the advanced classes she signed up for, Kimberly tells me that most colleges ended up rejecting her. She felt the urge to put all the blame on herself but tried to remember that it's a reflection of the systemic racism that has plagued this country's institutions. It's not always the brightest and the wisest who are set up for success; often it's the whitest and the richest. It's not a system built for "firsts" like Kimberly. And if she doesn't know this by now, it's likely she'll realize this in a matter of time.

"I thought I had worked so hard through high school for the outcome to be college," Kimberly says with frustration. "So, I felt like I failed myself and my family because I couldn't get into a college. Even though I had a good GPA, I was vice president, and many times I would go to school with two hours of sleep."

Yet her pride still manages to shine through the phone.

She just needs a little extra nudge to expose it. "A higher education is a higher education, no matter what form it comes in," she says. "I'm only nineteen, and there's still so much to know and look forward to. This is just the beginning."

BEING UNDER TRUMP

Donald Trump normalized hate, and hate is contagious, no matter how young you are.

Mere days after Trump won the 2016 election, the Southern Poverty Law Center reported that there were kids in classes chanting, "Build the Wall!" and "Trump, Trump, Trump!"— comments that were directed at their Latino peers. It didn't take long for media outlets and groups across the country to find that with Trump's rise there was also a noticeable increase in bullying across America's schools. In the aftermath of the election, the SPLC administered a study that surveyed more than ten thousand K–12 educators to understand the impact the election had in our schools. According to the report, 80 percent of the educators described that their students were feeling a general increase in anxiety and worry regarding the repercussions of the election. Four out of ten educators had observed "derogatory language" aimed at students of color. And, alarmingly, more than twenty-five hundred educators were able to point to specific cases of "bigotry and harassment" that could be directly linked to the divisive election rhetoric. As reported, these cases even included graffiti of swastikas.

During my conversations with Esperanza and Kimberly,

both alluded to feeling the effects of Trumpism. Often the most dangerous forms of prejudice are the ones that are expressed in disguised manners.

Esperanza recalls the first time she experienced this. It was during her freshman year in high school, in the midst of the 2016 election. One day, her teacher decided to bring up the topic of immigration, asking, "If Donald Trump, theoretically, were to deport immigrants, how would that affect our economy and our environment?"

A student responded with: "But what about my lawn?!"

Esperanza says, "It hit close to home because my godfather actually does yard work." Her classmate's comment served as a wake-up call—a sudden realization that the color of her skin could be weaponized as a tool of oppression. Seen as a mark of inferiority. Felt as a foreign object. Made unequal.

Prior to hearing those remarks, Esperanza explains, she was under the impression that all her classmates shared similar goals and morals. "But in that moment, it all clicked," Esperanza recalls. "That's not what's really going on in this world."

Esperanza became a victim of the Trump effect. After that comment was made, she felt she didn't belong in that classroom; she began to question her *own* ability to handle the AP classes she had enrolled in. And there it was, Trumpism doing what it does best: slowly chipping away at Latinx dignity, no matter how young the person is.

For Kimberly, the Trump effect looked like an ice-cream truck. As both of her parents are immigrants, Kimberly recalls feeling anxious when she found out that ICE raids were happening in her state. "I remember there was an ice-cream truck that passed by, and I remember I gasped," she tells me. She mistakenly thought the truck's horns were the precursors of an ICE raid. She didn't hear music; she didn't smell the different ice-cream flavors or hear her neighbors' laughter down the street. All Kimberly could hear were the sirens every immigrant family dreads most: ICE.

"Living through that fear," Kimberly tells me, "most people won't go through that."

They don't.

BEING TOO SPICY

Angela is still a teenager. This is hard for some people to understand. She doesn't beat around the bush but jumps straight into the conversation the second she answers my phone call.

"People always expect us to be a certain way. Or they think it's normal for Latinas to always be 'upset' or have an 'attitude.'" She's right. For years, people have sensualized Latinas, picturing us as "fiery," "fierce," and "aggressive." It's as if, when American society thinks of Latinx women, they revert back to an image of J.Lo singing "Waiting for Tonight" in that green dress, or they imagine Sofía Vergara in an episode of *Modern Family*, yelling to Ed O'Neill in Spanish: "*¡Ayyy, el Diablo!*"

"They sexualize us a lot," Angela tells me, "and they like that we have a 'spicy' attitude."

People often think of these adjectives as harmless, or even as cute compliments, but they are nothing more than internalized biases that lead to discrimination. For example, Angela tells me about the time she wore a crop top to school. "People were like: 'Oh my God, why is she wearing it?'" she recalls. "But then a white girl with a small size would wear something similar and it would be nothing." In other words, a white girl wearing a crop top is "cute," while a Latina wearing one is seen as "too much."

These microaggressions kept getting worse in school for Angela. "The students were looking at me different," Angela states. "I didn't feel comfortable there." After sophomore year, Angela tells me, she stopped going to school, which eventually led to her grades dropping, then to her failing her classes, and finally to her entering a state of depression. "I didn't want to go to school, and I would cry in the mornings," she says. "I just didn't feel like I belonged there."

How many times have young Latinx been in situations similar to Angela's? How many times have Latino students crossed friends in a hallway—mistaking insults for praises, sexism for flirtations, and racism for innocent jokes? With these types of microaggressions—especially the ones masked as flattering tributes—the lines between right and wrong become so blurred that they can easily be dismissed as harmless. And *that's* the danger: what doesn't make it overtly wrong is what normalizes biases.

Angela ended up transferring to another school where she seems much happier. "They care. They want you to be there." Sometimes that's all it takes, to actually show that you care for people.

Angela will have graduated from high school by the time of this book's release, something she couldn't even fathom a couple of years before.

BEING SHOT

I remember the first time I met Carlitos at the March for Our Lives rally in Washington, D.C., in March 2018. I was so amazed by his courage. I remember staring into a contagious bright smile.

It had been only a month since the tragic mass shooting at Marjory Stoneman Douglas (MSD) High School in Parkland, Florida, where seventeen people were brutally murdered. At the time of the massacre, Carlitos found himself hiding in one of the classrooms along with his fellow students as the gunman was firing. His close friend, Joaquin Oliver, was one of the victims. Shot in a hallway, right outside his creative writing class. And just weeks after the attack, Carlitos was one of the students leading a youth movement determined to end gun violence. In the aftermath, Carlitos also spearheaded a digital effort, "Stories Untold," to ensure that young communities of color had a voice within that narrative.

It had been a while since the Parkland shooting and since I had last seen Carlitos, so I called to check in on him. He picked up my phone call by saying, "I've had a pretty rough month emotionally. Sometimes I feel like I'm taking care of myself, but I'm really not. It's been over a year, and I thought I had it all taken care of."

He explained that even though he had friends and an incredible support system, feelings of loneliness and sadness kept resurfacing. This form of gun violence is a type of trauma many will never be able to personally experience, but as Carlitos speaks, he explains that there are many layers to this pain. In addition to the wounds produced by the gunshots and the loss, Carlitos's pain is exacerbated by other harsh realities that many of the Latinx community have to carry within them.

"There are also other stories that my family and myself are going through," Carlitos says. The Latinx story is *never* one-dimensional. In conversation, Carlitos points to the financial struggles his family is enduring. And he mentions that the dire socioeconomic situation in Venezuela, Carlitos's country of birth, is affecting his loved ones.

Violence is one of the reasons Carlitos's parents left Venezuela, only to face it again in the United States. But this time they were barely able to escape it.

"And I'm also taking care of other people," he mentions.

After the Parkland shooting, Carlitos felt an overwhelming sense of responsibility to shed light on the stories that were being left out. Part of that drive stemmed from the way in which the mainstream media were covering the Parkland massacre, focused mostly on highlighting Emma González, a Parkland massacre survivor turned gun violence activist, or on the perspective of MSD white students like David Hogg and Cameron Kasky, all of whom became the face of the #NeverAgain movement. Back in April 2018, Carlitos said, "More than thirty-three hundred students go to Marjory Stoneman Douglas, and we *all* were affected." So when he mentions that he is "taking care of other people," it's clear that he's still carrying a lot of weight on his shoulders. He's still trying to get our policy makers to understand that Latino children and adolescents are three times as likely to die from a gunshot as their white counterparts.

Even Carlitos recognizes what he's doing: "I'm so focused

The day Carlitos and I first met at the March for Our Lives rally in Washington, D.C., March 24, 2018.

on amplifying voices and giving a platform to other people instead of maybe saying: 'Wow, I need a second to breathe, to stop what I'm doing.'"

But I can tell he can't get those stories out of his mind either. Carlitos tells me about a recent trip he took and a student he met there:

"There was one specific student who really stuck with me," he says. Pensively, as if he's still trying to decipher what, exactly, touched him so much. "He's sixteen. He's a gang member. Coming from Parkland—a community where you normally don't see gangs—listening to that story really impacted me." Carlitos continues, "I started comparing my story to his, and he told me, 'No, don't do that. You have to own your story.' I needed that slap in the face," Carlitos says calmly.

What drives Carlitos is more than just telling stories. It's the fact that his pain is so deep that he's feeling others' pain, too. When I asked him about El Paso, he said, "The fact that change isn't as fast as we wish it could be affects me. It affects me. However, I understand that change isn't fast, and it's been slow historically. In the world we live in, there is urgency for these needs and for these issues. There *is* urgency. But in the system that we live in, it's always set to be slow."

This Latinx movement is about being able to take a look out a window and notice both sides of the view: the right and the left; the present and the past; what lies here and also all the way there. It's about not being afraid of taking that look. And that's precisely what makes this younger generation of Latinos "resilient" and "fighters," as the headlines love to point out. It's not just their ability to forcefully plow ahead. It's their capacity to *look back* at their pasts, their truths, and their pains. That's what makes El Paso's youth mobilize to vote for change after the massacre, what makes Carlitos hold his camera to tell untold stories of gun violence, what makes Esperanza go to therapy every week, and what makes Kimberly dream of graduating from college.

Because they've faced what's broken. They've confronted it. They've looked it in the face. And *now* they know they can come out the other side, truly unbroken.

The South

6

K'exel

Typically, when I think of "the South," I associate it with a time in my life when I went to a Christian camp in North Carolina.

It's still unclear to me how I ended up there, especially given that my parents are agnostic. But the truth is, I somehow managed to spend three summers deeply entrenched in what many would describe as "Bible camp." Surrounded by hundreds of white girls running across fields of green grass, eating sloppy joes, singing cheerfully at church, saluting the American flag every morning, and falling asleep to Jesus's commands every night. As a teenager who would then spend the rest of the year back in Europe with my mom, who lived in Madrid, I remember associating "America" with those summers in the South. Those white, Christian, good ol' hot summers did indeed feel very patriotic to my thirteen-year-old self.

The image I had of the American South as a teenager was completely distorted, though. Based on my Bible camp experience, where I was one of about four Latinas in the *entire* camp, I had the wrong image of what the South looked like. I certainly never imagined many Latinos living there. I was wrong. Between 2008 and 2018, the South saw the fastest Latino population growth of any region in the country. According to the Pew Research Center, during that period of time, the population there grew by 33 percent, reaching almost twenty-three million people. As I read that percentage, I immediately thought back to the Mayan woman and son I had met at the Arizona migrant shelter a few months prior. When I saw them, they had just been released from detention and were getting ready to head to their next destination in the United States. Like them, there were hundreds of other indigenous migrants dispersed across the country, settling into new cities. Where could they be? The answer is, they could be *anywhere* in the nation, including in the South. From what I would later find out on this trip, the American South wasn't such an unlikely destination for Mayan communities after all. In fact, it was a very likely one. Because what that twenty-three million figure doesn't capture is the fact that indigenous groups remain largely on the sidelines and therefore typically unaccounted for when we talk about the Latino community.

This indigenous community is extremely hard to quantify for a variety of reasons. For one, it's important to note that some people from indigenous communities do not necessarily identify with the term "Latino" or "Hispanic." Many see those terms as Eurocentric labels that erase indigenous people's identity while emphasizing Latin America's history of colonization. Additionally, although at least 25 percent of Latino adults in the United States consider themselves indigenous or Native American, often there's no box to check to represent how they truly identify. In the public's eye, indigenous people are assumed to be—and thus often unwittingly pass as—Latino. But claiming one's indigenous roots isn't just hard to navigate, it can also pose a risk, *especially* in the conservative South.

So I decided to return to the South. I was determined to find a face of America that had been buried this entire time: that of indigenous people. A face that had been concealed within generalizations, statistics, and labels that never captured its true colors. And that's one of the most powerful effects behind the Latinx concept: the recognition of our existence in the places you'd least expect. And if I'm learning anything from my return to the South so far, it's not just how vibrant the indigenous community is here but also how much this country has to learn from it, particularly when it comes to our own understanding of American patriotism and religion. That's right: patriotism and religion, two elements most white Americans wouldn't instantly associate with indigenous people.

The first stop I make is in Georgia, a state with some of the strictest anti-immigration laws in the nation. Yet it also happens to be a state that has historically attracted undocumented immigrants, who've found job opportunities in farming, construction, or agriculture. In fact, according to a report published by National Public Radio (NPR), there are currently more undocumented immigrants in the state of Georgia than there are in Arizona and New Mexico *combined,* among them many Guatemalan migrants who also poured into the state in the wake of the opportunities that sprang out of the 1996 Atlanta Olympics. And among many of the Guatemalans there were Mayans.

Dr. Alan LeBaron, director of the Maya Heritage Community Project at Kennesaw State University, known to some in Georgia's Mayan community as *el papa*.

One of the first people I met in Georgia was Dr. Alan Le-Baron, the director of the Maya Heritage Community Project at Kennesaw State University, just north of Atlanta. Like Blake Gentry, Dr. LeBaron had been working with Mayans for decades and, through the years, had become one of the strongest allies the community had in the South. So much so that, according to Dr. LeBaron himself, many in the community refer to him as *el papa*. The dad.

At this point, it's still hard for me to wrap my head around the fact that Mayans have a big presence in Georgia, so I jump straight into it: "How many Mayans are there actually in this state?" I ask. Dr. LeBaron tells me that he believes there are around twenty-five thousand of them throughout Georgia.

There are not hundreds but *thousands* of Mayans in Georgia.

FINDING PATRIOTISM IN GEORGIA

As Dr. LeBaron points out, many of these Mayans live in a small rural town called Canton, located in Georgia's Cherokee County, which Trump overwhelmingly won in 2016. Canton is situated in the foothills of the Blue Ridge Mountains. Not too far from where I went to camp. He immediately suggests that I head over to Canton, saying that if I go, I'd be able to witness something most people have never seen: Mayans honoring the United States, a type of patriotism most people aren't used to.

"Several young Maya had the idea to commemorate September eleventh . . . in a statement of solidarity with the homeland of their birth, the United States," he said.

My visit happens to coincide with 9/11, and it turns out that the Mayan community in Canton has an event planned to remember that terrible day in our history—though it isn't necessarily the first activity or interaction one might imagine when walking into the Mayan community. I was expecting to see more Guatemalan flags than U.S. flags or, truly, *anything* other than the stars and stripes. But I soon find out that's exactly the point: Mayans here are redefining what American patriotism and loyalty look like.

In Canton, I meet Candy, the main organizer of this 9/11 event. When I first see Candy, I instantly recognize that silence and shyness I witnessed at the shelter in Arizona. A slightly reserved young woman, somewhat timid, and with a smile that's always halfway open. She speaks English fluently, having mastered her own fluidity with language, seamlessly maneuvering her way through Spanish, English, and Q'anjob'al. That effortless ability to mold several backgrounds into *one* is characteristically Latinx. And it's not just a trademark millennial move but also a sign of the evolution of the Mayan community in the United States. A trajectory that has slowly turned silence into a command of multiple voices and identities.

Candy is a single mom in her midtwenties, and although she was born in Guatemala, she's been in the United States for most of her life, since the age of four. When her family came to the States from Huehuetenango, which is in western Guatemala, Candy's parents primarily spoke Q'anjob'al, an indigenous Mayan language. Candy's older sister did as well, which is what prompted her first schoolteacher to become alarmed and ask Candy's parents, "What's going on? I thought you guys were from Guatemala?" Candy recalls. Turns out the teacher was really confused that no Spanish was being spoken by her Guatemalan student. Though, as expected, through the years Candy and her sisters not only learned Spanish and English—adapting to society's calling— but started losing touch with Q'anjob'al and the indigenous traditions that defined their parents' roots.

American society lures us to believe that the future looks brighter the closer we hew to certain American ideals. For example, believing that the more English one speaks, the more one can assimilate and adapt to the surrounding norms. This was especially true for our parents' generation and for those that came before, often forced to believe that dreams sounded better, fancier, and more honorable in the English language than they did in the Latinx and indigenous native tongues. "Dreams" sounded better than *"soñar"* in Spanish or *"ajsn'ajs"* in Q'anjob'al.

But at some point in Candy's life, she realized there was nothing more important than staying true to herself, not losing sight of what made her *different* and *uniquely* her: being Mayan. And *that* realization and thought process was an emblematic principle of what made America *different* and *uniquely* hers: the ability to claim one's roots.

So I ask Candy, "Why is the Maya community coming together to honor 9/11?"

She responds with, "Americans, they all see us as Mexicans."

September 11 is one of the few days of the year when

Mayan children rehearsing for the 9/11 performance in someone's garage.

Americans choose to see ourselves as one, united as Americans and feeling it as the ultimate definition of patriotism. So Candy explains that she's leveraging this opportunity to force her neighbors into realizing how diverse the community is around them. She wants to drive home the point that they aren't all just "Mexicans" and "Central Americans" but also indigenous people. More than anything, this event is a way to show that you can be unapologetically Mayan *and* believe in American ideals. That you don't have to choose either one of those identities; you can be both. Candy wants her daughter and all the younger generations of U.S.-born Mayans to understand the importance of their indigenous blood. To not give in to that pressure of assimilation. "That's where we come from to begin with," Candy states, "and I don't want it to die with just me. So, that's why I want to also make sure my daughter knows."

In downtown Canton, I make my way to the local arts center, a beautiful building that stands out with its big white columns and brick structure. I feel as if I'm in a quintessential small American town. If you look at the center's regularly scheduled programming, on a typical day they'll host events ranging from gospel to cover bands playing the Eagles to 1960s-themed parties. This day, I walk up the stairs and find a sign that reads: "In Remembrance of 9/11, an event presented by the Maya Heritage Youth Group."

As I enter the building, I see Candy in the corner, talking to a group of young Mayan kids who are about to perform this evening. The first thing I inevitably notice is the abundance of color. This room is full of vibrant colors. The young girls are all wearing different beautiful indigenous *trajes*— garments that have been shipped all the way from the west-

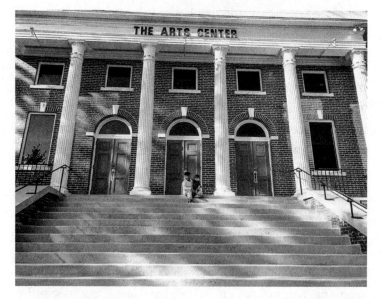

Mayan children, about to perform at a 9/11 event, in front of downtown Canton's local arts center.

ern highlands of Huehuetenango, Guatemala, meticulously woven by hands that keep traditions alive. *El huipil* (the shirt), *la faja* (the sash), *el corte* (the skirt)—the young girls are gleaming with the pride of a country they've never seen but only felt.

I take a seat in the back of the room. When the event starts, I watch kids onstage playing the marimba, a large wooden percussion instrument that was allegedly used by the Mayans in Mesoamerica way before the colonizers even arrived. For years, these kids have seen their parents and grandparents play the marimba at home, enclosed in living rooms and basements. But now it's their turn to play in public. In the right aisle, the girls stand in formation and, one by one, start making their way to the stage—their small feet moving to the Mayan beats and to rhythms that have ruled

Guatemala's highlands for centuries. The boys follow in the left aisle, sporting white shirts and red *pañuelos* tied around their necks, simulating traditional outfits worn by Mayan men. Together, the boys and girls go up the stage and continue dancing to the marimba, all the while glancing over to the audience in hopes of making their parents proud.

That's what I remain fixated on right now: where their eyes and their parents' eyes meet. Where two gazes start telling a story that can barely be articulated to the public, the evidence of everything that has been overcome by the community. As I look at the audience around me, a sea full of indigenous parents who cherish the potential of their children, I remember what Dr. LeBaron told me earlier: "A lot of them [the parents] suffer . . . they have pride, but they suffer from some feelings of inadequacy or fear. Fear of it, the fear that people are going to look down upon them for being too brown, too 'Indian looking.' "

And, looking directly ahead, I see a stage full of first-, second-, third-, and fourth-generation U.S. citizens, most of them natural-born citizens. I see gazes of Mayan children who want to liberate their parents from the fear and oppression they've carried for years. Gazes to inspire them to keep their head up, not low, and their voice up, not down. In other words, these kids are sending a clear message: to be Mayan *is* to *be* American. "They suddenly feel as though it's safe to say who I am," Dr. LeBaron reminds me. And that's as important for the parents to know as it is for their white neighbors to absorb.

When the kids finish the performance, applause erupts. I see parents who can't stop smiling and also some white local residents who are observing with curiosity. But when the center's doors open, allowing the breeze to come in from outside, reality starts to set in again. The vibrant colors inside don't look as bright anymore, and the pride that was oozing takes on a more subtle tone. A more cautious one. Across the center, I see a group of teenagers. They're all in a circle with their Polos, their practice shorts, baseball caps, and iPhones in hand. All of them are white. A reminder to the Mayan kids, who are looking over at them from the steps of the center, that not even thick skin and bravery can always overcome the cultural differences that lie between them and their peers. A young Mayan American who's in seventh grade tells me:

"I got bullied by one of my ex–best friends. I thought she was an actual friend, but . . . I stopped being her friend because she would always tease me and throw my lunch food. She would always bully me because I was a Maya. . . . Why do I look so dark, you know, and all this stuff. . . . And, I mean, to me it would be offensive because my mom always said if people bully you from where you are, they're probably jealous of you." The little girl then told me that, often, her younger sister also gets bullied in school.

When asked what advice she would give her younger sister on this topic, she says, "I mean, I would be like, 'Don't worry about it; you're a beautiful person. That's why you were born here. You were born here because you're a champion, and that you're really strong and that's why you are here.' " The little girl responds with words of wisdom you'd expect from a sixty-year-old, not a twelve-year-old.

True patriotism manifests itself in the most unexpected ways. As a kid, I was convinced it had to do with my ability to sing "The Star-Spangled Banner" and to perfectly recite the

Pledge of Allegiance. I was so off. Canton showed me that patriotism lies in the way you wear your *traje* with pride; it's in the way you choose to break silence and the way you tell your sister she belongs; it's in how you persevere in the face of biases and keep your head up high, at all times. That kind of patriotism doesn't waver. It doesn't change behind closed doors or in front of different-colored flags. It's grounded. It's real. It always stays true to itself. And that's because these young Mayans, like many Latinx across this country, are choosing not to be defined by single borders, identities, and languages. They can be everything at once.

That's America at its purest. And I found it in the most unexpected corner of the country.

FINDING FAITH IN SOUTH CAROLINA

As I drive away from Canton, I head to the Atlanta airport. This time I'm on my way to Greenville, South Carolina. Dr. LeBaron has urged me to meet the large Mayan community that lives there.

On the airplane, I'm instantly reminded of how deeply entrenched and present racism is among us. Before we even take off, the only black man in the entire plane is forcefully escorted off our flight owing to passengers' complaints about his alleged erratic behavior. Although he was apparently drunk, he certainly didn't seem to be bothering anyone. At least I didn't think so. On his way out of the plane, the man keeps yelling at us, "Y'all with Trump!" to which many people in the aircraft respond with, "That's right!" and nod proudly.

As this is taking place, I immediately text my friend

Denise Horn about the incident: "Girl, you'll never believe what just happened."

How naive can I be, though? Of course she can imagine this.

Denise simply texts back with: "Sis, I hated driving past the cotton fields in South Carolina. I was like 'Damn; my ancestors were there.'"

Welcome to Greenville, to the other foothills of the Blue Ridge Mountains.

Downtown Greenville is exactly what I pictured. A cute little main street, students frolicking around, families in line to get ice cream at the local store, and bars full of people watching football. A scene so seemingly unfazed by Greenville's deep-set racial divisions and its legacy with slavery—as Denise reminded me—that it almost fools me into thinking I'm inside a picturesque American postcard. The American illusion is very real, especially around this part of town. Because those I don't really see walking around me are the black and brown faces of the city—a community that's been pushed out of its own space.

Part of me wants to ask one of these preppy local pedestrians: "Hey, do you know where the Mayan community is congregating today?" But I know they'd probably look at me as though I'm crazy.

"Mayans, *here*?" they'd ask.

I drive across town, toward the fringes of the city, to introduce myself to the Mayan community there. My contact, Gilberto, is in his early thirties. He migrated years ago from Guatemala, and he's now a father and an employee at McDonald's. I finally arrive at the church where I am to meet him; it is said to be one of the first officially recognized Cath-

Mayans after Sunday church in Greenville, South Carolina.

olic churches started by the Mayans in the United States. When we think of Mayans, we don't necessarily associate the community with Western faiths—but Catholicism was enforced by the Spanish invaders. Now there's a large segment of the Mayan population that has managed to push the boundaries of religion as we know it, integrating spiritual indigenous beliefs *with* Christianity.

As I enter the church, I remember my talk with Dr. LeBaron about faith. During our conversation he recalled that a Mayan leader once told him, "I don't know why Christians just have to go to church to see God. God's everywhere. Go outside!"

That's the power of Mayan faith: it's limitless. And it means that God doesn't have to look or feel *one* way.

"I'll find you when mass is over," Gilberto tells me. Today's mass, he mentions, is in honor of San Miguel Archangel.

The churchgoers, some of whom speak Spanish and

many of whom speak Q'anjob'al, recite, *"Ángel de la Guarda, dulce compañía . . ."*

When I look up, I see four young Mayan women walking down the aisles. Outside this building, they look like ordinary American teenagers—wearing braces and blue jeans and holding their cell phones. But inside this church, these girls are dressed in their ceremonial *trajes*, each wearing crowns that represent different Mayan princesses. Princesses who carry the legacy of female warriors from the ancient Mayan civilization, who symbolize the culture of Guatemalan towns, and who honor indigenous blood.

As the mass ends, families exit the building and make their way to a fire ceremony that's taking place just outside the church. For Mayans, fire is just one of many manifestations of God. The smoke that comes out of the pit is used to cleanse, heal, and protect people. It's used to ascend one's

Mayans after Sunday church in Greenville, South Carolina, commemorating Saint Michael the Archangel.

spiritual life. Ashes waft on the wind. Mayan faith is not confined by any churches, scriptures, prayers, or summer camps. Faith follows the community members everywhere they go. It stays with them and lives within them. And *that* type of faith is the one that belongs in that picturesque American postcard.

Finally, I see Gilberto from afar. I thought I had lost him after mass. The first thing he tells me is, "Everything you saw in mass has a meaning. The clothes, the *huipil,* the crown. *Everything* has a meaning."

I immediately note to Gilberto that South Carolina is considered one of the most religious states in the country. In fact, *U.S. News & World Report* has it ranked as the sixth most religious state. According to the Pew Research Center, 74 percent of adults living in South Carolina say they are "absolutely certain" they believe in God, and 70 percent say religion plays a "very important" role in their lives. Gilberto could very well be part of those statistics and that narrative. But I wonder if Greenville locals would have trouble associating Mayan culture with Christianity and the type of faith they practice.

I ask Gilberto, "What are the differences and similarities between the way *you* practice faith and the way others do?"

Gilberto explains that, unlike popular belief, his Mayan community isn't a sect. "We are part of the Catholic Church, but with a different character," he clarifies. He tells me that Mayan philosophy migrated to the United States the same way his community did. "To a certain extent, we've simply conserved it. We've adapted certain things to mass and prayers, *our* way," he says. *"A nuestra manera."*

But it's the way Gilberto talks about the intangible that

really catches my attention. He describes what an outsider's eyes cannot see. "For us, when we pray or when we communicate with God, it's like having him in front of us. The same way I'm talking to you right now," he says while he points at me. "*That's* how we talk to God. *Everything* has his essence. It takes on a poetic form. Listen to this," he tells me. Gilberto slowly utters, "*¡Ay, Dios!*" in a serene, magnetic tone. It sounds as if he's singing a ballad. Almost like a song of love.

"You *see?*" He looks at me with a smile. "You can say it in a poetic way. Even though our kids may not understand the prayers in the Mayan language, the presence of God is felt."

In front of the Mayans, I feel history in a way I never have before. All of this speaks to the power behind this faith: it transcends.

"Let's take a walk in the park," Gilberto says.

We drive over to a big, beautiful park close by. Gilberto and his children and I start walking around the loop. As we're strolling, Gilberto abruptly stops. "*This* right here, where we are standing right now: this is our motherland. That's who feeds us. So, we also ask for her permission, and we apologize for all the harm we've caused, for all the disaster we've produced. Because our Mother Nature is the one that gives us life," he says. We then keep walking, and he adds, "We believe that land is our mother and that we must protect her, not exploit her."

Around us, I see other families and kids walking, their English contrasting with the Q'anjob'al Gilberto is speaking to his little ones. As we walk along, Gilberto looks at them and says, "They haven't gotten it right. They think nature is a product that can be exploited and from which richness can be extracted." Again, Gilberto's poetic manner has a way of brightening everything he touches. We continue our walk, with trees lining up by our side, shading us from the hot South Carolina sun. The sun is a symbol that's ingrained throughout Mayan culture, carved on altars and pyramids.

Gilberto looks up to the rays and says, "The sun is the first thing we salute. He's the first one that illuminated every human." He then glances over to the trees, all lustrously sitting under this light, and proceeds to tell me that each time Mayans have to cut down a tree, they ask for permission. "And you're *never* supposed to cut down a tree all at once. . . . You're supposed to cut it down in days and by pieces," he says.

Gilberto explains that if you cut a tree as a whole, steam emerges from within the trunk. The steam, like smoke, flows out and disperses into the surface. "*That's* the heart of the tree," he says. "It means the heart is dying."

Part of this entire journey with the Mayan community— from the U.S.-Mexican border to here in the South—has meant recognizing that their relentless drive to survive stems, partly, from *not* fearing death. Because at the end of the day, they see life when all others can see is death.

By the end of our stroll, as Gilberto's kids are running and playing with one another—now way ahead of us—he brings up a term in Q'anjob'al: *k'exel*. As Gilberto goes on to explain, *k'exel* refers to the idea that when humans physically perish, their traits don't leave the earth. They manifest in that person's descendants, so they live in their kids or their grandkids. Say if your grandfather was a doctor and he passed, the *k'exel* he leaves behind will lead *you* to be naturally gifted in the field of medicine. Consequently, the one

Gilberto and his kids, or his *k'exel,* in the park in Greenville, South Carolina.

you leave behind will lead your kids to *also* have that skill set. In other words, your spirit never really dies. It carries on.

Gilberto then looks at his kids and says, "It's probable that our ancestors are speaking for them. They will eventually come back through them, and they will be able to reclaim these lands."

Reclaim what is theirs, is what he means.

In the way Gilberto is staring at his children, I see the same gaze I saw inside the theater in Canton: the look of parents who are waiting for the next generation to set them free. Gilberto keeps pointing toward his young brown children: "*They* will identify as Mayans," he says, "as members of the original peoples, the native peoples. *They* will be our voices. They will be our messengers. That is the hope. They are our *k'exel,* so this never ends." Gilberto smiles.

As we head toward the parking lot and get ready to go back, we once again cross paths with several families, all of them white. They could have easily been one of the families I saw when I was walking around downtown Greenville. The picturesque ones. The postcard "American" ones. So, I turn to Gilberto and ask him if he's ever experienced racism.

"I can tell in their eyes, with their looks," he responds.

If only their eyes locked for just a few more seconds, these white people may have been able to recognize something that felt oddly familiar between them and Gilberto: faith. Like the patriotism I felt in Georgia, this type of faith also does not waver. It's steady and reliable, and it doesn't discriminate against skin color. If only these families were to look deeper into the history of these lands that surround them, they'd know that Gilberto belongs in the South just as much as they do.

On my drive out of Greenville, I roll down the window and let the air come in. From this view, the landscape loses all the labels society has imposed upon it. It's not "borders," or "national parks," or "towns," or "forests"—it's just massive lots of continuous land. Miles and miles of dust, grass, hills, and nature. I think back to a conversation I had with Lucia, a young Mayan woman I met in Canton. I asked her if she missed Guatemala. She told me, "Here, Maya people feel like they're in their hometown. We're surrounded by mountains and forests." It's a somewhat similar answer to what Gilberto told me about Greenville. He immediately referenced the trees: "There are trees here!" he said with excitement.

And it dawns on me during this drive that these landscapes must in fact *feel* like home to them because they're the same leaves, soil, and cliffs their ancestors were stepping on long before this continent was even discovered.

As I continue my drive by the Blue Ridge Mountains, I can hear Gilberto's voice again: "Being Maya is not a saying; it's a feeling."

His statement forces me to really think about my own views on faith and patriotism. Had I ever *felt* "American"? Did *I* even identify as such? I decide to go south, down the I-95 highway toward the city of my birth, Miami, to start finding answers to these questions.

7

Ground Zero

After spending much of my childhood in Madrid, I moved to Miami to finish my last two years of high school there. And when my classmates and I graduated from high school in Miami, we were doing something many before us hadn't done: we *left* the bubble. We took off while many of our parents and grandparents remained anchored. And I *really* left that time. I decided to root my life in the Northeast and saw Miami as nothing more than a vacation spot and the place I'd go to for family visits. It's almost as if I felt some form of resentment toward the city that gave birth to me, some kind of anger—perhaps irrational—for making me see the world *and* myself in such a one-dimensional way. In my eyes, Miami created an inaccurate representation of what the rest of the United States looked like. And, consequently, of what I looked like to the rest of the country.

After I left, I was so far removed from Miami that I lost touch not just with my old high school friends but also with some of my beloved Cuban cousins.

I came back to Miami only to visit. Usually, when I'm

down there, I zigzag through the city as if I'm on a mission—going from point A to point B, or from my mom's house to my dad's house, without any spare time to deviate from my route. But this time, as I drive through Coconut Grove and pass by my old high school, I roll down the window and let the heat creep its way into the car. Just like old times, Y100 is blasting on the radio, massive banyan trees concealing rays of light, zipping through the warm breeze of the ocean that fools you into believing it's summer any time of the year. To the far right, I spot young girls with their school uniforms and backpacks marching their way back through the school gates. That was me years ago. So perfectly secluded inside devious beauty.

To leave and come back home is such a strange feeling. There's a sensation of feeling completely changed in every way but still capable of falling right back where you left off years ago. Yet Miami feels different this time because its people have changed. We left and changed.

On that car ride, I wonder: What was it like for my high school friends and Cuban cousins to leave Miami years ago? For those who had the opportunity to go to college outside Miami, what was their experience like? Did they start questioning their identity, as I did? Were they, too, faced with myriad questions about what their background and nationalities meant, *outside* the "Miami bubble"? In a place where more than 70 percent of the population is Latino, with Cubans making up over half that number, it's somewhat shocking when you realize that the rest of the country looks, sounds, and feels absolutely nothing like the environment you grew up in. If you grow up thinking that speaking Spanish is the norm and that being from Cuba or Colombia is way more common than being from Ohio or Tennessee, then it's a strange feeling when you realize that's not exactly the case in the rest of the country. That's the "Miami bubble."

It had been years since I last talked to some of my high school friends, so I decided to reach out and get a big group together to talk through our collective experiences. The first question I ask is the question I could never really answer myself when I was in Miami: "How did you identify when you were growing up here?"

Perhaps the reality is that we never really *had* to answer that question as teenagers. Part of the privilege of living in Miami is that as a Latino you don't really need to explain who you are. You simply belong. That's why, looking back, I realize that I never really gave much thought to my identity as a Latina. Sometimes I would say I was Mexican, other times Cuban, other times that I was from Miami. I was a little bit of everything and fully nothing at the same time.

Terry Vazquez, from my high school graduating class, tells me that her parents used to tell her, "You're not Latina. You're not Hispanic. You're Cuban!" Terry tells me that even though she was born in the United States, she never called herself "American."

"I never said it, because we weren't here on purpose. We were here because we were forced to be here," Terry says.

Our Cuban families, forever visitors of this land: I can relate to that.

My cousins David and Katrina, who have always been tied at the hip, interestingly give me two different answers. David says, "Everybody else told me I was white. I wasn't black. I wasn't brown. I didn't fit in with them."

Katrina, on the other hand, firmly recounts, "I was raised Latina. I was taught as a Latina."

Cuban. White. Latina. So far, three different answers to a simple question: How did you identify?

Next, I ask them the question I'm really dying to know: "But, what happened when you left the Miami bubble?" When those words come out of my mouth, everyone releases a small, nervous laugh. Here's how they respond:

David, my Cuban cousin: "It was freshman year in Tallahassee. It was a culture shock, to say the least. It was there the first time that somebody was racist towards me. . . . In that moment, I said, 'Ohh . . . this is it.'"

Cristina, from Panama: "They'd ask me if I spoke Mexican."

Laura, from Cuba: "In my circle of friends in New York, I became the brownest of my friends."

Terry, from Cuba: "They'd say, 'You're Cuban, right? Why are you so white if you're from Cuba?'"

Luisa, from Colombia: "People didn't know how to spell 'Colombia.'" [It's Colombia, not Columbia.]

Katia, from Nicaragua: "In New York, that was the first time someone said, 'I wanna call you little mama.'"

Katrina, my Cuban cousin, gives me the flip side: "When I got to college, I met a lot of people who were coming from other Latin American countries. And they told me, 'You're American. You're not Hispanic.' I was brought up with people telling me I was Latina, and then they told me, '*No*, you're not.' "

Again, multiple answers to that question, but one clear underlying theme among all of us: We were *never* what Miami told us we were. We realized, once we left, that we were someone else.

I have one last question for the Cubans in the group. As we were growing up in this city, "being a Republican" went hand in hand with "being Cuban." That's the party that consecutively won the heart and the trust of the Cuban exile community, especially after President John F. Kennedy's failed Bay of Pigs invasion. So I ask: "Did you ever depart from that conservative Cuban mentality? Or did you stick with it?"

The first thing my cousin David says is, "Castro was Voldemort." That's exactly what most of us who grew up around here were raised to believe. Many young Cuban Americans were expected to follow their family's conservative voting record. Yet the election of Barack Obama shed light on the beginning of a generational divide that started erupting among us: it was the *first time* in history that a Democratic presidential candidate had won the Cuban vote in Florida, and that was, in great part, due to the younger voices that slowly started forming opinions of their own, memories and histories of their own. Seeing not just the past but the present that unfolded among us every day.

When I pose that question, my cousin Katrina tells me that although she considers herself an Independent—which falls in line with the political voting trend among many younger Latinos—she still takes her Cuban grandmother's

Conservative Cubans put up this poster in downtown Miami: "No Socialismo, No Comunismo, Somos Capitalista."

opinion into consideration every time she casts her vote. David also recalls signing up to vote for the first time and feeling his grandmother's presence *everywhere.* "I felt my grandmother standing over my shoulder saying, 'Did you put Independent?! . . . No, no, put Republican!'" David goes on to explain: "Leaving Miami gave me an opportunity to find my own voice, to find what I liked, to find who I followed because I was no longer following my parents."

All of us needed to leave Miami in order to find *ourselves.*

Interestingly, every single person I talked to had returned to Miami for good. Once they left for college, found jobs in other states, and attempted to make a life elsewhere, they all eventually packed their bags and got a one-way ticket back home to Miami. And I don't know if they *see* what I'm seeing, but every single one of them came back changed. Terry, Cristina, Luisa, David, Katrina, Laura. Every single one of them *feels* different. Many left thinking they were white and came back realizing they were not. Left undefined, came back Latinx. Left loyal to the Republican Party, came back open to change. Left as a local and came back as an immigrant. Left extremely privileged and came back with renewed self-awareness.

In other words, all of us needed to *leave* Miami in order to *see* Miami. The *whole* Miami.

Because when *you* change, the city you come back to starts to look different. You start to see the things, the corners, and the people who were standing next to you *all this time* but were simply never part of the fantasy you grew up with.

THE NEW AMERICAN

"*Abuelo,* do you remember when you first became a U.S. citizen?" I ask my grandpa Carlos.

It was 1970 when he officially became a citizen. He laughs and immediately recounts one of his favorite anecdotes from that time. It has to do with his Cuban friend Mariano. Apparently, when Mariano took the U.S. citizenship exam, the examiner asked him if he could name a president of the twentieth century. "But Mariano, who was the person that *least* knew English in the world, thought that the examiner was asking him for twenty dollars as a form of bribery!" my grandpa says. "So, he put his hand in his pocket, took out a twenty-dollar bill, and gave it to the exam administrator. The administrator ended up accusing Mariano of bribery and suspended his exam. Years later, Mariano successfully passed. He died soon after," Grandpa says.

Every single immigrant has a memory about how they

or those around them became a U.S. citizen. Everyone remembers *something* about that day. My grandpa remembers Mariano's story. My Mexican dad remembers how he got his U.S. passport the same day he got his citizenship. The day after, my dad flew for the first time as an American citizen. He tells me with joy over the phone, *"Al día siguiente viajé como ciudadano de los Estados Unidos."* It's a feeling you must never forget: finally, legitimately, *belonging* in America (at least on paper). But the reality is that there are more individuals than you think who were born into citizenship but are just now uncovering what it feels like to be "an American." Many who are now finding themselves navigating an identity and a system that was theirs to begin with—by blood and *on* paper—but was never really theirs to belong *in*.

I'm talking about Puerto Ricans, a community that is as American as it gets. Puerto Rico has formally been a U.S. territory since 1898, but one that has often been ostracized, *otherized,* its residents treated as second-class citizens by the mainland. For example, nearly 50 percent of Americans do not even know Puerto Ricans are fellow citizens through their territory status. But if you're born an American, do you automatically feel like one? As they step onto the mainland, these are questions many young Boricuas are grappling with now. Approximately thirty thousand to fifty thousand Puerto Ricans moved to Florida after Hurricane Maria swept through the island, leaving nearly three thousand dead and unimaginable destruction in its wake.

So, I drive down to Florida International University (FIU) to talk to three Puerto Rican students. Two of them, Gabriel and Javier, are currently on campus taking undergraduate summer classes to make up for the semester they lost on the island owing to Hurricane Maria.

They are athletic, tall, serious, and poised. They feel present. Javier tells me he's studying biochemistry to be a veterinarian, and Gabriel says he's pursuing biology to become a doctor. Gabriela, the third student, has been on the mainland longer, and she's the president of the Puerto Rican Student Association. But I soon gather she's become much more than that title: she's the leader who's giving voice to the post-Maria students on campus. I can tell by the way Javier and Gabriel look at her and defer to her.

Like Javier and Gabriel, many others feel the same way, displaced but grappling at a new home. After the hurricane, roughly one thousand Puerto Rican college students transitioned to Florida public universities. And according to the Florida Department of Education, more than eleven thousand students from the island were enrolled in the state's public school districts by 2018. As Gabriela reminds me, the post-Maria migration was driven by youth. The mainland indeed has a younger face now.

Maria is deeply ingrained in their psyches, and the trauma informs the direction of their new steps. "I woke up to things I had never seen in my life," Gabriel tells me.

Javier remembers, after Maria struck Puerto Rico, the stress he felt as he was waiting in line for hours in the supermarket to get ice for his grandmother's insulin. "We needed to keep the insulin cold," he says. They both tell me about the eight-to-ten-hour-long lines to get gas, about the way they waited for water, and about the giant posters people held up along the dirt roads. Some read, "We need help." Others, "People are killing themselves, help!" Those are memories

Gabriela, Gabriel, and Javier, all Puerto Rican students, at Florida International University's campus.

they cannot forget. As Gabriel and Javier tell me, the opportunity to come to Miami in 2018 after the hurricane offered mixed emotions—they felt immensely privileged to get to finish their studies but also had reservations about leaving their loved ones behind.

Neither one of them had been to Miami before. Like many people, they saw Miami as a vacation destination, not a place one actually *lived* in. "I've always been an extrovert, you know. I talk to people. But it was hard with the gringos, with the Americans," one of them tells me. Even Miami, the nation's mecca for Latinos, required them to assimilate. Eventually, Javier and Gabriel found their natural crew with their fellow Boricuas, as well as with a group of Venezuelan and Cuban students. But they are quick to tell me that there were several post-Maria students on campus who simply couldn't get used to life on the mainland and made their way back to the island. "They left because they couldn't assimilate . . . they couldn't stand being alone."

When I ask the boys about their recent visits back to Puerto Rico, their eyes light up.

"Every time I go back to Puerto Rico to visit, I don't want to leave the island, but I come back," Javier tells me. "It gets easier every time."

"Is your intention to return to the island? To go back? Or is Miami home now?" I ask.

There's silence in the room when I ask that question. No one can give me a straight answer. "Yes . . . No . . . Maybe . . . ?" And that in itself is the answer: Miami was becoming a place they called home. Even if it's reluctantly.

"It gets easier every time," they say again.

There's something even more significant about that answer. For example, unlike the majority of Cubans and Venezuelans currently in Miami, people who are fleeing political unrest and violence, many Boricuas like Javier and Gabriel *do* have the option to go back to their island and settle down. In a way, that door is still left open for them. But who they are in Miami is shifting into much more than just "post-Maria students." They are becoming much more than labels defined by pain, trauma, and natural disasters. They are, in effect—unwittingly or not—reclaiming their title as "Americans" and using that voice to include Puerto Rico in the American narrative, recognizing that the best way to love their island—to fight for their beloved Boricuas—is by being active members of America's mainland. By becoming *present*, visible, and seen. No longer victims of a hurricane but, now, advocates of their people.

"In order to be able to represent our power in Puerto

Rico, and the best interests of the island, we have to represent ourselves here. If we don't—if we don't strengthen the
diaspora—then we won't have the power to help the island.
That's the link we need to strengthen," Gabriela tells me.

As she says this, Javier and Gabriel are nodding their
heads, still looking at Gabriela with admiration. It *must* be
admiration, because Gabriela has helped them both uncover
the unique power they hold in Miami. As Javier recalls, it was
Gabriela who pushed him to acknowledge how important
his vote was in the United States. "Your voice in Puerto Rico
almost doesn't count," she'd remind him. (Since Puerto Rico
is not considered a state, Boricuas on the island *don't* have
a right to vote in presidential or congressional elections.)
Eventually, Javier changed his voter registration to Florida.

"I said to myself, You know what? I'm going to vote here,
because at the end of the day, if I can motivate other people
like me, we can make our interests heard. So many of us are
here after the hurricane that we can force politicians to take
us into consideration," Javier tells me.

"We represent the people on the island," Gabriela affirms.

There are thousands of young people who were forced to
come, then stayed and are now swapping their voter registra-
tions. At least, thanks to the efforts Gabriela has put in place,
they are contemplating that change. And this shift is much
more powerful than you may think, because it's a proclama-
tion of belonging. Of a right, a presence, and a status Puerto
Ricans were always entitled to. Since birth.

I ask, "How do people see you?"

"Well, we are part of the United States, right? But, at the
same time, American society doesn't see us that same way.
They look at us like strangers," Gabriela responds. She tells

me that there have been many times where people have asked her if Puerto Rico is part of Mexico. "So, you're Mexican, right?" is something that she's heard quite a bit.

"It's so weird to me that Americans don't know their own history," Gabriela tells me.

This is a new generation of post-Maria Boricuas who are seizing this opportunity to be *seen*.

To change the face of what this nation's citizens have always believed was "American."

In this battleground state, young Puerto Ricans have amassed new voting power. Although Florida has always had the largest community of Puerto Ricans outside of the island, Puerto Ricans in the state have traditionally shown lower voter turnout than other Latino groups. That pattern may start to change with people like Gabriela, Javier, and Gabriel, though. Their power lies not just in their numbers but in the message they are trying to send with every new voter's registration and ballot cast: they matter as much as any American; their island matters. And from what I've seen on this journey, that determination to turn tragedy into hope is an overarching characteristic of the Latinx community.

Before I leave the school, Gabriela has one more thing to tell me: "I'm running for office." She then immediately clarifies that she won't be running on the island. She's running on the mainland, in Florida. And, I suspect, people like Javier and Gabriel will be knocking on our doors for votes.

THE NEW VOTER

"Dad, do you remember the very first time you got to vote in the U.S.? What did it feel like?" I ask.

"It's the first time I felt one hundred percent American," he responds. He remembers how badly he wanted to vote in person that day. He wanted the whole experience. To stand in line, to touch the machine, and to cast his ballot. But because of his travel schedule, he had to do it by mail. He reminds me that it was an important first vote for him. "The U.S. was coming out of two wars."

Soon, more people in Florida will get to feel this, too. Not just Boricuas like Javier, Gabriel, and Gabriela but also thousands of formerly incarcerated people across the state who will be able to use their right to vote, many for the first time in their lives. Florida used to be one of the few states in the country that kept individuals with felony records from regaining their voting rights after they'd served their sentence. It was the culmination of post–Civil War efforts that sought to enact felony disenfranchisement laws to continue silencing the voices of people of color. But thanks to the work of activists, there was a ballot initiative in Florida during the 2018 midterms to reverse felony disenfranchisement and automatically restore voting rights after incarceration. Florida's Amendment 4 was not only approved but passed overwhelmingly with nearly 65 percent of the vote, repealing that 150-year-old statute that had permanently denied felons their civil right. As a result, approximately 1.4 million people with felony records in Florida are now eligible to vote. Yet, as I write these words, there are fervent GOP efforts in place to revoke that eligibility.

Angel Sanchez is one of those former 1.4 million felons with a new voice and newfound dignity. He's a millennial, has a Cuban dad and a Venezuelan mom, and grew up in Miami.

Angel in downtown Miami, by Brickell Avenue.

I first meet Angel in Miami's swanky neighborhood of Brickell—surrounded by fancy condos, bougie cars, and hip coffee shops with tall glass walls. Angel, who looks like an actual angel, has a clean-cut shave; he's wearing white jeans and an orange shirt, perfectly blending into Miami's elite.

We talk for what feels like hours. I ask him, midway through our conversation:

"Angel, what's going on in your mind right now?"

Angel looks around us. He looks left and right. Staring at the pedestrians who are walking by us.

"I'm thinking, how many of them would believe that I'm a convicted felon, that I did twelve years in prison?" he says.

He continues to look around at people—that couple making their way to their apartment, that girl walking her puppy on the street, or that guy who just zoomed by us in his Mercedes. "I'm the person you fear," he says calmly. "I think my ability to be here and be *just* as normal as anybody else serves as an example—as an ambassador for others that are locked up—that, if given the opportunity, they could be here and be just as normal as anybody else."

At one point during our conversation, Angel starts waving his arms at someone who just recognized him. I ask who it is, and he tells me that it's one of his law school classmates. Angel is a law student at the University of Miami, one of the state's best colleges. As far removed as he was from this Brickell neighborhood during his upbringing, it's now a place that's not uncommon for Angel to frequent during the weekends when he goes out with his school buddies or hangs out in one of their fancy condos.

I ask him if he feels like he's part of the "club" now, Miami's cliquey bubble so many get sucked into. "Yeah, and sometimes I feel survivor's guilt," he says. But there's one thing Angel does that's unusual to see around here, especially among flashy streets like these: he *always* tells you who he is; he always stays true to himself.

Every time Angel introduces himself, he says, "I was born in Miami; I grew up in prison; I went to school in Orlando; and now I'm back in Miami to go to law school." He intentionally wants you to hear the word "prison" in that sentence to ensure that any and every stereotype you ever had about felons is immediately shattered. "That way there's no doubt about my story," Angel affirms.

It's *that* introduction—that intentional insertion of the word "prison" among ordinary nouns, verbs, and pronouns—that is creating change in Miami, giving people a second chance to prove that they belong to these sunny streets and not behind bars. But that requires having faith in yourself, and that's something Angel didn't always carry, *especially* when the system was betting against him.

The Miami neighborhood of Little Havana, where Angel grew up, has provided many Cuban exiles with a sense of faith for years. The bulk of life in that neighborhood has been concentrated on 8th Street, the famous Calle Ocho. There, countless Cubans have found corners, cafés, and sights and smells—enveloped in nostalgia—that gave the community members enough reasons to believe they could, one day, go back to their island. It was a type of faith that convinced people that something *better* was in store for them—a faith not in a God or in any higher being but always in themselves. In their ability to carry on. Yet while those streets in Little Havana brought so much joy to many, they are also the streets that sentenced Angel to jail.

Angel didn't grow up with that type of faith in the future. He was brought up on 10th Street, just two blocks away from Calle Ocho. While Miamians may have known the neighborhood as "Little Havana," he corrects me and tells me that it was more common for locals to nickname it "Little Managua." As Angel says, in the 1980s, the Contra revolution erupted in Nicaragua, and many Nicaraguans ended up rebuilding their lives in Miami's Little Havana. When Angel was a teenager, most of his neighborhood friends were boys with single mothers who came from low-income families like his. Families that worked hard to make ends meet. But slowly, through the years, "neighborhood" was coined "hood" by the system and "friends" were labeled "gang members" by the police. Tags, ironically, that actually gave these teenagers more pride, belonging, and self-worth than anything else ever had. A type of status they yearned for.

As Angel says, when you're treated like a gang member, you act like a gang member. When you're met with aggression, you react with violence. And when you're told you're "nobody," you believe it. Especially when no one around you is there to tell you otherwise.

"We started doing everything that gangs did," Angel recalls. As he tells me, he remembers trading Super Nintendos for guns, being celebrated by his friends for every gunshot he'd fired, and getting street cred every time he was arrested by the police. "I started becoming what they were saying I was: the worst of the worst," he states. Slowly, even though Angel was still a minor, coming in and out of jail and getting tried as an adult became his norm. One of the times that he was out of prison, Angel got rearrested for an armed robbery. That time, he ended up being sentenced to thirty years in prison. When Angel says this to me, he has a calm voice, as though it were always part of his plan.

And it's interesting how people can find their identity in Miami. Pride takes on many different forms in this city. For example, Angel—confined to thirty years behind bars and far removed from freedom—eventually came face-to-face with a different part of himself he wasn't able to see outside of prison bars. He found pride and strength *inside* there. And that's the thing about identity: if you do find it, it gives you purpose.

"It was one of the first times that I felt so proud of being Latino," he says with a smile, "because Latinos had respect in prison." Being Latino took on a different meaning for Angel.

He tells me that one of the first things other inmates would ask him when he got to his prison cell was, "You talk Spanish?" or, "*¿Tú eres Latino?*" Questions that immediately signaled camaraderie among them. That's also what drove Angel's interest into his own community's history, leading him to learn about colonialism, indigenous communities, and his Cuban and Venezuelan roots.

"It was there, for the first time, where I started realizing that I wasn't a menace to society," Angel tells me. "That I wasn't the scum of the earth—but a product of my environment—and that I had a lot to be proud of."

And what happened when he found pride? Angel's not the only one who changed. The city, too, changed *with* him. Although Angel was released before his thirty-year sentence concluded, he still spent twelve years in prison. As soon as he got out, Angel knew there was *one* thing that he needed to avoid: going back to Miami. Under *no* circumstances would he return to 10th Street, those troubled blocks that tore his future apart. Tenth Street was crossed out, just like an ex-girlfriend. With his eyes set on starting a new chapter and searching that call to justice he found in prison, Angel ended up spending four years in Orlando, and not once did he look back at his hometown of Miami. However, Angel was recently presented with an unexpected opportunity to intern for a judge and go to law school at the University of Miami, something he simply couldn't decline. As he tells me, Angel tried looking for housing everywhere around Miami—tiptoeing his way around 10th Street and Little Havana. He tried everything possible to avoid those streets—yet he'd continuously get turned down by skeptical landlords who'd zone in on Angel's criminal record.

So, I ask: "Where did you end up landing?"

He laughs. "Tenth Street," he says.

He tells me that 10th Street was the *only* place in Miami that took him back. "I would have never imagined not only going back to Miami but going back to the blocks where I had been incarcerated," he says. "Out of all places. And just like me, that place has completely changed."

I ask him what type of change he notices around Little Havana these days. Angel tells me that he sees fewer people hanging out on the streets, which is an indication that there are other places for them to be in. He notices more after-school programs and fewer opportunities for kids to trade Nintendos for guns. He sees change. But, unbeknownst to him, the *real* change 10th Street is experiencing is Angel's return to his old block. A return that is defying the odds and paving the way to a brighter future for everyone who's following in Angel's footsteps. Among many things, Angel is committed to restoring faith in his community—and that starts with understanding that he has a voice to make change. Angel was one of the activists who fought for the passage of Amendment 4, which gave formerly incarcerated individuals like him the power to vote.

So I ask Angel a question similar to the one I asked my dad earlier: "Do you remember the first time you registered to vote?"

His eyes get watery.

Angel responds, "Wow, most people wait till they're eighteen to register to vote for the first time. I had to wait till I was thirty-six, you know? I had to wait twice as long." He continues, "In this time, I learned how to mobilize. I learned how to advocate. I learned how to organize. I learned how to research. I learned the history of this whole thing, and now I appreciate it much more. Now, I'm going to make my vote count. So, it's very special to me."

After we say good-bye, Angel picks up his Lyft scooter and zooms out of Brickell.

(REDISCOVERING) HOME

Windows still rolled down, tropical heat still creeping in, volume all the way up—another thing that immediately strikes me during this drive is just how elitist Miami's Cuban-exile community had been. Almost like an exclusive boys' club. Without a doubt one of the bravest and most hardworking groups I have ever known, but also one whose status, success, and recognition were very much determined by the lightness of our skin. I think back to my trip to Cuba in January 2014. Walking up and down La Habana Vieja, crossing paths with people who were so many different beautiful shades of black and brown. They, too, were the people who made up the island that consumed our stories all these years. They, too, were people of Cuba. But where were the Afro-Cubans in the Miami I grew up in?

"We're trying to paint this picture of something that actually isn't realistic," Leyanis Diaz, an Afro-Cuban from Miami, tells me. "Cubans come in all shapes, colors, sizes, and I don't really feel like the population in Miami is actually reflective of that." For instance, a lot of people are surprised to hear about the Chinese Cuban community. Albeit dwindling, they are present. In the mid-1800s, more than

Afro-Cuban man hanging out in Miami's Little Havana.

one hundred thousand Chinese, mostly men, were brought to Cuba to work as laborers in sugarcane fields. It is said that at one point Havana had the largest Chinatown in Latin America. Today there are approximately 114,000 Cubans with Chinese ancestors living on the island. So, yes, Cubans can look many different ways.

Leyanis, for example, is a millennial who was born in Cuba and came to Miami when she was three years old. I should really introduce her by saying that Leyanis was "Miss Black Florida USA" in 2017, a telling title that captures a snippet of her journey in Miami: it was black people, not necessarily Latinos, who embraced her first. And while it took me eighteen years and a move away from Miami to face basic questions about my identity, Leyanis had to look no farther than this city to face an ugly reality.

As she tells me, when she was in elementary school, one of her classmates came up to her and asked, "Where are you from?"

She said, "I'm a Cuban."

"I've never seen a black Cuban before," the boy responded.

Leyanis recalls being shocked by that response. To be honest, that little boy's impulsive reaction could have been mine. He was merely speaking to an image that contradicted the whitewashed face of the Cuban diaspora many of us grew up with. An image that assured those with light skin that they belonged and told Leyanis she did *not*. Leyanis says that soon after that experience she started alienating herself from her culture and thought to herself, I'm done with this. I don't want to be Cuban anymore because no one thinks I'm Cuban anyway.

By the time Leyanis went to high school, she was able to find pride again. Through conversations with her mom and grandmother and through her own research, Leyanis found power in her history and beauty in her Afro-Latinidad. Yet self-love, as we know, doesn't necessarily translate into public approval. *Especially* when it comes to standards of beauty. For years, Miami has set the tone on what "Latina beauty" means, sexualizing fair-skinned skinny women with, *con perdón,* big busts, lots of makeup, and superhigh heels. That's why, as Leyanis began her journey in Miss Florida's beauty pageant system, she always felt out of place. Leyanis tells me that often she would be the only black person competing and would find herself straightening her naturally curly hair to assimilate with the other women.

"I think there was always this *hush* to kind of look less black than what you actually were," she says. Leyanis *kept* competing in the contests and *kept* losing by one or two points. She was great, but not great *enough* in their eyes; talented, but not talented *enough;* beautiful, but not beautiful *enough* for them. Always one or two points behind that woman with lighter skin, lighter hair, and looser curls. It was a struggle she knew all too well. Growing up in Miami, she was either too black to be Latina or too Latina to be black.

Until one day it hit Leyanis that she simply wasn't competing in the right beauty pageant. Instead of giving up, Leyanis tells me, she entered the Miss Black USA system, a platform that felt way more open and inclusive of women of color. A platform that allowed Leyanis to disrupt beauty standards, binaries, and biases, leading her to become the *first* Latina ever to win the Miss Black Florida USA title. She earned that crown—not with straight hair or with *one* identity but with natural curls that found force in *two* identities: black *and* Latina.

Even though Leyanis and I didn't go through the same struggles when we were growing up, I assumed there was one thing we truly had in common: Castro. At the end of the day, there's often one stereotype that's true around this town: if you're a Miami Cuban, chances are you despise Fidel Castro. As my cousin David said, "Castro was Voldemort."

Or was this image accentuated by the bubble I had grown up in, which cast all Miami Cubans as anti-Castro? As an Afro-Cuban, did Leyanis feel differently? I didn't see Leyanis on the streets of Little Havana cheering with the crowd on November 25, 2016, the day of Castro's death. It felt as if almost all of Miami were out on the streets that day. Hundreds and hundreds of people gathered outside the Versailles Restaurant, marching through the streets with tears running down their faces. Tears of resentment for the years that were lost outside the island, tears of vengeance for the abuse of human rights, and tears of joy for thinking that freedom for Cubans was an inch closer.

I didn't see Leyanis that night because she wasn't there. Yes, she saw Castro as a dictator and a tyrant, but she also saw another side of him that many of us refused to acknowledge or even see. "The way black Cubans see Fidel is a lot more positive than white Cubans do," Leyanis tells me. "And that just goes back to history."

As Mark Sawyer, a professor of political science and African American studies at UCLA, put it during an NPR interview, "I think we need to look at Castro's mistakes of not allowing black pressure groups, not pursuing more rigid antidiscrimination policies, as failures, but that he came as close as anybody has ever come to eliminating racial inequality in a place that had had plantation slavery." That's *it*: for many, Fidel came as close as anyone had ever come to fighting for racial disparities on the island, and *that*, in and of itself, meant his death carried various legacies, not just the one-dimensional one I had grown up with. Those legacies meant that, understandably, people would have different reactions to his passing, including celebrating *and* mourning his death and everything in between. "Fidel was not perfect . . . but I think what he did for black Cubans may not be a lot, but they're able to eat, able to have homes, and at least have access to basic life necessities."

With a heavy feeling of betrayal toward my own family, I do see Leyanis's point. It's not a matter of agreeing or disagreeing with her. It's *her* truth, *her* lived experience, and *her* reality in *her* skin. It's a recognition that not even a villain like Fidel Castro was ever so black and white in Miami.

After I finish my conversation with Leyanis, I get back in the car and continue my drive. I now start noticing a tale of two cities in the city of Miami. I see a city filled with hypocrisies. A city fueled by immigrants, yet one that rejects its sanctuary status; a city full of wealth, yet one with the nation's highest income inequalities; a city governed by Cubans, yet one that raises the bar for other Latin Americans. But I also see a city full of new opportunities, ones capable of shifting the balance of power around it.

That's because I see, more than anything, a Miami where history is repeating itself. Where the same cycles our families went through generations ago—the fleeing, the trauma, the starting over—are still taking place. This time, however, the story doesn't have just one protagonist. There are many. It's not just the Cuban exiles anymore. There are the Puerto Ricans who are building new futures after Hurricane Maria and the Venezuelans who are escaping oppression. There are also the locals who were given second chances and the younger generation of Cuban Americans—like my high school friends—who came back to Miami completely changed. Together, these are the new Latinx voices rediscovering what it means to become an exile, a voter, an American, and giving a whole new meaning to it.

That's why this city is ground zero, because Miami's *ground* is changing—its land and its people are evolving. Part of finding Latinx in my travels is understanding that newfound identities also have the capacity to change the environments surrounding us. Through the Latinx movement, we're not just finding ourselves, we're rediscovering places, seeing them through a different lens of brown people as though we never saw them before.

THE NEW EXILE

With Castro's passing also came the death of dreams. Thousands of Cuban exiles realized that it was too late to go back to their beloved island. Too many years had gone by. But when one villain dies, new ones come to light. When illusions fade, new ones take over. And that's why the anti-Castro chants I grew up with are slowly dissolving into forceful anti-Maduro rallies.

Venezuelans are populating new enclaves of Miami's exile community. The Venezuelan story in Latin America has a tune similar to the Cuban novella, with a final chapter ending in socialism's triumph over the people's freedom. Hugo Chávez, Venezuela's former president, rose to power in 1999 with a promise of revolutionary change, restoring hope and turning a new page in history. He held on to that title for decades, with many analysts arguing that his populist platform—though liberal on paper—was also authoritarian in nature. Chávez did nationalize industries, heavily expanded his country's social programs, and uplifted the poor. But he also abused the state's power and violated basic human and civil rights. After Chávez died in 2013, his successor, Nicolás Maduro, assumed presidential powers and led the nation into an unprecedented crisis. Venezuela used to be a prosperous country, with the world's largest oil reserve, but it has now collapsed into a poor, dangerous, and chaotic state—one experiencing not just an economic crisis but a complete humanitarian emergency.

Venezuelan migration has been steadily increasing for years, even before Maduro took power. But since 2014, more than four million Venezuelans have fled the country, with approximately three hundred thousand of them fleeing to the United States. In Miami, there were about one hundred thousand Venezuelans at the time this book was written. Around town, it's common to hear people say that Venezuelans are the "new Cubans." Not only does their journey and pain evoke the Cuban experience but their voice in Miami is starting to feel present in every corner, organizing with every opportunity and *loud, loud, loud*. They are reminding us of the abuses that are happening on their *tierra*.

The Cuban diaspora Miami knows best was defined by unique historic protections. Cubans long benefited from the "wet foot, dry foot" policy, which granted asylum to pretty much any Cuban who touched U.S. soil. And although that rule was recently revoked, Cubans still face a shorter pathway to permanent residency than any other nationality through the 1966 Cuban Adjustment Act. In short, for years Cubans were the first in line to get citizenship and basic legal protections.

It's true that Venezuelans stand tall and vociferous in Miami, exuding the same type of confidence Cubans have for decades, but without the same protections, Venezuelans carry a fear that never really seeped into the streets of Little Havana—a fear of being removed from their land not *once* but twice. Not just from Venezuela but also from the United States. It's a fear of being told, "You don't belong here." The type of fear you may not notice in the anti-Maduro chants, the public rallies, or the headlines, but one that is changing the core of Miami's exile community into a humbler one.

"A hypocrisy Cubans live—and one that many Latinos live—is that unless it doesn't affect you, everything is an illusion," I'm told by Helene Villalonga, a Venezuelan activist in Miami. That's because her son, Juan, exemplifies the full range of emotions and legal limbos Venezuelan exiles can face in this country: one day he was taken in by the United States; the next day he was growing up like an American; the following day he was deported to a nation he barely knew; and finally he was granted asylum and U.S. citizenship. Juan had the very same dreams newly arrived Cubans often have in Miami. But he's the perfect reminder of the differences that exist between Cuban and Venezuelan exiles who dream: for Venezuelans, as opposed to many Cubans, illusions can die hard, even in Miami.

Juan's story begins the same way my grandparents' did: as a visitor to this country.

"The United States was a visit," his mom tells me. "It wasn't a place to settle in or for your kids to grow." Faced with violent threats under Chávez's regime, Helene and her loved ones were forced to flee Venezuela and seek temporary asylum in the United States. Yet plans of coming back to Venezuela were soon dashed, and their time in Miami quickly turned into an endless visit with no foreseeable return ticket. This city ended up becoming Juan's home—where he spent his teenage years and built his first memories. But Juan was exposed to Miami's subtle hypocrisy: he felt both at home and out of place. Both part of the "bubble" and out of it. Miami has an unparalleled way of charming Latinos, of luring one with its language and making one feel the same warmth that was once felt abroad—but Juan's immigration status served as a daily reminder that this city was never *his* to fully claim.

Juan and his mother, Helene, the new faces of Miami's growing exiles.

"Since we came here, I was never able to deepen my roots with this country, because I never felt secure with my status," Juan tells me.

By definition, Juan was as much of an exile as any of my Cuban family members were. But on paper, as he awaited to close his open case for political asylum, Juan's undocumented status was a reminder that he was still missing the legal stamp of approval to remain in the United States without fear. More than ten years after he moved to Miami with his mom as an eleven-year-old boy, Juan was stopped and arrested by a highway patrol officer as he was driving his way across the country to attend college in Canada, where Juan was offered access to several scholarship funds. During the drive, he tells me, he called his mom to say, "Mom, there's a cop behind me." Shortly after his arrest, Juan was sent to a corrections facility for six weeks, placed in an ICE detention center for three weeks and eventually deported on a plane back to a Venezuela he never knew, barely even recognized. When you ask him, Juan perfectly remembers that moment of his life with pain: he remembers reading more than twenty books in jail, writing more than 170 pages behind bars, feeling lost in Caracas's airport, and uncovering a deep resentment toward a president he'd once admired. "I supported President Obama, and getting deported during his administration is something that really frustrated me."

It's important to hear about these stories because these are the people who are walking around you on Miami's streets today. Young people, like Juan, who have already lost their countries more than once. He tells me, "First I lost my country when I became an exile at eleven years old, and then I lost it again when I was twenty-one. This [the United States] was my country in every single way a country belongs to a human.

"One of the things one loses first is identity," he continues. "Imagine growing up with an American mentality, with a feeling of freedom and independence and grit. And then coming back to a country where simply speaking English made me a target. People would stare at me."

When Juan was deported to Venezuela, he was supposed to stay there—separated from his family—for at least ten years. But thanks to his mother's tireless activism in Miami, Juan was granted asylum in the United States two years after his removal, and eventually returned to Miami in 2011. The incredible thing about Juan's journey is that after such a roller-coaster ride, he recently became a U.S. citizen. That final step toward citizenship is what eventually glued it all together for Juan, slowly picking up the broken pieces that were lost along his journey.

"And how do you feel now?" I follow up.

"Until two or three weeks ago when I actually became a U.S. citizen," he tells me, "I had never felt secure in *any* place."

Sometimes, it's easy to take security for granted. Many Cuban exiles who have lived in Miami for more than fifty years have lost touch with the fact that they, too, were once refugees struggling to find security. Juan's journey to citizenship was filled with uncertainty and fear that clouded over him for years. When you pick up all the broken pieces you come across in Miami, what springs from the traces of lingering insecurity, pain, fear, and trauma is a different profile of a new American citizen—one with courageous humility and a renewed sense of self. And when you line up all those pieces, you start seeing the image of the new Miami. All those pieces are what make Juan a different type of citizen— one who doesn't take his citizenship for granted.

Security is often a feeling we're all constantly searching for. When you actually feel it, it must mean you're done feeling like a visitor in your own land.

THE NEW GROUND ZERO

"Grandpa, do you remember the first time you touched land in Miami?" I ask.

"Your grandma took the ferry in February of 1961. She left Cuba crying, and she arrived in Miami crying. I, on the other hand, was very happy because I was going to reunite with your grandmother and your mom, as well as with my mother and siblings," he says. "I'll never forget that scene in the airport when your grandmother and I reunited. I got there September ninth, 1961. I was the happiest person on this entire earth. *Era la persona más feliz de la tierra.*"

The thing is, the Miami of sixty years ago is not the same one it is today. An important part of understanding the way Latinos in this country are changing is by paying attention to our environment, because it says a lot more about us than we may think. Subtleties such as how the sun shines, the wind blows, and the oceans rise impact how we live our lives. It's no coincidence that climate change has become one of the top concerns of Latino voters across the nation. Latinos tend to live and work in places that make them particularly vulnerable to the health and economic threats presented by climate change. The majority of Latinos live in states like California, Texas, New York, and Florida, which are among the most affected by extreme heat, air pollution, and flooding. Almost 80 percent of Latinos say they are worried about global warming, and more than eight in ten believe global warming is happening.

Climate change *is* happening. And in Miami, that couldn't be truer. Climate change is impacting every corner of the city. In fact, some say that Miami could be underwater in one hundred years. As local activist Alexander Zastera (aka "the Climate Crusader") tells me, "This is an emergency. It's a climate emergency. And we're not acting as if our house is on fire." The Latinx lens forces us to break with those stereotypical images of Miami as a vacationer's paradise.

I decide to take a walk up and down Brickell Avenue. I walk by the same buildings and roads I've been passing most

The Climate Crusader and his team. They educate the community about the growing threats of climate change.

of my life. My friend Cristina's old house to my right, the stupid traffic light where my mom almost got in an accident to my left, and those same palm trees that always greeted us before entering my grandparents' building still lie straight ahead. It seems as familiar as it always has been—except, if I close my eyes, I feel the heat of the sun pounding on my skin more than it had before. That warmth I missed in New York City is almost suffocating now in Miami. If I take a couple of steps, I stumble upon a puddle of water, even though everything else is telling me that it's a perfectly sunny day. But you'd never know if it rained a second ago or three days ago, because the signs of floods are everywhere now. Plants that have been soaked in water for days, pavement colors that have been washed away, and the overflowing drains. Everything is so subtly constant—the heat, the floods, the storms—that it's almost impossible to notice the difference.

I get back in the car and drive to the CLEO Institute, one of the leading nonprofits in South Florida that's tackling climate change, to talk to their executive director, Yoca Arditi-Rocha. Essentially, I'm here to ask her, "What. Is. Happening? Can you break this down for me?" Immediately, Yoca tells me that Miami is in fact ground zero for climate change. Miami's sea levels are rising, storms are becoming increasingly stronger, and our oceans are warming. The warming tides are, in turn, also plaguing our coasts with some of the worst blue-green algae crisis we've seen in history, and the high sea levels are causing saltwater intrusion into the city's drinking water supply.

"And what about this insane heat I always feel these days?" I ask Yoca.

Yoca tells me that hot days of more than one hundred degrees are slowly becoming the norm and that by midcentury, triple-digit heat will be more common than not. "It can become the perfect storm. With a few inches of sea level rise, the impact is going to be exponential," Yoca states.

Exponential? If we do nothing, this city could be gone. Sunk. Unlivable. Buried. But if you start looking around you, you'll notice that some of Miami's people are *already* gone.

People have vanished from the homes that saw them grow old, the streets that took them in, and the corners that housed their fondest memories. Pushed out—not just by death or those crippling heat waves or devastating hurricanes but by the slow gentrification of Miami's neighborhoods that is putting a price on the cost of human life. Places like Little Havana, Liberty City, and Little Haiti—low-income, high-elevation neighborhoods removed from the coast where Latinos and people of color have laid roots for decades—are being transformed by big developers into fancy safe havens for the privileged. Rich people who traded their waterfront condos for "hip" inland properties are sucking the life out of these zip codes, driving out the soul of these blocks.

Around here, even climate change can discriminate.

And that's what drove people like Adrian Sanz, a Miamian from Venezuela and Nicaragua, to fight for affordable and sustainable housing in Miami. For him, climate change is about displacement. It's about the way people are being pushed out from their homes. He tells me that as an organizer in Miami, knocking on people's doors, he learned that housing was the number one issue that kept coming up.

"The fact that they were living in slum conditions so that they could afford housing, the fact that they were homeless, the fact that they had very few options when it came to figuring out their future in the city," Adrian explains. That's why one of his main focuses now is addressing Miami's climate gentrification, so everyone—not just Miami's 1 percent—can have access to resilient infrastructure and new developments.

If those big blue ocean waves crash this city, *who* gets to survive? *What* would happen to Miami? In many ways, those climate disasters are the moments of urgency that test Miami's resilience. A resilience that relies not only on Miami's technical ability to tackle climate change but in its ability to come together as people. Its willingness to find strength together. To fight as *one*.

Adrian tells me about his experience with Hurricane Andrew. He was about four years old when Andrew hit Miami on August 24, 1992, with those category 5 winds that tore through South Florida. The trees had fallen down, the electricity was out, and cars were destroyed. There were piles of debris everywhere and countless homes without roofs.

"Our family lost everything. We lost our entire apartment building. It was destroyed, and we had to find a new place to live," he says.

That passion Adrian holds when he talks about housing rights makes even more sense because he himself knows what that type of loss feels like.

"At no point in time did it ever feel like we had a community that was really looking out for us," he tells me. "It felt like a very lonely time, you know? The family was just really struggling very hard to get by, and it would have been great to be able to lean on some other people, but everybody was going through their own shit."

For years, everyone *was* going through their own shit in Miami. Everyone was battling their own fights, dreaming their own stories of returning to their home countries, or living in the Miami bubble. We rarely thought about what this city meant, who we were, and what *we* wanted, collectively. But after walking through ground zero, I cannot help thinking that today, Adrian might have a whole community looking out for him if another Hurricane Andrew strikes Miami. Everybody may still be going through their own shit, but we're noticing that our struggles have more in common than we ever imagined. Miami is not just ground zero, it's a city that is being rebuilt from the ground up by people who are now stepping into who they are.

De abajo a arriba.

8

Erased

Tucked away in another corner of Miami is Allapattah, traditionally a working-class immigrant neighborhood with a
vibrant Dominican community. Some even consider this
part of town the *last* blocks to be untouched by Miami's gentrification. As I drive through the area, I see no tall skyscrapers, no hip bars or cool coffee shops. I park the car at Tipico
Dominicano, an old restaurant started in the 1980s that has
long served as a refuge for newly arrived Dominicans.

I walk out to the restaurant's patio and into a large crowd
that's gathering to discuss race and culture among the Latino
community. The first thing I hear is a group of organizers
asking the assembled crowd, "When you see a Latina, *who*
do you think about?"

Everyone on that patio stares at one another in silence.

In my case, my mind immediately took me to the TV
screen I grew up around: Univision. I remembered the tall,
skinny women with huge busts from *La Usurpadora* and *La
Dueña*, my two favorite telenovelas from the 1990s. I also
remembered the anchors and reporters who appeared in

my dad's newscast—most of them wearing tight dresses, some of them dolled up with pounds of mascara, and all of them with their hair completely *alisados,* straightened. I then thought about Eva Longoria. And then about Sofía Vergara. And, finally, my mind couldn't stop picturing J.Lo, wearing those baggy white pants and tank top, dancing in her "Jenny from the Block" music video.

Then someone followed up with, "And what about immigrants? *Who* do you see when you think of immigrants?"

My mind took me to the border.

I thought about the Central American and Mexican migrants I had met in McAllen, Texas, a couple of months prior. I could perfectly remember their faces as they stepped out of the shower at the respite center—their *first* hot shower since they had crossed the border. I thought about the countless Latinos I had met throughout my work—the farmworkers, domestic workers, students, and artists—all of them people with titles, but all of them immigrants first. And I thought about my own family. My mind took me to Cuba and Mexico.

An older woman from the back of the patio, with weary skin and eyes, raised her hand. She said, "We ·are very hardworking. I started here cleaning houses, and now I'm a cashier Monday through Friday. I work very hard in this country for a better life," she said. "For a better United States." She was saying this as if she had to prove a point to us, almost as if she were begging for approval.

Everyone on that patio paused when this woman spoke, and I fear it's because many of us had the same realization in that moment. Nowhere in our minds did this woman surface: the image of an Afro-Latina. In Latino communities, brains are so conditioned to linking the words "Latino" and "Latina" to light-skinned people that the notion of anyone darker is obscured by stereotypes and social constructs that we can't even see ourselves. In Latin America, governments and Western civilization erased all trace of Latinos who are of African descent; as a result, those who share bloodlines with enslaved Africans, who survived at the mercy of colonialism and lived in the shadows of history, haven't always had a place in their own countries.

During the colonial period of 1502 to 1866, more than eleven million enslaved Africans were forcibly shipped to the New World, and a number of them ended up in the Caribbean, South America, and Latin America. As has been reported by the historian Henry Louis Gates, Jr., many Latin American countries enacted policies to "whiten" their states after they received enslaved Africans into their land. To increase their white population, governments encouraged migration into their countries of white families and also encouraged interracial mixing as a means to whitewash the darkness. Yet even centuries after this period, Afro descendants in Latin America were barely recognized as human. It wasn't until the 1980s and 1990s—in large part because of local social black movements in countries like Brazil, Colombia, Panama, and Honduras—that governments across Latin America started adding racial data to their national censuses. That fight is far from over now. The Mexican government has yet to unanimously recognize Afro-Mexicans in its national constitution. The more than one million Afro-Mexicans who live in the country aren't even *guaranteed* constitutional rights as of now (pending final congressional approval). In fact, it wasn't until 2015, when the government included Afro-Mexicans in the official national census after being pressured by activists, that the country even bothered to recognize the existence of this community.

But, no matter how hard you try, you cannot truly erase facts and history. According to the Pew Research Center, "In Latin America's colonial period, about 15 times as many African slaves were taken to Spanish and Portuguese colonies than to the U.S." That's why today, centuries later, there are approximately 130 million people with African roots living in Latin America. Per Princeton University's Project on Ethnicity and Race in Latin America, that's about one-quarter of the continent's population.

The challenge for many Afro-Latinos is that the public simply doesn't know how to categorize them. On the one hand, Americans don't see them as African Americans. On the other hand, Latin Americans don't see them as Latinos. People are accustomed to seeing blackness through one lens.

Back in Allapattah, one of the event's main organizers, a young woman in her twenties, raised her hand at the front of the patio. She wanted us to give her all our attention, and looking straight into the crowd, she said forcefully, "Fifty thousand Haitian immigrants are at risk of immediate deportation after Trump ended Temporary Protection Status for Haitian refugees. These are the images we have to keep in mind, and the people we have to keep in mind, because our media is not accurately articulating who are some of the most affected populations in the immigration debate."

She was absolutely right.

When the organizers at Tipico Dominicano initially tossed the word "immigrants" at us, my vision was so hyperfocused on the U.S.-Mexican border that I left everyone else behind—the black undocumented immigrants coming from the Caribbean, the Afro-Latinos who were neglected in the migrant caravan, or all the immigrants who crossed borders not by feet but by plane or by sea, in the air, and over waves.

Immigration, too, it dawned on me, was a story centered around a very specific backdrop in the United States, a very specific landscape, and a very specific series of protagonists: starring the border and featuring brown people. But what about those who *never* made it on the screen? What about the lost voices overshadowed by their own darkness? The ones that were dismissed as "too black" to be Latino or "too dark" to even get in the back of "the immigration line"?

The very intent of the event I was at was exactly *that:* to push the audience to ask these questions, to challenge our own biases, and to expand our understanding of our very own people. That afternoon, we found ourselves in the backyard patio of Tipico Café, a Dominican restaurant in Allapattah. Then, as people were waiting to watch Omilani Alarcón's documentary, *LATINEGRAS,* I sat quietly in the audience and observed my surroundings. To my right, a young Afro-Dominican was telling her friend how she was taught as a young girl to *always* walk in the shade in order to avoid getting any darker. To my left, I overheard a black Nicaraguan indigenous woman say: "People think we are weird." And right behind me, a young black Puerto Rican girl recounted how, as a kid, her parents would always straighten her hair so she wouldn't have *"pelo negro."*

All these women were part of the Latina community. Yet

at some point in their lives, they had faced discrimination because the color of their skin never quite fit inside the "Latina box."

And *who* was defining that "box," anyway?

Everyone in that crowd knew the answer: we, the light-skinned Latinas, had for years.

I asked Omilani how she came up with the idea behind her film, *LATINEGRAS,* a documentary that explores her journey of self-love as an Afro-Latina. She told me that for a while she had a hard time explaining her identity to people. Yes, she was from Nigeria, but she was also Boricua. In fact, she grew up in a black, Puerto Rican, and Filipino household—all backgrounds she was proud of but that were easily reduced to "black." In people's eyes, she was a black woman. As she told me, in an effort to do her story justice and honor the entirety of her roots, Omilani wrote a song, "Latinegra." The original lyrics started with: "I was told Latina ain't black, so stop with that. But when I walked out in the street, what did I see? Morenitas just like me." The song ended up becoming so popular—eliciting so many online responses from fellow Afro-Latinas—that Omilani turned it into a film.

"Why should we feel ashamed, you know?" Omilani told me. "Let's reclaim our identity."

Shame stems not from our own reflection but rather from the void in which that image sits. So many Latinos and Latinas had to assimilate, fake it, or pretend to be something they weren't. The thing is, Afro-Latinos don't get to blend in or hide, which is why visibility and representation can serve as superficial antidotes to shame. It's no substitute for the

Omilani Alarcón, Afro-Latina documentary filmmaker, in Miami.

real structural changes that are needed to truly value the lives of black and brown people. But as psychologists often point out, the more you see yourself, the more you love yourself.

So if you don't see yourself on the screen everyone is watching, how do you find pride?

After the event at Tipico Café wrapped up, I went back home to catch the newscast on Univision.

As I turned on the TV, I recognized how powerful the image that lay in front of my eyes was: my father, a light-skinned journalist from Mexico, sharing space with Ilia Calderón, a black journalist from Chocó, Colombia's pre-dominantly Afro-Colombian region, which sits right on the Pacific coast. Ilia had become the first Afro-Latina to anchor *any* major television newscast in the nation. In that moment, as I was watching her, I imagined how many *more* Latinos suddenly saw themselves reflected on that TV screen. From Chocó to Univision—I wondered how Ilia must have felt about this experience. What was that journey like?

The following day, I asked Ilia if I could come chat with her at Univision.

"I grew up being black and feeling very proud about being black," Ilia told me. I immediately noticed that she affirmatively used the word *"negra"* in that sentence, a word that has long been a taboo in the Latinx community. Each time anyone I knew had ever used that word in the past, it was always done in the form of a whisper with a derogatory connotation. Ilia, this time, said it loud and clear, as if she were reclaiming its meaning: *"Yo crecí siendo negra."*

Unbeknownst to most tourists who visit the scenic Cartagena beaches, Colombia has the second-largest African-

My dad, Jorge, and Ilia Calderón anchoring their nightly newscast on Univision.

descendant population in Latin America. Ilia grew up in the predominantly black, low-income region of Chocó, an area where blackness was the norm. Yet although Ilia felt immense pride about where she was from, society tried to inject a different message through mainstream media: "I grew up watching telenovelas where black people were always either the slaves or the service people." A contradiction that was also felt when Ilia left the Pacific coast and ventured into Colombia's cities—this time exposed to a type of humiliation that lived not just on TV but also in real life, in front of her face. "Even though I was proud, that pride teaches you a form of survival and to also keep yourself really quiet," Ilia said. "You learn to almost go unnoticed. But, what's the limit, right? How much can you take?"

The thing is, Ilia was born *to* be noticed. She was born to pave ways, create paths, and break ceilings. Ilia eventually forced millions of light-skinned Colombians to welcome her into their living room every single day. In doing so, she was also affirming to more than 10 percent of the population—Colombia's Afro-Latino community—that they, too, belonged in their country. They belonged not just as slaves or as marginalized people but as prestigious journalists. As stars. As people worthy of taking the stage. Ten years after Ilia left Colombia, another Afro-Latina eventually became a prominent national news anchor, following in Ilia's footsteps.

When Ilia first got to the United States in 2001, she followed the track many Spanish-language journalists do. She first joined Telemundo and later Univision, hosted various programs, and, in 2017, finally rose to become a coanchor of the most watched Spanish evening news program in the

United States. A role that until that moment had been previously occupied by fair-skinned people.

"How did it make you feel?" I asked Ilia. "What does this new role symbolize for you?"

She very humbly told me that the success wasn't about her, it was about others. "For me, what's important about this role is to echo other people's voices and leave a door open for other young girls that are just like me." She followed with: "It's about me retiring or leaving this post and the door not closing on them. It's about them feeling that they can do it."

The rise of Ilia Calderón is considered an anomaly—a "first of its kind"—but that's only because we have made it one. Every telenovela, newscast, story, or mainstream broadcast that has ever featured only light-skinned Latinos has fooled us all into thinking that our community held only one color. But if you actually look around you, Afro-Latinos have always been among us. Part of us. Leading us. According to a 2016 Pew Research Center survey of Latino adults, one-quarter of *all* U.S. Latinos self-identify as Afro-Latino. That's at least one million people in this country. I say *at least*—and stress this—because the Afro-Latino identity is a very complex one. Not only is it rarely offered as an option in polls and surveys but it also lies at the intersection of two backgrounds—blackness *and* Latinidad—that have historically faced deep discrimination.

Why put two targets on your back when you could have just one? Why tick two boxes when you can blend into one? As the columnist Jomaira Salas Pujols wrote in *HuffPost*: "It is not surprising, then, that in the 2010 census, only 2.5 percent of Latinos selected 'black' as their race. For many

Latinos, selecting 'white' or 'some other race' in the census is aspirational."

Culturally, Latinos have made it aspirational to assimilate to whiteness, to pass and suppress our darkest shades. We've always striven to be the Sofía Vergaras of the world. And we have to ask ourselves: Why? Why did we choose that image? Where did that fascination come from?

As Mijente executive director Marissa Franco told me: "There is such internalized racism" among our community. And that's one of the reasons Mijente, a national Latinx and Chicanix organizing platform, recently partnered with Alicia Garza's Black Futures Lab to launch the largest-ever Spanish-language census geared toward Afro-Latinos living in the United States. The purpose is not just to accurately count Afro-Latinos but to lead them toward *wanting to be seen.* Wanting to be counted. Wanting to have a voice. "One of the greatest sins of much of the Latinx organizing history in the United States has been questions around race and gender," Franco added. And as there continue to be efforts in place to reverse some of the damage we have done to our own community, scholars are starting to notice a trend among millennials and Gen Zers. As Dr. Adolfo Cuevas, an assistant professor at Tufts University, told me: "The younger generation has been acknowledging their African ancestry more than ever before."

Again, imagine growing up with the image of Ilia Calderón on your TV screen every night. What effect would that have?

Ilia got a little teary eyed, looked outside her office window, and told me the story of her cameraman's daughter. A couple of years prior, Juan Carlos brought his dark-skinned young daughter to Univision one day. The second they stepped into the office and walked around the hallways, offices, and desks, the girl looked at Juan Carlos and asked him why no one in Univision looked like her. Juan Carlos saw Ilia leaving the makeup room and turned to his daughter, saying, "Look, here she is! Her name is Ilia Calderón, she's my friend, and she's Colombian just like me!"

Ilia told me that when the little girl looked at her, she saw how her eyes became wide-open: "I hugged her and started crying."

Ilia then proceeded to tell Juan Carlos's daughter all about her journey, about how she got to Univision and what her work entailed every day. Ilia recalls Juan Carlos telling her, "You are the image my daughter wanted to see, and the one she was hoping to see. It means a lot to the both of us."

That's what change looks like for Ilia.

Ilia's legacy has already been set in motion. Not just through Juan Carlos's daughter, but through the other hundreds and thousands of young Afro-Latinos in the United States who no longer see a massive barrier between themselves and their screen. Thousands who can now *see*—not just dream or imagine—themselves sitting in a chair inside a TV studio. They now know what that looks like, feels like, and sounds like—and it's a beautiful image that has been missing from the picture for far too long.

Ilia was the first Afro-Latina to anchor a major national newscast in the country, and she surely will not be the last. And that's because it's part of a culmination of big and small acts of courage, big and small gestures of valor, and big and small milestones that are slowly breaking down the systemic barriers that have erased, neglected, and held back Afro-Latinos for centuries. All around us, there are countless Afro-Latinos who are paving their own paths toward justice, the same way Ilia did from the coastline of Chocó in Colombia to the offices of Univision in Miami.

So what do these changes in our Latinx community look like? How far do they go? Who is leading them? I take a look around me and see the changes already starting.

9

Dark Shadows of Freedom

Enrique and I were never supposed to face each other. We were never meant to be in the same room, at the same time, sitting inches apart from each other. That's because Enrique Tarrio goes against everything I believe in. My morals, my values, my own existence. He's a young Afro-Latino who not only supports Donald Trump but does everything in his power to ensure his victory.

On paper, Enrique and I were meant to be friends, though. For starters, I had imagined that as an Afro-Cuban—someone who shares not one but *two* identities that represent marginalized communities—he would consider his own history differently. After all, Enrique was the descendant of enslaved Africans and part of a community that had endured a long legacy of suffering on the island. Systemic racism has historically been ingrained in Cuba's societal structure. By the nineteenth century, Cuba had become the world's largest producer of sugarcane, turning the island into the Caribbean's largest market for enslaved Africans, who were exploited on the plantations that produced sugarcane. By the time Fidel Castro came to power in 1959, marginalized communities had something to hope for in revolutionary plans that promised more opportunities for the underserved. And although some Afro-Cubans saw progress in their lives—as Leyanis pointed out to me—Fidel's promises never truly translated into real, lasting change for the community.

According to a recent study, the racial gap in Cuba, created by skin-color racism similar to that found in the United States, has remained a wide chasm that leaves the dark-skinned ancestors of this historical slavery at a disadvantage. For example, 70 percent of black and mixed Cubans don't even have access to the Internet. Only 11 percent of black Cubans have access to a bank account, and they are less likely to have college degrees than their lighter-skinned counterparts. This reality of black Cubans on the island, which somewhat mirrors the struggles black people continue to face in America, led me to naively believe that someone like Enrique Tarrio would be more sympathetic toward the United States' Democratic Party—which had attempted to center its agenda around people of color.

Beyond the political assumptions, Enrique and I were both born in Miami to families of exiles. Both of us are first-generation immigrants. His *abuelo,* like mine, was forced to flee communist Cuba as a political refugee and eventually found his new anchor in a neighborhood that's just a couple of miles west from where my grandparents ended up settling. Enrique grew up in Little Havana. I grew up watching my *abuelos* sip their *cortaditos* in those same corners of Miami. Chances are I may have seen Enrique around before we met for the first time. I imagine that we may have even crossed paths before, never noticing each other. Always roaming around each other's peripheries, but far enough away to remain complete strangers.

But if there is one main lesson to be learned from this Latinx journey so far, it's that it's always important to break with the assumptions that lie on papers. Our biases are quick to create stories for our minds. In Enrique's case, the color of skin—a black *and* Latino man—read like the antithesis of Trumpism. Yet to look at people through a Latinx lens means to understand that no one, *including* Afro-Latinos, is meant to fit into boxes, narratives, and labels. It means giving people the space to be whoever they want to be, even if that means being a black and Latino Trump supporter. *That's* Latinx: turning stereotypes on their head. Sometimes all it takes is to step outside of our own shadows to do just that.

One morning, I was browsing the Internet and came across an article from the *Daily Beast* titled "Why Young Men of Color Are Joining White-Supremacist Groups." In that story, I read about Enrique for the first time:

"Tarrio, who identifies as Afro-Cuban, is president of the Miami chapter of the Proud Boys, who call themselves 'Western chauvinists.'"

The Proud Boys is a national organization with various local chapters, founded by Gavin McInnes, one of the original cofounders of VICE Media, during the 2016 presidential election as a right-wing fraternal group. Their main slogan is: "Western chauvinists who refuse to apologize for creating the modern world." The easiest way to describe them is by having you picture a "bros-only drinking club" that's tied by a common bond over hard-core patriotism, love of conservatism, and obsession with the First Amendment. Over the years, they've closely aligned themselves not only with President Trump but also with political crooks like Roger Stone and extremists like Richard Spencer, who's become an icon for white supremacists.

But organizations like the Southern Poverty Law Center view the Proud Boys as much more than that. They consider them a hate group made up of de facto white nationalists. Among other things, the SPLC points to the group's anti-Muslim and misogynistic rhetoric. In them, they see dangerous violence disguised as political incorrectness. The group has been spotted at extremist rallies across the country, in brawls against protesters, and posing alongside groups like neo-Nazi skinheads in photos. Although it'd be incorrect to say that the Proud Boys are single-handedly responsible for initiating attacks, their strategy is certainly to incite them. Beyond the SPLC, there are many other hate-monitoring organizations that are wary of the way in which the Proud Boys use their freedom of speech. From Facebook to Instagram, the Proud Boys' social channels have been banned and categorized as "hate speech" and "hate organizations." But the Proud Boys have aggressively contested all these allegations and started proceedings to sue the SPLC for their "hate group" designation.

Enrique Tarrio, an Afro-Latino—a millennial wearing a "Make America Great Again" cap in the streets of Miami, a city built by immigrants—is their national chairman, the spokesperson of a group that promotes "Western values," which have traditionally neglected people who looked exactly like him: dark skinned.

How could that be possible?

Enrique Tarrio, smoking, by his house in Little Havana.

ENRIQUE'S SHADOW

In Enrique, you see a man whose name has been tainted by perceived extremisms:

"Chairman of the Proud Boys . . ."

"President of Latinos for Trump's Florida chapter . . ."

"Banned from Twitter . . ."

He's seen online, posing with Roger Stone here; the sound of his voice as he chants, *"You fucking communist!"* to Speaker of the House Nancy Pelosi at an event there. Enrique has publicly denounced white nationalism, yet he was spotted at the Unite the Right rally in Charlottesville, Virginia, in August 2017, a violent march that led to the death of thirty-two-year-old Heather Heyer. Article after article points to a phenomenon known as "multiracial white supremacy" to attempt to explain people like Enrique: individuals who are hyperfocused on pushing undocumented immigrants out of the country rather than actively embracing whiteness. He spent almost a year in federal prison after being involved in a scheme that sold stolen diabetic test strip kits to people. This dark side of him is further infused with the smell of cigarettes Enrique likes to smoke.

Although the United States moved on from its fixation with the Castro regime and into a post–Cold War era, it seems Enrique was never able to let go of that battle. Anywhere you look around Enrique, you see reminders of a past that once denied his people freedom. His grandfather sweetly rocks in a chair on Enrique's front porch—back and forth—carrying wrinkles of his exile. His neighbors—up and down the block—with humble exteriors decorated in the Cuban blue and white stripes, all rumble in an accent that never left the island. His house is full of old kitschy portraits that trace back family trees.

Yet Enrique is on guard. His mind replays the moment communism turned its back on the Cuban people. That's why, where others might see incredible stability and calmness around them, Enrique sees the imminent danger of Marxism. *Especially* when he hears mention of someone like New York Democratic representative Alexandria Ocasio-Cortez. For him, Ocasio-Cortez represents the Democrats' main problem: a party that is leaning dangerously toward the Far Left, away from America's democratic ideals. A Left that, in his eyes, resembles Cuba's communism. In fact, Tarrio is so allergic to what Ocasio-Cortez represents that he's sold T-shirts labeling the congresswoman an "idiot" and "communist."

"Don't you think you're being kind of paranoid?" I ask Enrique.

"I think that it is a safe paranoia, because we're so used to living in peace here in the United States. . . . It's a slippery slope because humans are prone to error," he tells me.

This paranoia overshadows all of Enrique's moves. Outside his house, you can almost feel the same breeze that hits the Cuban coast, which lies just about one hundred miles away from our Florida shores. Enrique mentions that it was "rough" while he was growing up in Miami, mirroring a forgotten truth many Cuban immigrants endure in the United States. Up to 15 percent of Cuban families live in poverty. But Enrique, like many first-generation Cuban Americans, seems more fixated on what lies on the other side of the ocean than what's happening here. He's only one hundred miles away from the stolen revolutionary dreams and corrupt government that oppressed his family. Just one hundred miles away from the political prisoners, imposed maximum wages, and controlled goods that reign in Cuba. In that sense, Enrique could be doing what a lot of first-generation Cuban Americans tend to do: internalize their parents' trauma. Growing up with those stories of the past allows them to feel more real, as if they also happened to *you*. Their trauma can become yours.

Enrique holds on to the U.S. Constitution with disruptive force. If you browse online or observe some of Enrique's signature moves, you'll find him citing the Constitution as a way to justify his extreme views:

"The Second Amendment was made just in case there's a tyrannical government. For the people to take up arms against the government," he tells me with assurance.

Yet as I talk with him, this extremism presents as a cover

for the fear of losing the only thing that truly belongs to Enrique: his rights. Now, a potentially controversial conversation about the Second Amendment sounds more like a plot for basic survival: the anticipation of corruption.

The amendment reads: "A well-regulated Militia, being necessary to the security of a free State, the right of the people to keep and bear Arms, shall not be infringed." There are some gun rights advocates that interpret the term "militia" as "private citizens' ability to arm themselves in an effort to free the country should the United States ever fall into the hands of tyranny." Many argue that's exactly what James Madison inferred in *The Federalist Papers*. That's why there are some individuals, like Enrique, who see guns not only as a means for hunting, recreational sports, or protection against burglars but as weapons that can save humanity against tyranny. For many people like Enrique, this is a plausible reality. The government once stripped his family of their freedom. How can he ensure that won't happen again?

The same lens of thinking applies to other controversial issues. Enrique is always anticipating the government's overstep. For example, when we discuss whether abortion should be legal, he tells me that, for him, the issue centers around how much we should allow the government to control our private lives. His fight is with the government's infiltration of human privacy, not necessarily with a woman's right to choose.

"My issue with Planned Parenthood . . . is how they get money from the government," Enrique says. In this same conversation, he regurgitates Democratic sound bites: "yes" to decriminalizing marijuana; "no" to the Dakota Access Pipeline; "yes" to marriage equality. Based on this conversation, some people would call him a "Republican," a "Libertarian," a "Trump supporter," and even a "liberal," but the reality is that no box has been crafted for him.

For Enrique, the pendulum swings not as much toward polarized ideologies as toward enshrined values that test the limits of rights. It's not about being for or against, pro or anti—it's about defining paradigms of equality that cannot be coerced by force or by governments. And for Enrique, the biggest testament to that untouched liberty lies in his words. In his ability to provoke you, enrage you, and instigate you as an act of principle rather than defiance. Freedom of speech is a sword he uses to awaken the masses' senses, pinch them out of their numbness, and remind them of the degrees of separation that stand between them and oppression.

Enrique will write "Michelle Obama is a tranny" on a poster. He'll call an African American actress an "ape." He'll print T-shirts that say "Pinochet Did Nothing Wrong" or "Roger Stone Did Nothing Wrong." He'll appear at a local Women's March rally in South Florida with a megaphone so loud it disrupts the songs they're chanting. He'll go to a college campus to enlist students into "Western Chauvinism."

Enrique needs all this to remind himself that he is, in fact, alive in a democracy.

" 'I prefer dangerous freedom over peaceful slavery,' " he says. "I've always liked that statement."

All this at *whose* expense? *Who* pays for Enrique's freedom? I ask Enrique if he understands how his actions can be seen as a dangerous form of hate speech.

He responds with, "Victimizing yourself is the worst thing that you can do, because it doesn't prepare you for the real world. The real world is ugly, and we're both trying to change and make it a better world to live in."

"But this type of language *can* incite others to act violently," I stress.

That's one of the most palpable effects of the Trump presidency. I remind Enrique that in 2017, the FBI reported that hate crimes increased by 17 percent. By 2018, the FBI found that hate crime violence and threats had reached the highest level in the United States in the last sixteen years. Particularly, they uncovered that the number of anti-Latino hate crime victims rose by more than 21 percent.

I keep pushing Enrique on these points. Eventually, he tells me that he's not responsible for other people's actions. "I'm not responsible for anyone. I'm only responsible for my own. I feel like it's healthy . . . to have a bully in your life because they teach you how bad the world can be and how evil people can be."

When Enrique says that, in my view, it sounds as though he is feeling a lot of resentment toward the real world. I believe that it's a world he desperately wants to fit into but one that hasn't always fully welcomed him in—a young Afro-Latino who, throughout his life, has walked the lines of fire as a means of survival and assimilation. When others never saw him, Enrique made sure to be seen, heard, and felt.

Who's had Enrique's back all these years? *Who's* been looking out for him?

Enrique belongs to *no one*. No concrete definitions, no labels or set structures. On the left, progressives immediately think Enrique looks like their base: a young, black,

Latino man. "One of us," they claim, but soon they dismiss Enrique as an extremist. On the right, Republicans are very attracted to the idea of having the "token brown conservative" on their side, then give no tangible power to people who look like him.

"I feel like the GOP . . . hasn't helped us out. They've been playing politics their entire life that they forgot the middle class," Enrique tells me.

Forgotten? I think about Miami's iconic Versailles Restaurant, an obligatory stop for presidential and congressional candidates who are trying to win the hearts of Miami voters like Enrique. I think of the countless photo ops that have taken place inside those walls. The TV cameras, local radio stations, and customers snapping picture after picture on their iPhones. They come in and they go out. Enrique's house is not too far from the Versailles, but I wonder *who* took the time to walk down the block to greet him. Who knocked on those doors when no one was watching?

"All right, Enrique," I say, "so help me understand *why* Donald Trump, though? *What* did you see in him?"

The simplicity of his one-word answer explains what many academics have tried to do in three-hundred-page books. "Because *calle*!" he says.

"Sorry, what did you say?"

"¡*Calle*!" he says back. *Calle* means "street" in Spanish. "He had *calle*!" Enrique reiterates.

In Trump, Enrique saw a billionaire who looked *nothing* like him and possessed *nothing* like him but spoke a language that was everything like *his*: street talk, *calle* talk.

"[Trump] is not well-spoken. He's not polished. He's not a great speaker. He's actually a really crappy speaker, but

Latinos for Trump rally in Miami.

because of that it resonates with everyday Americans," he explains.

There is truth in that statement. Trump's magic weapon has always been his language. His ability to appear to be speaking without bullshit and political correctness. Liberals and progressives may not like how he sounds or what he says, but there's no doubt that he cuts through the noise for those Americans who think like him. In the midst of the 2016 primaries, *The Boston Globe* did a fantastic piece analyzing the Republican contenders' communication strategies. The piece, "For Presidential Hopefuls, Simpler Language Resonates," stated that Trump talked to voters using fourth-grade-level language, and they found that strategy actually *worked*: "The Republican candidates—like Trump—who are speaking at a level easily understood by people at the lower end of the education spectrum are outperforming their highfalutin opponents in the polls. Simpler language resonates with a broader swath of voters in an era of 140-character Twitter tweets and 10-second television sound bites, say specialists on political speech." Politics is about reaching people on an emotional level, and Trump can incite emotions in people. It's that simple. Sometimes all you need to do is say simple words like "beautiful" and "huge" to win people's hearts.

It happened to Enrique. Enrique felt that someone understood him. We may call that underlying attraction for Trump's misogyny and sexism, but at its core it also reeks of an immigrant's desperate journey to be accepted in this country. Accepted for who he is, even if he's rough around the edges.

How, then, can Enrique reconcile Trump's harsh stance on undocumented immigrants with his own family's history of seeking refuge in this country? The Cuban exile community, more than any other, has benefited from the United States' embrace. For decades, U.S. immigration law has given Cubans faster paths to permanent residency and citizenship over other immigrants. For decades, Cubans have been called "humans" and "refugees" instead of "illegals" and "aliens." Enrique's instinct, when we start this conversation, is to retreat behind his shield—still wreathed in cigarette smoke. His answers point to defending "legal immigrants over illegal immigrants" and to "the wall." But when words are rid of politics and partisan slogans—when nouns become real stories instead of abstract statistics—contention starts to slowly dissipate. Each time we managed to put politics aside, the tone of our conversation felt less tense. We also, unexpectedly, started seeing eye to eye on some things.

"Well, they should be able to come in if they are fleeing gang violence," Enrique tells me.

To make sense of it all, I asked Dr. Eduardo Gamarra, a Latin American professor of politics at Florida International University, what a Latino like Enrique Tarrio has to gain in a "Western chauvinistic" world. A world that has historically benefited the white elites and built power structures around their clenched fists. Where does Enrique even fit in this world?

"I think it's false consciousness. This view that somehow you can move into white society," Dr. Gamarra states. "They identify as a negation of their background."

As Dr. Gamarra says this, I think back to the first time I hung out with Enrique and some of his Latino conservative Proud Boys friends during a VICE shoot with James Burns, Justin Green, and Jonny Kapps. There were probably more than ten of them. Cubans, Peruvians, Argentinians . . . sitting around in their boys' club fraternity room. Fathers and husbands, old and young, but all of them unequivocally "Latino" to the mainstream eye.

One of the very first things I asked the group was, "How do you all identify?"

They immediately yelled back at me with, "We are American first!"

One followed with, "I'm an American who *happens* to be Latino."

The other one said, "I'm an American of Cuban descent, but I'm American first!"

Last, I heard, "I don't identify as a Latino man!" from the back of the room.

For me, pride stems from my ability to respond to that question with, "I'm Latinx." For them, it's their right to spell out "American first." Yet whether their response can be seen as pride or as an outright negation of their Latino background, as Dr. Gamarra pointed out, the ultimate testament to their truths is how they identify when *no one* is looking. It's how they view themselves outside the public eye, when their intrinsic character overrides any form of social expectations. Because then, there is *no* escaping who you are.

Enrique is a man who is fighting against no one other than himself. "When you go to prison, people segregate themselves," Enrique tells me as he recalls the year he spent incarcerated. He explains how, while he was locked up, people tended to group themselves according to the color of their skin. He remembers how black people congregated by their own chairs, how Latinos were in another section of the room, how Puerto Ricans had one corner, and how white people were on another side.

"I feel like it's natural to go ahead and resort to that," Enrique tells me.

"And where did *you* go, Enrique?" I ask him. "What group did you associate yourself with?" I wonder if he went with the white group.

He pauses. "I went with the Latinos," he responded.

Enrique is someone who has spent his entire life breaking people's biases and living his life outside the boxes and labels that have attempted to tell his story. When I first approached him for this conversation, everything in me wanted to believe that Enrique was an outlier among the Latino community—someone who could in no way represent us. At the end of the day, I was wrong. My story on Enrique was wrong. We don't see eye to eye on almost anything, but we do agree on one thing: everyone is entitled to build his or her own narrative. And that, in and of itself, is a Latinx story.

The Northeast to the Midwest

10

The Act of Being Ordinary

As I make my way north from Florida, leaving behind that place of nostalgia for me, I'm reminded that one of the underlying threads of the Latinx community is the important role our ancestors played in developing our story. Part of our essence as a community is that the majority of us can look back and trace our origins in a faraway land. None of our journeys began *here;* they started south of the American border. Our stories, like our ancestors, migrated to the United States—and that's a unique trait we carry with us. But my conversations in Miami with the Afro-Latino community made me think twice about that: if people are barely recognized in their home country—barely captured by its census, history, and society—then how do we tell *full* stories? How do we capture the beginning of their journey?

It's proven shamefully hard for Latin American governments to recognize their Afro-descendant communities, so imagine how hard it must be to track their movements and stories elsewhere. If you're not seen by your home country, then how can you expect the United States to trace and account for you? That's one of the reasons we barely picture Afro-Latinos when we think about the contentious immigration debate in the United States or when we talk about the eleven million undocumented immigrants living among us. Afro-Latinos are typically unaccounted for. But they, too, transcend borders. Just as all our ancestors have.

For example, according to a Pew Research Center analysis of the U.S. Census, there were approximately 4.2 million black immigrants in the United States as of 2016, mostly hailing from the Caribbean, Latin America, and Africa. Of those, about six hundred thousand are undocumented. And although they are underrepresented in the system, undocumented black immigrants are disproportionately targeted and deported by ICE. According to the National Association for the Advancement of Colored People, black people in this country are incarcerated at more than five times the rate of white people. As we know, they are more likely to be stopped by officials, to be arrested and, therefore, put in jail. This means that black immigrants, who of course present as black people, are then more vulnerable to facing deportation. Criminal backgrounds are a straight entry point into ICE's hands. A 2016 report published by the Immigrant Rights Clinic of Washington Square Legal Services, Inc., at NYU Law School found that "black immigrants are much more likely than nationals from other regions to be deported due to a criminal conviction." But don't take that statement at face value: America's criminal justice system—which sets up black people to face incarceration—serves as the *best* pipeline into the immigration system.

You see? You're damned if you do, you're damned if you don't. Black immigrants face double punishment in this country. No matter *what* they do, they can be criminalized by the color of their skin or the stamp on their passport. But one of the biggest punishments black immigrants face in this country is forgetfulness. They are very likely to be forgotten by American society, just as they are in their own home countries. Out of sight—blended as black Americans here—out of mind.

During one of my pit stops along the road as I was driving to Washington, D.C., I was flipping around newscasts on TV when I heard a woman with a Cuban accent. She was pleading to have her brother removed from a U.S. detention center in Louisiana. In the segment, the woman was telling MSNBC news correspondent Morgan Radford, "When they get there, it's like arriving to a cemetery. You don't have an exit. There's no answer."

She spoke just like my grandmother, *con ese acento cubano.* I was also surprised to see this woman on TV because it's pretty uncommon to hear stories about undocumented Cuban detainees; the general story of Cuban immigrants told globally tends to be one of privilege and success. But then it all clicked: the woman's brother was Afro-Cuban. He was a black doctor who fled the Castro regime after the government beat him up. He came to the United States in search of better opportunities but instead ended up in ICE's custody in the Deep South. By the time I saw the report on TV, the man had been inside for ten months. Unlike most Cubans I knew, this darker-skinned one was neglected, untracked, and unaccounted for. Forgotten in the Deep South.

In that moment, I wondered how much longer he'd be inside those walls. Other than his sister, who's thinking about him? I thought to myself.

Jonathan surely was.

I was traveling to meet with Jonathan Jayes-Green, a cofounder of the UndocuBlack Network, one of the few national networks in the country that look after undocumented black immigrants. Jonathan is a queer, undocumented, Afro-Panamanian Deferred Action for Childhood Arrivals (DACA) recipient. D.C. is the hub of immigrant rights power players, incredible people who work tirelessly to bring justice to the most vulnerable. But at times, that circle of activists can get somewhat tight-knit and out of touch. At times, they're one-dimensional. They sound like brilliant policy nerds, swapping real sentences for sexy yet robotic political talking points. I have done that countless times myself. Yet Jonathan has managed to humanize advocacy by cutting through all the bureaucracy that typically surrounds D.C. politics. That means not only exposing the untold stories of undocumented black immigrants in the United States but also *healing* the owners of those stories. *Acknowledging* their agony. *Recognizing* their trauma. Even as I sit across from Jonathan—with that huge, optimistic smile of his—I can sense he feels somewhat uncomfortable with all the attention focused on him. But for him, opening up to me is an act of resistance in itself.

The story of undocumented black people in this country isn't just one of immigration—it's a story compounded by centuries of colonialism and institutionalized racism. It carries the oppression that lies on the other side of the U.S.-Mexican border and also the injustices with which blackness is then further stigmatized on *this* side of the fence. It's a story that says you're invisible *there* and criminalized *here*. Neglected *one* day, targeted the *next*. Jonathan is talking to me not just for himself but also for the rest of the Latinx movement. It's for *them,* too. It's to break *their* silence. To rid them, if only just an ounce, of the burden they carry.

Until 2016, when UndocuBlack really took off, there wasn't a space where undocumented black immigrants were represented. To explain its conception, Jonathan takes me to the streets of Baltimore, not far from where he grew up in Montgomery County. It's April 2015 and Jonathan is marching with the thousands of other people who are protesting the death of Freddie Gray, Jr., a twenty-five-year-old black man who died from injuries suffered in police custody. At that point in his life, Jonathan had already become somewhat disillusioned with the system through his previous work in Governor Martin O'Malley's administration, where he served as the administrator of the Governor's Commissions on Hispanic and Caribbean Affairs. As he explains, working in such a high-level position was an immense privilege that gave Jonathan the opportunity to represent and fight for his community. Yet at times it seemed that flashy photo ops with high-level politicians and stakeholders outweighed substantive policy solutions for the state's black and immigrant populations. So in the face of disillusionment and Maryland's history of mass incarceration, Jonathan walked into the Baltimore riots, which began in April 2015, with a long trail of anger that had been building in him for decades. And so did countless other black people. Not just in Baltimore but across the nation—an uprising that unleashed fervent anger against a system that prefers to see black lives buried rather than alive.

Unlike many of the other marchers, Jonathan was not born in the United States. But just like them, as an Afro-descendant, Jonathan shared the lived experience of being discriminated against in his own country. In March 2020, the representative of Afro-descendant women in Panama (Red de Mujeres Afrodescendientes de Panamá), Cecilia Moreno, said during a conference, "In Panama, we've been denouncing the fact that poverty's face is indigenous and Afro-descendant." Unsurprisingly, in Panama, where approximately 15 percent of the population is Afro-Latino, inequality hits Afro-Panamanians the hardest. And yet despite the degrees of separation with the United States, during the Baltimore riots Jonathan was marching alongside black Americans, all under one banner—all under the same blue sky. Because if you're black and undocumented in America, there is no escaping this death trap: even if this country doesn't see Afro-Latinos as one of theirs—they're still automatically sucked into its brutality against black and brown people, still just as at risk of being wrongfully typecast and profiled, of becoming the next Freddie Gray, Jr.

In the midst of that scene, as he's marching down Baltimore's streets among the masses, Jonathan makes eye contact with an older black woman who's sitting on top of a car. She looks straight at Jonathan and says, "This is for you."

"I felt like she was looking at my soul," Jonathan tells me. He pauses. His eyes get watery.

Those words affirmed that he belonged. They affirmed his blackness, which was always questioned as an Afro-Latino. It affirmed his dignity as an undocumented person, which was often neglected in the mainstream political narrative. It affirmed his place in the country, which was demonized by some. It affirmed the need for the immigrant rights movement to show up for black people. And more than anything, it affirmed the pain and anger he carried inside him. How many other Afro-Latinos across the country were feeling that way that day?

"I was really angry with what I was experiencing in Baltimore," he tells me again. A painful reminder of the deep injustices black communities across America were enduring. Shortly after the Baltimore riots, Jonathan posted a status on social media expressing his anger. Slowly, people started commenting on his post. "I'm angry, too," his cofounder Jaime wrote. Eventually, they decided to turn this online outrage into a small meeting for black undocumented immigrants across the country. But given the huge interest and attention it received, what was meant to be a ten-person gathering turned into a seventy-person assembly. That's when it dawned on Jonathan that there was a much bigger community that needed to be seen and talked about. "The call was getting stronger for us to occupy our space— our rightful place in the movement. It's very clear to me that getting papers doesn't erase years of trauma that folks are under."

The story of undocumented black people is much more than about immigration. It's not just about the reality of living in this country without papers and status; it's also about being a black person in America. That reality says that black people are more than twice as likely to be killed by police than are white people; it says that 21 percent of black people live in poverty, compared with 10 percent of white people; that black women are twice as likely to die giving birth as are white women; and that black students are three times more likely than white students to experience gun violence on their campuses. So the story of undocumented black folks is one that's still finding the necessary words to heal all its wounds. And that's one of the reasons why the creation of UndocuBlack in 2016 was so groundbreaking: it originated out of an organic need to heal instead of a calculated political strategy to win. Through the years, UndocuBlack has turned to policy issues, from advocating for the American Dream and Promise Act to calling for the reversal of the 1996 Illegal Immigration Reform and Immigrant Responsibility Act. Now Jonathan finds himself sitting in fancy, powerful conference rooms all around D.C. and the country. But even when Jonathan and I find ourselves discussing policy, he manages to bring me back to the heart of it all: that quest to find inner peace.

"There's so much trauma that our folks are under," he reminds me. "What are the levers that we can push to move us all towards a collective healing?"

Jonathan is thinking big. His vision extends beyond the borders of this country and into the horizons of the lives that have been forgotten in America's jargon around blacks and immigration. Words that can now touch the forgotten. The neglected. The untracked. The same way that older black woman told Jonathan, "This is for you," during the Baltimore riots, I can now imagine Jonathan repeating that back to his community: "This is for you."

Even as he does so, he reflects, "At times, I don't want to be your extraordinary *negro*. Like, I just want to go to work, you know? Have fun, you know? I want to include immigrants' ability to be regular."

There is nothing more human than being regular. Than being allowed to live your own life and make your own mistakes. And, after all, that's exactly what Jonathan wants for

Selfie with Jonathan in Washington, D.C.

Jonathan in Washington, D.C.

undocumented black immigrants: to be seen as nothing more and nothing less than regular people.

Throughout my career, including my time on the Hillary Clinton campaign, I've spent so much time in Washington, D.C., going in and out of offices, conference rooms, and meetings with fancy people—highly educated, highly important in their fields—all of us scratching our heads to come up with brilliant messaging, groundbreaking policy solutions, and punchy press releases around immigrants and Latinos. Washington, D.C., in a strange way, makes one feel it's essential to be both an "extraordinary person" to operate in all those high-level, high-stress environments and the constant producer of "extraordinary work." So many people who walk those halls carry impostor syndrome, and I worry that it truly forces us all to overthink and overperform. And, as I'm talking to Jonathan, it dawns on me: maybe, this entire time, we were missing the picture. We've spent so much time trying to paint immigrants and Latinos in this nation as extraordinary beings; maybe the key is to show how regular we are, too.

There's no doubt our ancestors were extraordinary people—that's the story we love to tell, because it's part of the fire that lights us every day. But the reality is that they were also ordinary people, just like any other American. And in the Latinx community, one sees both: the exceptional and the ordinary.

11

Invisible

Fifteen years after I first moved to New York City, I'm just now realizing how easy it is to lose sight in the most visible places. That was never my intention, though.

One of the main reasons I decided to move to the flashiest city in the world was to never lose sight of my surroundings. Part of my thought process was that moving to the Big Apple would unearth parts of me that had once felt suppressed. I had heard my mom talk about her days in the Upper West Side at Barnard College, about living on St. Mark's Place, and about how she would find her favorite independent movie theaters in the East Village. Through her stories, I could always picture her walking around downtown, stepping into the Angelika, and sitting in Washington Square Park in the sun. It always seemed so liberating. And in my young eyes, that's exactly the effect I thought New York had on its residents: it prevented them from *ever* feeling invisible. I wanted that.

After I said the longest goodbye to Mom on 116th Street

and Broadway, survived my first solo subway ride (I vividly remember this woman yelling at me from the back as I climbed up the stairs: "Why are you so fucking slow!"), and figured out how to master my "New York City fast-paced walk," I felt truly loved by this city. I was a teenager who was being seen for the first time. At least that's what it felt like. New York City became the first place where I lost fear of holding hands in public with my crush. It's where I kissed on a lawn—*outside!*—for the first time. Where my clothes and outfits started garnering stares of admiration rather than judgment. Where my legs walked with endless curiosity, unbound by brakes to step on or traffic lights to wait on. It's where my best friends were a gay black man from Seattle and an Indian woman from New Delhi. Where I could dance the night away to French electro and cumbia, under one roof. And where my various accents, identities, and complex family histories became part of that famous pot that slowly melted us all into one.

Fifteen years since I first moved here, New York City and I have both grown. Together, we legalized same-sex marriage, marched for World Pride, celebrated our sanctuary status, and moved to the beats of AfroPunk. We saw Hillary Clinton become the first female nominee of any major U.S. party, we witnessed the rise of Alexandria Ocasio-Cortez, rallied in front of Trump Tower, and protected undocumented immigrants. But we also grew apart with the deaths of Eric Garner and Layleen Polanco. We grew apart every time we overheard racist slurs in the subway, each time the income-inequality gap widened, and every night a Latinx family could no longer afford their rent. These were years that formed me, molded me, and challenged me—years that forged the patterns of my life, my daily routines, and those quirky, unexplainable tics I've developed with age.

Then I realized I hadn't been seeing the other people who were changing—or remained unchanged—with the city. When was the last time I *really* looked around me? How many times was I looking down at my phone instead of up at people's faces? Had I ever changed my morning commute? For every subway ride I shared, every block I walked, every patch of grass I sat on: who, around me, was invisible to my eyes? *That* was the original question I came to this city for, and it dawned on me I had completely forgotten to find an answer.

I decided to take a walk around the city I thought I knew so well. But instead of following my daily routine, I decided to travel New York with that same endless curiosity I'd had as an eighteen-year-old who had just moved into her dorm room.

Instead of being led by the inherent presumptions that had built up around me throughout the years—moving my feet like two motorized toys—I'd stray from my original lane.

In forty-eight hours, here's what I see around me:

STOLEN *VIDAS*

Vida means "life" in Spanish.

When you first see Vidal from afar, you'd never think that his life has been stolen from him multiple times already. Not once but twice. Not one year but *many* years of his almost thirty years of life have been ripped away from him. You'd never know with that bright smile of his, though. If you accidentally make eye contact with Vidal from across the block in Harlem, you'd probably fixate on his tattoos and then unconsciously turn that glance into a stare. But that's exactly what Vidal is used to: long stares of suspicion.

"I grew up in an era of 'stop and frisk' . . . when police would stop you three to four times," he tells me.

"Stop and frisk" was a policy exploited by Mayor Rudy Giuliani that essentially allowed the New York Police Department to detain and search pedestrians without reasonable suspicion. The same year I was graduating from college in 2009, the New York Civil Liberties Union recorded that the NYPD stopped 581,168 people. Eighty-eight percent, almost all of them, were found to be innocent. While some of us, just down the road, were walking with a diploma in our right hand, some men of color like Vidal were walking with hand-cuffs on both, spending their hours being stopped a couple of times a day, harassed by the police, and placed in an arbitrary "gang book."

Over the years, the NYPD has been quietly building a controversial database of suspected "gang members" in the city. The department has been using arbitrary measures to affiliate people—mostly young men of color—with gangs. Anything from being subjected to "stop and frisk" to having a low-level criminal offense on record can get someone in that database. From 2013 to 2018, it's been reported that more than seventeen thousand people were added to the "gang book," almost 100 percent of them Latino and black. As of today, there are about eighteen thousand people in New York City whose names are inscribed in that book.

Vidal was written off as a gang member way before he even became one. And that's because, as our system stands today, much of our future is predestined at birth.

"I just mirrored whatever was around me," Vidal says.

As toddlers, we barely hold on to any memories, but Vidal remembers the days his mom's stomach wouldn't stop growling. "The days where you look at certain moments and say, 'You know, what happened to the land of the free?'" he says. Like many immigrants, Vidal's mom came to the United States from the Dominican Republic with a set of ideals and aspirations. Yet instead of living under a roof, Vidal ended up living under a staircase with his siblings and his single mother. With homelessness and poverty as his backyard, opportunities for Vidal looked less like extracurricular activities and more like selling drugs and adapting to life in the streets.

"I think what happened was that I went on survival mode, right?" he explains.

By the time Vidal was fifteen years old, he was a member of the Bloods, one of the oldest and most notorious gangs in the United States. At sixteen, he was arrested for the first time and sent to Rikers Island, New York's main jail complex, and was later sentenced to seven years as an adult.

Before 2017, New York was one of only two states across the country that prosecuted sixteen- and seventeen-year-olds as adults. Vidal was a victim of that system—one that never presented him with role models, pictures of success, or chances to thrive but, instead, punished him for approaching life as a teenager with a blindfold. "I mirrored people who all their life were influenced by the drug dealers, pimps, and gang members," he recounts. "In reality, what I really needed was not incarceration but actually a solution to come home."

As a sixteen- and seventeen-year-old at Rikers, Vidal

recalls being treated like "an animal" and fighting for his life every single day behind those bars. "Being incarcerated, physically and mentally, what it does to you, it's like you have demons and you are fighting them every single day. How do you operate?" he tells me. Vidal was released from Rikers on probation after two years, but life outside wasn't any easier than it was when he was first arrested. Vidal states: "I was traumatized, and I didn't know how to return to society."

Job opportunities were denied him, police harassment and profiling continued, and Vidal got sucked right back into gang life. Mirroring the high recidivism rates that plague this country's broken criminal justice system, Vidal eventually reentered the system at nineteen and remained locked up for another five years of his life. From Rikers Island, he was sent to the Greene Correctional Facility, where he was put in solitary confinement many times. But it was during the second time he landed there that Vidal made a promise no one had ever suggested he consider before: to believe in himself.

"I had to ask myself: What am I doing? How can I change the conversation around me? What can I do?"

After solitary confinement and several death threats, Vidal made it out. And chances are you've probably seen him on your TV screens, in newspapers, or somewhere online by now. After his long journey, he became one of the leading voices in the criminal justice reform movement. He successfully advocated for the "Raise the Age" policy, which effectively changed the criminal responsibility age in the state of New York to eighteen years old, and Vidal now has his eyes set on ending mass incarceration.

But Vidal is doing something else that has often been missing at the national level: including Latinos in the con-

Vidal and me outside the
JustLeadershipUSA offices in East Harlem.

versation around criminal justice reform. "People think that
the criminal justice system is just an African American problem. It's not," he tells me. We know that black and brown
men are disproportionately represented in the system. We
know that in 2017, Latinos accounted for more than 20 percent of inmates in this country (even though Latinos account
for only 16 percent of this country's adult population). This
means that one out of six Latino men will likely spend time
in jail at some point in their lives. And we know that there are
countless Vidals on the streets of New York—criminalized at
birth, incarcerated from puberty, traumatized for life.

Yet it's still extremely hard to find accurate data on Latinos
affected by the system. Researchers and policy makers agree
that there hasn't been enough effort to collect the necessary
information that would allow us to understand the full pic-

ture. Very simply, criminal justice has never been seen as a "Latino issue." The Latinx lens is starting to change that narrative.

For one thing, there's often not a clear ethnicity box to check for Latinos. But more than anything, as a community, we haven't made it our collective fight just yet.

"I know we are fighting so many different fights. Our identity, what we are going through . . . and I think in reality we just gotta find out what exactly it means to meet at the bridge, right? Create a bridge where we all are fighting together," says Vidal.

Before I leave, I ask him: "If you could go back in time, what would you tell six-year-old Vidal?"

"To love yourself," he responds very clearly.

I immediately think about Karolina in Arizona, because I suspect that if I'd asked her this same question, she would have given me the same answer: to love herself. Actually, I believe I would have gotten the same answer from countless people I've met on the road so far. For decades, that love was easily found in religion. We could turn to *Dios,* Jesus, or *la Virgen* to seek that unconditional love that was missing elsewhere. But even church doesn't seem to be enough these days. In fact, by 2014, the Pew Research Center found that almost 25 percent of Latino adults were now *former* Catholics.

So, *what* or *who* is replacing this void?

ALLAH AND *FRIJOLES NEGROS*

Twenty minutes away from New York City, I meet with Salim Patel, a member of the Passaic City Council in New

Jersey. Seventy percent of Passaic's residents are Latino (many of whom had been forced to leave New York because of increasing rent prices), and Salim tells me that the Latino community is "yearning for some type of spiritual enlightenment."

He goes on, "Through their unique experiences, their contacts, their relationships, whether at school or at work, they're exploring and finding Islam in a multitude of ways."

Latinos are yearning for something else. Salim tells me how, as a kid growing up in Passaic, he doesn't remember ever coming across Latino converts. But that's changed. He tells me that through the years, he's witnessed an exponential growth of Latinos turning to Islam.

"And why is that?" I ask.

"If you speak to each and every one of them, they're coming from a past that they may not necessarily be proud of. . . . Whatever religion they were following wasn't resonating, and they found something within Islam that just made complete sense," he answers.

Back in New York City I continue my walk, now searching for answers to questions I didn't even expect to be asking: Are Latinos finding themselves in Islam? Did I somehow miss this movement around me? Evidently, I did.

It's spring in the city, which means that New Yorkers have officially ended their hibernation mode. During this time of the year, everything sounds different around here. The radio oozing from those cars with the windows rolled down, the petals blooming in the park, and the cheer that erupts every time someone scores a goal or makes a basket in the outdoor courts. With spring, the city's layers start to slowly peel off and we can hear things more clearly again. If you listen, you'll hear the morning prayers at dawn, the evening prayer at sunset, and the joy that comes with the breaking of the fast every evening.

But if you listen closely, the morning prayers have Boricua accents, the mosques are filled with Dominicans, and the fasts are broken with *arroz y frijoles negros*.

It's officially Ramadan in the city.

Don't be surprised, because Latinos are actually the *fastest*-growing demographic within U.S. Muslims. Per a report published by the Institute for Social Policy and Understanding, only 1 percent of Muslims identified as Latino in 2009, but by 2018 that proportion increased to 7 percent. Today there are approximately 250,000 Latino Muslims across the United States, and the community keeps growing and growing.

So I make my way to a gathering to meet Puerto Rican members of the Latino Muslim community. My first question for everyone is, "What made you turn to Islam?" And they all give somewhat similar responses. It's pretty simple: when you're *actually* given space to *choose* your faith, Islam becomes the clear answer for many.

Aldo Perez, a local community organizer, tells me that the moment came to him when he realized he had been indoctrinated for years. In his eyes, Latinos' historic ties with colonialism mean that the community has always been *given* a faith rather than the option to *accept* one. "You know, it's our parents who make us Christians and Jews," he affirms. "My free will and choice to choose was actually to be a Muslim." Similarly, after time exploring the Koran and drawing their *own* conclusions, people like Danny Salgado and Wesley

Lebron, a former Catholic and a Christian, were eventually persuaded by the idea of *one* God over the concept of a mysterious Trinity.

"My God, my God, why hast thou forsaken me?" Psalm 22.

Throughout his journey to finding Islam, Wesley Lebron remembers questioning that very Bible verse. A while back he asked a Christian: "*Who* is that someone crying to God?" as he referred to the verse. The answer he received was, "Son, you just have to believe"—an underwhelming response many take for granted and follow blindly. Instead, Wesley Lebron searched for his own answers and ended up turning to Islam.

"People read the Koran as a form to attack Muslims and, in that journey, they end up finding this beautiful thing," he explains. The same thing happened to Wesley's Latina mom. More than two decades earlier, she kicked him out of the house when he began converting to Islam. But two years before our conversation, she told Wesley, "Son, I've been watching you, and I want to be Muslim."

Being Muslim and Latino may seem like two identities at complete odds. That's perhaps why people like Wesley's mom have those initial reactions at first: "You're converting to what!?" "*¿¡Qué!?*"

So I ask the community, "What's the biggest misconception Latinos have of Latino Muslims?"

Aldo doesn't even blink, he immediately responds with, "Terrorism."

Danny says, "That we're no longer Latino by being Muslim."

Wesley Lebron has to remind me, "I'm *still* Puerto Rican

Aldo, one of the leaders of New York City's
Latino Muslim community.

de sangre y de corazón." That Latino blood and heart can
never leave one's side.

The more time I spend with the community, the more
I'm realizing just how much overlap there is between these
two identities.

After my conversation, I end up going to a local iftar dinner to join Latino Muslims as they break the fast during this
Ramadan season. When I enter, I see Korans in Spanish, a
stand with information to benefit the victims of Hurricane
Maria, and, of course, loads of food waiting to be served.
The energy one feels around here is one that seems oddly
familiar. A welcoming one. It's one of giving, love, and compassion.

"The brotherhood and sisterhood . . . that's something that appeals to Muslims *and* to Latinos as well," Danny points out.

"Upon studying Islam and studying the traditions of the Prophets, we find that there are huge synergies [between the two cultures]: how you treat your partners, your parents, your guests—all of these different things synergize," Wesley tells me.

But I don't want to intrude in their space during iftar. I want to be respectful as they're observing this sacred holiday, so I decide to sit at one of the corner tables. Although I soon realize there *is* no such thing as "them" and "me" here. It was a mistake to make that assumption in the first place, because everyone is *familia* around here. A young woman approaches my lonely table and tells me, "Sister, come this way and sit with the other sisters." I smile and immediately follow her. We leave behind the men, who are all seated to the left of the room, and join the women, who are all gathered on the right.

After the prayers are done and the sun finally sets, we all break fast with the *arroz con frijoles,* the fried chicken, and the cake that's waiting for us. I'm surrounded by women I had never met before: a Mexican immigrant who left her family behind in la Ciudad de México in search of Islam; an Afro-Panamanian Muslim mother; a Dominican Muslim Trump supporter. The list goes on. *Abuelas,* mothers, and daughters. *Primas* and *tías.* All Latinas with their hijabs unveiling truths this country has never heard before, crossing intersections this nation has never walked in before, and breaking stereotypes. But all of them, at some point, speak-

My plate from the iftar dinner, which included delicious *arroz con frijoles* and fried chicken.

ing a familiar language we, as women, know all too well: resistance.

Our tranquil iftar dinner became an impromptu women's roundtable—a safe space. It almost sounded like a *chismería* session:

"We need to speak up for ourselves," one said.

"*Hay que decirlo,* [the men] feel like we should be at home," another woman mentioned.

"Come to our weekly meetings," someone else told a new member of the community.

It felt not at all like a reproach of the men to our left but rather like the symphony of a women's chorus that was starting to find its own voice.

Before I leave, one woman comes up to me and says,

"[The men] didn't introduce you to me at any point, right?" She's the woman who was leading the *chisme* session at the table, pushing the other Latina sisters to reflect, ask tough questions, and see themselves as a *unit.*

"You're right," I say, "they didn't introduce us. But now I know who you are."

We give each other a hug and formally introduce ourselves.

Next time, she'll be the first person I look for in a room.

THE OCASIO-CORTEZ EFFECT

Ever since I was young, New York City has always exuded power to me. There is something about the massive skyscrapers, Wall Street, City Hall, the constant buzz . . . that feels inaccessible and powerful. No one in this city would have known that a woman called Alexandria Ocasio-Cortez, from the Bronx, would change the very meaning of power, first in this city and then in the entire nation.

For decades, Latinas didn't really know what political power looked like or felt like. We knew it was concentrated in the white hands of a few and that every now and then congresswomen like Nydia Velázquez, Hilda Solis, and Ileana Ros-Lehtinen would shine in the spotlight. Even though they paved unprecedented paths for many of us, and even though their appearance had a satisfying familiarity—the slight accents, the fierce resolve, the contagious sense of humor—power, for many, still felt distant. We perhaps saw ourselves reflected in their *platforms,* but not necessarily, entirely in *them.*

After Trump's election, our marching feet eventually led

to unimaginable change in our nation's capital. Following the 2016 elections, Latinas didn't necessarily start to march, advocate, and fight; we continued to build on that march for justice that Dolores Huerta spearheaded with her *"¡Sí se puede!"* chants in the 1970s. Now, with even more force. I remember how, the day after Trump's inauguration, Carmen Perez, president and CEO of the Gathering for Justice and a national co-chair of the 2017 Women's March on Washington, was among the leaders who stood on a stage that faced a crowd of more than half a million people gathered just blocks from the White House. Amid that massive crowd—and in front of millions more who were watching on television—Carmen opened her speech with:

"I stand here as a Chicana, Mexican American woman."

She then paused, almost as if she wanted all of us to let that sink in. Carmen eventually continued with her five-minute remarks.

"Remember, when you go back home, think about why you marched. And organize, organize, organize!!" Carmen said right before ending her speech.

And with her fist to the air, she closed with: *"¡Sí se puede!"*

Carmen's voice on that stage was a subtle nod to all Latinas who were making history without even knowing it.

Months after the march, I was able to talk to Carmen about her experience. She told me that prior to the 2017 Women's March, Latinas didn't necessarily see themselves in leadership roles. There weren't many stages we were standing on or megaphones that were willing to amplify our words. "What the Women's March has allowed us to do is to see women in different shades, different body types. . . . And now there are so many more young people saying: 'I am her and she is me,' " Carmen said. That was the preamble to the Ocasio-Cortez effect.

When Alexandria Ocasio-Cortez rose to power, finding her seat in the House of Representatives, millions of Latinas were able to say for the first time: *I am her and she is me.* That's partially because the 2018 midterms officially went down as the return of the "Year of the Women." There were many reasons for that headline. For one, an unprecedented number of women were elected to office, leading to a record 131 women serving in both chambers. Among them, women with last names like Ocasio-Cortez, Escobar, and Garcia started to swarm the busy halls of Capitol Hill. *The Washington Post* reported that the election had produced "one of the most diverse groups of politicians in American history." Similarly, women, as they have in every midterm election since 1998, voted at higher rates than men and they also overwhelmingly chose the Democratic Party, which was viewed as a referendum on Trump. Latinas drove a lot of those trends. Generally, they not only outvoted Latino men but voted blue more reliably, with 73 percent of Latino women voting for Democrats compared with 63 percent of Latino men. And in important battleground states like Nevada, 75 percent of Latinas voted for Democratic candidates in the Senate race compared with 54 percent of Latino men. In other words, Latinas across the United States spoke up.

Propelled by the march-goers, the #MeToo protesters, the farmworkers, and the younger generation, Washington, D.C., started to look different. It suddenly became possible for a twenty-eight-year-old Boricua bartender from the

Bronx to become the youngest congresswoman in history. Once broke #AF (that stands for "as fuck"), with radiant red lips, big hoop earrings, and no prior experience in politics, Congresswoman Alexandria Ocasio-Cortez now effortlessly strides through the halls of Congress.

As with Carmen Perez, Parkland student Emma González, and activist Mónica Ramírez, in Alexandria Ocasio-Cortez hundreds of thousands of Latinas are now able to see themselves.

Many feel passionate about the policy issues she's advocating. From abolishing ICE and uplifting Medicare for All to architecting a Green New Deal, she enables a new generation to feel heard for the first time. But in many ways, Ocasio-Cortez represents not just a voice for the young but also a call for justice on behalf of the older generations of Latinos who have paved the way for us. And that's something many first-generation Latinos can relate to: their win is really their parents' win as well, building on their generations of struggles to get us to this point. On the week Ocasio-Cortez was sworn into office, she wrote on her Instagram:

> Mami mopped floors, drove school buses, + answered phones. She did whatever she needed to do, for me. When my father died, she was left a single mother of 2, and again she had to start over. After he passed we almost lost our home, so we sold it and started over. & over. & over.

Ocasio-Cortez completely shook the status quo, but the barriers she broke were as much hers as they were her mother's—and that resonates with a lot of young people, even if very subtly. So yes, we don't see ourselves just in Ocasio-Cortez's looks or in the policy platforms she proposes. In fact, many don't even agree with her politics and quite a few reject her as a "socialist." But it's her aura that we cling to. It's the unabashed persona that we recognize. It's the confidence that feels familiar to us. Because it projects a courageous image that, at times, we've all been too afraid to step into.

Now we know what that image of power looks like. It no longer feels unreachable.

The power of that projection is best measured outside Washington and the hearing rooms of Capitol Hill. It lies in its ability to awaken people who are outside the traditional realms of power. The Ocasio-Cortez effect does that: it makes many of the Latinx community feel that anything, even running for office, is possible.

"OUT" AND THE CITY

One thing I've also never been able to forget is Prides in New York City.

Pride in New York, marching down Fifth Avenue, passing by the Stonewall Inn, and dancing into the West Village. Rainbow flags covering endless blocks across Manhattan, unfolding like squishy red carpets beneath our feet. Pride embracing you with a freedom, an openness, and a love that honors the roars of the liberation movement and the bravery of the unsung heroes of the Stonewall riots. You stomp proudly for *them*—for Marsha P. Johnson and Sylvia Rivera,

Trans-Latinas, led by Liz Chavez, in front of the Stonewall Inn in New York City.

the overlooked transgender women of color who led the uprisings of 1969. During Pride, the invisible become visible.

"It's like a fantasy," Francisco tells me. Francisco is his pseudonym.

Kendra says, "It's a day where we get to express ourselves and where people support us. But, two days after, those are the very same people pointing fingers at us. We live in a world where there are two morals." Kendra is also a pseudonym.

"It's the most progressive city in the world!" they tell you. But you soon find out that's not always the case.

I don't think Francisco and Kendra had met before this day, but their stories have similar beginnings and progressions. Every single day—whether in the morning, afternoon, or evening, whether before or after each goes to bed— Francisco and Kendra experience a similar pain at some point during their daily routines. Unknowingly, their paths cross almost every day.

Francisco came to New York to be an openly gay man, escaping the homophobia he experienced in Mexico. Similarly, Kendra came to the city to feel free in her skin as a transgender woman, leaving behind the violence and persecution of Honduras. As the story goes, neither has been able to find that absolute freedom they were craving. While Kendra hasn't been able to land a job, Francisco, at least, is able to earn a stable income.

Francisco tells me that once he got to the city, he became a construction worker. "I can't really be open around them because they would bully me," he says.

Kendra, on the other hand, has been forced to do sex work. "I don't like to do sex work," she tells me, "but I have to do it to be able to survive, live, dress myself, and feed myself. How *else* would I be able to live? *¿Cómo podría sobrevivir?*"

That's a fair question. How else does she survive?

Even though Kendra and Francisco live very different lives, this is where their experiences converge, in the simple act of walking down the street:

KENDRA WALKING DOWN THE STREET

Close your eyes and picture a very slim transgender Latina with long, straight hair, big hoops, and a huge smile walking down a crowded intersection in the immigrant-heavy neighborhood of Jackson Heights, Queens. Even though this is an immigrant-filled area and one of the country's most diverse neighborhoods, being a trans woman still puts you at risk of incarceration, violence, or even death. As reports indicate, over the years, the NYPD has been arbitrarily profiling trans women and targeting them with prostitution-related charges based solely on their appearance and gender identity. In 2018, prostitution-related loitering arrests increased by more than 180 percent in New York City, with the majority of them taking place in Queens.

Kendra describes to me how she receives stares from random pedestrians. "Oh, look, it's a man dressed as a woman" or "This person looks weird" is written on people's faces as they pass by Kendra. Then Kendra quickly regroups with her friends, because they have learned the hard way that it's unsafe for transgender Latinas to walk alone outside, even in the streets of New York City, all of them carrying a fear of coming across an aggressive person who will harass them. Eventually, they do stumble upon that person—not once but multiple times throughout this walk.

At one point, someone throws a water bottle at them; at another turn, someone insults them: *"¡Maricones! ¡Se creen una mujer!"* Faggots! You think you're a woman! A little farther down the street, someone tries to snatch their bags; and then there's that person who tries to put his hands up their skirts. Physical aggressions may come to an end in this walk, but the terror is endless.

FRANCISCO WALKING DOWN THE STREET

Now, just one block down the street from Kendra, Francisco walks down the street.

Although it's significantly easier for him to assimilate into society as a cis gay man, his days at work at the construction sites usually involve some form of verbal harassment by his colleagues. But during this walk, things are different.

A person comes up to him and starts punching him in the face while yelling racist comments. Francisco's eyebrow is immediately busted open. When the attack is over, Francisco follows his aggressors—an African American couple.

"At least tell me why you're doing this to me," Francisco asks his attackers.

"Because I hate Latinos, motherfucker. Don't you understand?" one of them responds.

Kendra's and Francisco's accounts are real. Both of them are lived experiences.

"Those words will always stick with me," Francisco says.

"They say New York is a very open-minded city, a very generous one. But the reality is another one. Especially if you're a person of color, if you don't understand English well, and if you're trans," Kendra tells me.

This city is so full of light. There are streetlights shining down at night; there's the glow of the skyscrapers looming over all the boroughs and the countless tiny windows radiating fluorescent light. *How* do we miss this every day?

Before we leave the Make the Road New York offices in Brooklyn, where we've been chatting for hours, I ask Francisco and Kendra to talk about their dreams. "What are they?" New York City is many things, but one thing that it's known for worldwide is as a place that allows people to dream big and have big aspirations for themselves. But that's not the answer I get.

"All I want is for everyone to be able to walk down the street without having anyone offend us," Francisco says.

"One day, I want to get on a train without having anyone pointing at me. I want to go to a restaurant without having anyone talking about me simply because I'm gay."

When he says this, it's like a wake-up call.

Francisco reminds me that maybe, all this time, New York has had me dreaming way too big. My eyes have been set on the horizon, and at times I've neglected the way freedom and I have interacted throughout all these years. Did New York City really feel free? At times, I've unconsciously chosen to *not* hold hands with my partner as we walk down the street. I've unconsciously chosen not to kiss her in public or be affectionate with her during a subway ride. Was I truly as "free" as I thought I was all this time?

"LITTLE OAXACA" AND PRINCESS DONAJÍ

The last stop in New York's Metro-North train is one that few people get off at: Poughkeepsie. I don't know exactly why, but I remember that during my college years Poughkeepsie always had a bad rep. It was known as an industrial, crime-ridden, "ugly" city. As a place with little to no reason to visit (unless you had friends at Vassar College). It always seemed like one of those abandoned ghost towns you saw on TV. Over the years, I had gone to New York State's beautiful Hudson Valley plenty of times for small getaways from the city, but I never bothered to make a detour into Poughkeepsie.

It turns out that Poughkeepsie transformed itself into "Little Oaxaca," a vibrant community of indigenous Mexicans that completely revitalized this forgotten American city.

You would expect to see Oaxacans settled in Los Angeles

or New York City, but never in a town that goes by the name of Poughkeepsie.

Oaxaca is a state in the southwestern part of Mexico, and it's one of the poorest in the country. Approximately 60 percent of the population lives in poverty, 20 percent in extreme poverty, and 35 percent don't have access to food. Because of its rural location, most of the region has traditionally survived on agriculture. Most important, Oaxaca is also one of the country's most ethnically diverse regions. There are sixteen indigenous tribes in the state, including the Zapotec and Mixtec people. It's a place where it's as common to speak Spanish as it is to speak in one of its various indigenous languages. Imagine majestic mountains, Pacific waters, and forests overlooking lands marked by the souls of indigenous ancestors. The land of mole, *mezqual,* and *tlayudas. That's* Oaxaca.

It is well known that the three southern states of Guerrero, Oaxaca, and Chiapas have the highest poverty rates in the entire country, partly (but not entirely) because of their high indigenous populations. As reported by the *HuffPost*'s analysis of an Oxfam report, indigenous people suffer from poverty levels four times higher than the national average. The rate of extreme poverty is also three times higher than the national average. And word of mouth is that the small town of Poughkeepsie actually has the *largest* population of Oaxacans outside Mexico. But out of all the places in the world, *why* did they migrate to Poughkeepsie?

That's the thing about immigration—the shortest answer to the most complex questions about this debate is often *love.* No matter the borders, no matter the policies, big walls, or strategies, people will always continue to migrate out of love. That's an unstoppable force. Poughkeepsie became home for many Oaxacans simply because that's where *their* loved ones were. That was the only similarity between the two towns. During the 1970s and 1980s, many Oaxacans started migrating from Mexico to New York City, looking for jobs. Instead of giving up when they couldn't find opportunities in the Big Apple, many of them took New York's Metro-North train all the way to its last stop and ended up in Poughkeepsie. It was the station no one else would get off at—the most remote and foreign one to them—but it ended up becoming the town where Oaxacans slowly found jobs in factories, restaurants, and the textile industry. It was where they found a new home and, eventually, what became "Little Oaxaca."

"You go where your people go. . . . That's how it happened," says Susie Ximenez, a young Oaxacan Poughkeepsie resident who came here with her family years ago.

And it was indigenous Oaxacans who helped rebuild this town. Susie recalls how Poughkeepsie's Main Street was completely burned down after the Rodney King riots of 1992. An uproar that was felt not only in the streets of Los Angeles but also in Poughkeepsie and across the entire nation. "Nobody knows this story," Susie reminds me, "but the Latino community and the Oaxacan community were the ones that stayed when Main Street was nothing, and they have pushed it and thrived. And every other business since is built off the Oaxacan community."

Felipe Santos, another Oaxacan local, remembers a similar before-and-after picture of Poughkeepsie. "The streets were like a garbage can when I first arrived here," he says, "but now there are small businesses and the community is thriving. That's how we can conquer hearts."

It's hard to believe that I'm here and not walking around an Oaxacan pueblo. During a stroll through Poughkeepsie's Main Street, the majority of the stores you see are in fact run by Oaxacans. The "Chapulin" kiosk stands out, selling *chilacayota, horchata,* and *agua de Jamaica.* There's also *diablito* on the menu, that sweet tamarind-flavored shaved ice with Valentina and Tajín. Seeds, fruits, and fresh waters everywhere, just like the ones you find at the Mexican *zócalos.* Everything so fresh, so meticulously garnished and curated with love. But it's not just the food that strikes you in this town, it's the way in which the Oaxacan community has been able to channel the richest parts of their Mexican indigenous culture in such a powerful manner.

It feels as if by holding on to their roots, Oaxacans are reclaiming a piece of the United States that belonged to their indigenous brothers and sisters, the Native Americans who settled in Poughkeepsie long before Europeans ever did. In fact, the word "Pough-keep-sie" actually derives from the Wappinger Indian people. And when you start to look at Oaxacans through that lens—not as immigrants but as natives—the city of Poughkeepsie takes on a whole other meaning. The things you believed were "out of place" are exactly where they're meant to be.

More than ten years ago, Felipe Santos re-created "La Guelaguetza" right by Poughkeepsie's riverfront. La Guelaguetza, which means "offering" in Zapotec, is the state of Oaxaca's most notorious annual festival. It honors the region's rich precolonial indigenous history through tradi-

Felipe and me talking by Poughkeepsie's riverfront, where La Guelaguetza takes place every summer.

tional dances. Today, thanks to Felipe and the local folkloric group he started, that celebration has also landed in Poughkeepsie. Once a year, the vibrant clothing, the artifacts, and the sounds of Oaxaca take over the town with pride. As Felipe sees it, it's a way not only to offer the city a beautiful gift but also to pass on traditions to the new generations of Oaxacans living in Poughkeepsie.

With its colors and melodies, it seems impossible to miss La Guelaguetza around here. But unless your eyes are opened wide and accustomed to seeing Oaxacans as one of "us" instead of one of "them," it'll go unnoticed.

The mayor of Poughkeepsie, Rob Rolison, who's lived here more than half his life, hadn't known about La Guelaguetza until recently.

"I lived here for thirty years and I didn't know about it!" he tells me. "Which is sort of symptomatic, that . . . a lot of people that live in this city don't know that it's going on."

So I ask the mayor: "What was it like the first time you actually saw the Guelaguetza festival? What did you think?"

"It was mind-blowing," he responds.

This city is breaking even more stereotypes than the ones I originally foresaw. I have to admit that when I first met Mayor Rolison, I unjustly wrote him off as an out-of-touch Republican. Since he took office as mayor in 2016, Rob Rolison has become a crucial voice in strengthening the ties between his constituents and the Mexican state of Oaxaca. He wants his local residents to be in touch with their culture, not to suppress it. He wants them to be proud of where they come from, not ashamed. To be out, not in the shadows. He's currently working on building an exchange program between the two local governments and is committed to making Poughkeepsie a safe place. "Just because you left Oaxaca," he tells me, "you didn't leave your culture there. So, we need to let you know that we feel good about the fact that you're here and that you're Oaxacan."

Sometimes you find answers you were always looking for where you least expect them. This small Republican town, removed from the national headlines and D.C. spotlight, has something figured out: how to lead with love.

It almost feels like a fantasy. What if you don't believe in all these traditions? Or, as a young person, what if your American, Latinx, *and* indigenous identities don't fit perfectly into *each* box? How do you navigate it all?

Susie Ximenez is a millennial who migrated from Oaxaca at a young age. Susie spent most of her life in Poughkeepsie and was ashamed to embrace her indigenous roots until recently. For years, Susie hid her indigenous name, "Donají," from most people.

"What were you so ashamed of?" I ask Susie.

As she recalls, American media would always paint the state of Oaxaca and its indigenous people as an impoverished, dirty community. And that's one of the many reasons Susie decided to hide her indigenous name from Poughkeepsie locals and her own Oaxacan people. Yet, as she tells me, once she really began to learn about her home state of Oaxaca, the richness of her culture, and the ways in which Oaxacans had *literally* revitalized Poughkeepsie, she started to see the real power behind her identity. There's one specific moment Susie recalls: when she looked around her surroundings and confirmed that the backbone of Poughkeepsie's economy was built by strong Oaxacan women.

Today, when you ask Susie what her name is, she'll tell you: "My indigenous name is Donají, which means 'the People's Princess.'" She doesn't beat around the bush anymore. Susie came out not once but twice.

First, she came out as Donají, not only by accepting her name but also by truly honoring the power that comes with it. As the legend goes, Susie is the descendant of an ancient Zapotec princess who sacrificed her life for the people. No matter how far away she is from Oaxaca, that's a responsibility Susie carries in her soul these days. Second, Susie came out as a queer woman, something that hasn't always been easy to navigate in a community that values tradition.

In fact, when I bring up the La Guelaguetza festival, Susie quickly tells me she *never* went as a kid while she was growing up in Poughkeepsie. I ask her why. "My parents tried to

Princesa Donají in Poughkeepsie.

keep us far away from that because we were made fun of so much," Susie says. She recalls how she and her brother would be constantly bullied because of their sexual orientation—some would call her *"marimacha,"* others *"Juanita."*

"It really sucked hearing all of these negative things from the community you're supposed to call your people or your home," she tells me.

I know how much that sucks. But there's something about our generation that really differentiates us from our parents: we don't compromise our truths. Contrary to what others may think, for Susie, being queer is *not* an insult to her indigenous roots but a testament to its beauty and richness. "There are so many queer icons in our indigenous history—why can't we acknowledge it?" she tells me.

I ask, "What's an indigenous legend you admire the most, Susie?"

Centuries ago, there were two male warriors who fell

madly in love. They would go into the valley—away from everyone and everything—to hide their love. "They would wait there for each other because that's the only place they felt comfortable in," Susie explains. They waited, they lay next to each other, and they loved each other, eventually morphing into two continuous mountains that are now part of Oaxaca's horizon. Now so intertwined in Oaxaca's history and culture that you can barely notice.

I have no doubt that the next time I come back to Poughkeepsie, those mountains will be replicated somewhere in the Hudson Valley. And thanks to Princesa Donají, we won't be afraid to say their names out loud either.

MISS RIZOS

When I finally come home to my apartment in Brooklyn, De'Ara, my girlfriend, is brushing her hair in the living room. Her hair is black and curly. Her hair is one of the first things that caught my eyes.

When De'Ara and I started dating, so much of the beginning of falling in love happened while we weren't even paying attention—while we were mindlessly performing our daily routines. Except that what was routine for me was not for her, and vice versa. She'd see me brush my teeth and leave the cap off the toothpaste every night; and I'd see her wear her silk nightcap to bed and apply deep conditioner to her curls. Now, because I've memorized her routine after all these years, I know that each time we land in a foreign city, one of our first stops will be at the local supermarket so we can find the best shampoo and conditioner for De'Ara's

De'Ara, smiling.

curls. I also know that, usually, when I'm in charge of picking that hair product for her, I always get it wrong.

De'Ara loves her hair. But don't take that love for granted.

I see how much maintenance her hair takes. I see how much care it requires. How much energy is needed. And, more than anything, I see that it takes love. But I need to understand that the beauty I see in De'Ara's hair hasn't *always* been accepted by Afro-Latinas. Loving their hair hasn't always been as straightforward as we may think. When social norms, mainstream media, and traditional professional etiquettes all tell the masses to straighten their hair in order to "look good" and "presentable," curls become the curse of that image. When white people get to set beauty standards—dictating what's acceptable and what's not— curls are to be suppressed. And when the color of one's skin can make them a moving target, curls must be hidden from the eye of the beholder. Tamed as much as possible. It's true that it's a lot more common to see Afro-Latinas like Amara La Negra posing on magazine covers with their glowing natural curls, but this hasn't always been the case. That liberation, too, is still being fought for.

Now that I'm back in New York, I decide to get in touch with Carolina Contreras, an entrepreneur who's also known as "Miss Rizos" or "Miss Curls."

Carolina is a young Afro-Latina from the Dominican Republic who opened the *first*-ever beauty salon for naturally curly hair on the island. Carolina is now on her way to opening another salon in Washington Heights. I had already heard about Miss Rizos before I met her. One of my sister's close friends from college, Shaday, has often sworn that Carolina sells the "best hair products" for curly hair. For as long as I've known Shaday, I've *always* seen her rocking those beautiful curls of hers. That's exactly what Miss Rizos envisioned when she launched her business: for Afro-Latinas to feel proud—not ashamed—of themselves. And that's not something Carolina always felt. Carolina learned to love her curls.

When I sit down with Carolina, I ask her to take me back in time to the first relationship she had with her curls. As with all relationships, love goes through phases—resistance, pain, evolution, then maybe even acceptance.

"I remember my mom pulling my hair . . . it was instilled in me from being little that it was a problem," she tells me.

As Carolina explains, without any general knowledge about how to handle curly hair, her mom resorted to what countless Afro-Latina moms did: relaxing Carolina's hair.

Relaxing one's hair was synonymous with having an easier time in school, an easier time finding jobs and navigating reality. It was, as she says, the normal thing to do and a positive reinforcement that was code for "feeling beautiful." As her mom taught her, Carolina passed on those very same traditions to her sisters—fixing their hair, relaxing their curls, and literally causing pain for the sake of assimilating.

"I would burn their scalp with the relaxer," she states. "Literally, that's what I did to my sisters, and that's a violent act."

Trauma, Carolina reminds me, can be hidden in many forms.

She continues, "I was physically causing harm on them [her sisters] and making them cry. I was thinking that I was also doing them a favor by making them more beautiful and by also having them conform to what's normal. I was assimilating to become more Eurocentric," she states. And that pressure to assimilate to European standards was felt both on the island and in the United States, as Carolina and her family moved from the Dominican Republic to Massachusetts when Carolina was very young.

"And, at what point were you able to see this pain for what it was?" I ask. "At what point did you realize what was happening?"

As she tells me, the consciousness of how her hair was an extension of her skin color dawned on Carolina when she was in high school. "It was then that I started to think a little bit more about what I was doing with my hair in relation to being black," she tells me.

As she got older, Carolina began educating herself about race, leading her to find pride in her blackness, to find a voice in advocacy, and to start questioning a lot of the assumptions she grew up with. Although by the time she got to college Carolina had grown increasingly skeptical of the norms that were ingrained in her as a child, she still couldn't let go of the practice of straightening her hair. As we all know, routines are really hard to break.

"I just felt that it was so normal to straighten my hair. I compare it to brushing your teeth. It felt like showering. It felt like if I didn't relax my hair every two months, I felt dirty." Carolina did explore leaving her hair curly a couple of times in college and even upon graduating, but each time she either was overcome by fear or thought it was too impractical.

At some point down the road, things really changed.

As with so many others in the Latinx community, there was a specific moment that marked Carolina's transition. It was the moment she realized that there seemed to be a disconnect between the values she preached and the actions she took. As she recounts, one day she found herself sunbathing in the Dominican Republic when suddenly her friend told her, "What are you doing in the sun? Get out of there; you're going to get dark like a Haitian! *Te vas a poner prieta como una haitiana.*"

Carolina recalls feeling angry and confronting her friend for making such a derogatory comment. But here's what Carolina didn't expect: her friend's response.

"What are you talking about? You straighten your hair."

Carolina tells me that in that moment, she didn't know how to defend herself because she couldn't get herself to genuinely say that it was *her* choice to straighten her hair.

"I didn't have the language then because it wasn't the case," she states.

The next day, Carolina cut her hair. The next week, she cut a bit more. The next couple of weeks, even more was gone. By the end of the month, Carolina had chopped off most of her hair. Everything she was holding on to, gone.

I ask Carolina how she felt after she cut off all her hair. She tells me she went through a lot of emotions. At times feeling like a boy, other times feeling like *un pollo,* sometimes feeling beautiful, and most times feeling ugly. But eventually, she felt liberated. And that very feeling—that discovery and unearthing—was the beginning of the birth of "Miss Rizos."

"I think without those feelings, I probably wouldn't have the same journey towards discovering Miss Rizos and being able to help other people, because I lived it."

After blogging about her journey and developing a big online presence, Carolina became one of the most influential voices in natural hair care for Afro-Latinas. From selling her own beauty products to answering hundreds of questions from followers to seeing customers in her living room—people from all over the Dominican Republic were seeking Carolina's advice.

"Little by little, I started feeling that there was something really special about what was happening," Carolina says. And years later, in 2014, Carolina successfully opened Miss Rizos, the island's first hair institution dedicated exclusively to natural curly hair.

But the thing is, Miss Rizos is more than just a salon. Miss Rizos has become a space where people find a type of support they're unable to grasp elsewhere. Where they find a beauty they didn't know they had or a power they didn't even know belonged to them in the first place. Where all of a sudden, they feel understood. As Carolina says, a woman may come in wanting to detangle her hair, but she leaves knowing what to tell her husband each time he says he doesn't like her natural hair. She may come in for a simple treatment, but she leaves in awe of a body she just discovered. She may come to learn how to handle a burned scalp but leaves with a box of tissues because she now knows that it's okay to feel pain from trauma. She may come alone, but she leaves with a group of women who now support her and her daughters and granddaughters.

With each chop, treatment, and conversation that takes place inside those walls, it's not only strands of hair that fall to the floor but years of abuse. Of pain. And of trauma. And with the past death of each curl comes newfound birth. Now,

Carolina, "Miss Rizos," in Washington Heights.

stronger than ever. More resilient than ever. Healthier than ever.

"It's a special place, you know?" Carolina says. Now, Washington Heights can expect the same.

Carolina, like everyone else I've met throughout this walk, is working tirelessly to ensure she is being seen.

Corners where we pass by Vidal, trains where we sit next to Kendra, tables that we share with Wesley Lebron, and air that we breathe with Princesa Donají. Every single one of us has had that moment where we decided to look away instead of straight at whoever was in front of us and when we walked past without any hesitation to stop.

New York City is still the same city my mom and I fell in love with decades ago. It's still the same city that lit up my dreams every night. And I can still close my eyes and contour the skyscrapers that tower over me. The only difference now, after these forty-eight hours of wandering, is that this city looks so much more magnificent than I had ever imagined.

12

Home

Believe it or not, America's Midwest actually feels like home to many Latinx.

Where you least expect it—removed from the border towns, the sunny southern cities, and the West Coast—the Midwest is a place many Latinos can call home. This place they've labeled as "Middle America," seen by so many as "the land of the white," is really the land of the brown, home to millions of Latinos who have been silently laying brick after brick there. It isn't readily apparent until you start paying attention. But when I finally did, I realized it's the closest to home I'd felt in a long time. That's partly because the Latino presence in the Midwest goes way back. Way before the mainstream history books even knew about Latino history.

Rebekah Crisanta de Ybarra, an indigenous Salvadoran Latina artist from St. Paul, Minnesota, tells me, "Part of the problem in academia is that everything needs to be referenced, and it's been wrong since the beginning." In her eyes, what the history books fail to mention is that ancient indigenous communities from the Paleolithic era, like the

Latin American Lenca tribe that originated in the highlands of El Salvador and Honduras, had been migrating across the Americas for as far back as we can remember. In fact, Rebekah's tribe can find ancient traces and connections to the native Dakota people's sacred sites in the state of Minnesota.

Cultural existence then starts to rely on the indescribable intimacy certain spaces naturally evoke in people. Like when you meet someone for the first time, but it feels as if you've known them forever, as though you've met them before this lifetime. That's what a remote place like Minnesota can feel like for some Latinos like Rebekah. Indescribably familiar. Rebekah tells me that visitors will often look at her and say: "You guys have a different vibe here in Minnesota; it's something I *can't* put my finger on."

For Rebekah, the answer is simple. "I think part of it has to do with this deep foundation of the alliance of tribes," she says.

Whether it was in the Paleolithic era or just a century ago, Latinos' presence in the Midwest is *not* a new development. And while not nearly enough academics or researchers have looked into this, young scholars like Sergio González, who grew up in Milwaukee and is now an author and professor, are reviving pieces of history that have remained lost in translation for far too long.

"This is *not* a new history," Sergio assures me.

Sergio stresses that if we focus only on the border when discussing Latino migration, we risk missing the entire picture. I have to admit, until recently I *was* one of those people who would drive through the Midwest without giving it any pause. Without any urgency to detour into the farmlands, the tiny towns, or the south sides. However, it's been recorded that during the first three decades of the twentieth century, more than one hundred thousand Mexicans settled in the Midwest. From Wisconsin to Iowa, Minnesota, and Illinois, people were driven not only by jobs in farming, manufacturing, or meatpacking but also by their need to escape political and social unrest happening in Latin America, like the Mexican Revolution.

"We often think of Latinx people solely within the context of being workers. Latinos have come to the U.S. for a variety of reasons . . . this diversity of experiences is often lost," Sergio says.

Although only approximately 9 percent of all Latinos across the nation live in the Midwest today, the community there keeps growing. To give you an idea, as the overall Latino population overwhelmingly grew across the United States from 2000 to 2010, the U.S. Census confirmed that this growth was *mostly* felt in the South and in the Midwest. As they found, during this ten-year period, the Latino population increased by almost 50 percent and was "more than twelve times the growth of the total population in the Midwest."

Suddenly, this midwestern land starts to feel more like ours.

FOLLOWING THE SMELL OF FOOD: CHICAGO

I hadn't been in Chicago since I worked on Barack Obama's reelection campaign in 2012.

Even though it had been so long, my feet were still accustomed to a routine that wanted to take me to our old campaign headquarters overlooking scenic Millennium Park and deep blue Lake Michigan. From high up in the Prudential Building, where our offices were, I remember feeling as though we campaigners were on top of the world. As though we had the power to help everyone who had ever felt left out. That was our promise for "Hope and Change." But sometimes it's necessary to leave that high altitude in order to understand what you're missing on the ground— yet I couldn't recall how many times I had actually physically left the Prudential Building in 2012.

So instead of treading old ground, I asked my taxi driver at O'Hare International Airport, "What should I do here?"

He didn't think twice.

"You have got to go to Restaurant Nuevo Leon. *Todo está bien rico ahí,*" he said. Everything is "so good" there. He started recalling to me how his mother would make him pozole and mole back in Mexico. As he told me, it had been twenty-four years since he was last in his hometown.

"I'm sold. Please, take me to Nuevo Leon," I said. And during this car ride, imaginary smells of corn, chili peppers, and pork took us both across the border.

When I get to Nuevo Leon at eleven thirty A.M., it's already starting to get crowded for lunch, and that's because they call themselves the "best Mexican cuisine in the Midwest." Next to me, a crew of construction workers sing to a José José song playing on the radio, and in front of me, owner Emeterio Gutierrez greets every single person who walks into his restaurant: "*¡Hola!* Hello!" he says with charm. He's seventy-four years old, and for decades he's seen the community grow, transform, and suffer. "If you don't have anywhere to eat, you go find it," he assures me. Since 1962,

Restaurant Nuevo Leon has served as a place where Latinos found refuge.

When Emeterio was sixteen years old, his parents opened the restaurant with just six small tables. Like the majority of immigrants who had just arrived from Mexico during those years, the Gutierrez family saw the restaurant simply as a way to get by. And they ended up finding success in Chicago the same way they once did in their Mexican hometown of Sabinas Hidalgo: by cooking for others. In their newly opened restaurant, they served *machacado con huevo, caldo de res, frijoles sabinas,* and *tacos sabinas.* Emeterio recalls that during the 1960s, the restaurant's clientele turned into a tide of immigrant men who had just left their families behind in order to get jobs and get settled before bringing their wives and children to the United States. Lonely men who, far from their loved ones, found comfort in food. But all those dishes soon became much more than mere ingredients for them, slowly replacing nostalgia with aromas and yearning with spices.

"That wasn't a restaurant; it eventually became an institution," Emeterio says with pride.

Eventually, the men's wives arrived in Chicago from Mexico. And one by one, new generations blossomed inside Nuevo Leon. As I look around me, sitting in a corner with my Mexican Coke and *tacos sabinas,* I still manage to see stillness amid all this change. Through the last seventy years—right outside the restaurant's doors—Chicago prospered, grieved, segregated, and hoped. And *inside* these doors, the men started sharing tables with new generations of sons, daughters, and grandchildren—but also with their Polish neighbors, black families, white tourists, and undoc-

Restaurant Nuevo Leon staff in Chicago.

umented immigrants. Everything changed over these years, but everything also stayed exactly the same thanks to recipes that lent consistency, security, and ease to a place that once felt distant to so many immigrants. The Gutierrez family transformed a restaurant business into a sanctuary.

As I leave Nuevo Leon, Emeterio yells from the back: "Hope you come back, *mija!*"

Just around the corner, the smells of *paletas,* churros, mangoes, and roasted corn follow me. Small-business owners line up across the block as they wait for hungry students to get out of school and tired parents to leave work. I don't know if they realize it, but they have immense power in their humble hands: to feed people with memories. To make them feel they belong. Around us, headlines show how Chicago police brutality skyrockets, gentrification pushes peo-

Don Abel on the left, his granddaughter, and his son. Three generations of Panadería Nuevo León owners.

ple out, bullets go off like firecrackers, and poverty glooms
over the city's south and west sides. But from these food
stands—small refuges from reality—time manages to pause
the same way Emeterio manages to keep time still inside his
restaurant.

But when recipes *do* eventually change, they start to tell
new stories about us. New smells, new ingredients, new
serving sizes, and substitutes are all signs of a changing narrative.

I decide to follow the scent of butter and sugar that's been
calling my name since the morning and eventually end up
in Panadería Nuevo León (not related to Emeterio's restaurant), a bakery in Chicago's historic Pilsen neighborhood
that has been in business for more than forty-five years. Don
Abel, the longtime patriarch of this establishment, grew his

small business by crafting a menu around his community's demands. "Oh, you don't have *pan de muerto*?" clients would ask. "Can you start making it?"

Slowly, the bakery became an oasis that reflected the distinct tastes that traced Mexico's different provinces—from north to south Mexico, every type of bread was represented here. When I walk inside the *panadería*, I'm greeted with unending *conchas*, but the one that immediately catches my attention is the one I least expect: *vegan pan*.

In my head, veganism is not synonymous with Mexican food. What would my Mexican grandmother Yuyu think of this! I ask myself. I stop for a second and ask the young Latina across the counter, "But, why *vegan pan*? How did that happen?"

She tells me, "Veganism is growing in the Hispanic community. With Pilsen changing, it's also given us an opportunity to challenge ourselves. It's keeping us creative."

To now get to *be* creative and break from our traditional molds is a gift our ancestors have given us. Something Don Abel himself probably couldn't have dreamed of back in the day. A sign of hard-fought freedom.

Xiomara, it turns out, is Don Abel's granddaughter, and she now helps run the family bakery. As she explains to me, vegan options are on the menu because her *own* journey as a vegan prompted her father to bake breads that would satisfy her new palate. But this newfound veganism is also a reflection of the new faces that are coming in and out of the bakery's doors. It used to be older Latina mothers who would buy stacks and stacks of bread for their children and big families. Now many of their clientele are younger, individual customers who buy one or two pieces of *pan* for themselves.

Street food vendor in Chicago, selling *mango con chile y limón*.

"People now want to take pictures, so we have to make the breads look cute," Xiomara tells me.

"Have you heard of the *manteconcha*?" she asks with enthusiasm. (I definitely had never heard of that.) "It's a muffin in the bottom and a *concha* on top! With that, business is going well." From selfies to fancy plant-based products, these new Mexican breads are more than just millennial and Gen Z trends: they are glimmers of the choices our parents never had. Ingredients that are starting to carve out their *own flavors* in America. Businesses that are starting to make inroads with new customers.

Before I say good-bye, I once again mention how amazing it smells inside (they must get this *all* the time).

Xiomara laughs. "I'm so used to the smell, I don't smell it at all. This is what I grew up with."

"Wait," I say. "You can't smell *this*?"

"No," Xiomara responds.

I suppose it's like coming home after a long time away. The smell from the kitchen strikes you with force at first, but then you quickly become accustomed to it. You stop missing it, because you're in it. You're home.

But the ability to lose one's sense of smell is real around here. It can mean that you've lost a part of you. Around this town, the numbness is, unfortunately, more familiar than many of them realize. If you look closely while you're walking down a Chicago street, you'll end up making your way to La Catrina Café.

The second you walk inside, it feels different. As I'm distracted by the countless colorful skulls that pay homage to the Day of the Dead, I *still* can't put my finger on why this place feels distinct. But when I meet the owner, Diana, and her businesses partner and daughter-in-law, Paola, it immediately hits me: it's the *realness*. Just as food has an ability to create refuge, it also has a magical ability to help us shrug off our problems and drown our sorrows. Comfort food, they call it. But Diana and Paola seem to have a different take on this. They don't serve *chocolate caliente* just to bring back childhood memories, they serve it to confront the taboos the community is escaping from, like drugs and opioids. With every bite, sip, or conversation around these tables, it's almost as if Diana and Paola want you to face death so you never forget what it feels like to be alive.

And that's because Diana's twenty-two-year-old son, Gabriel, left this world too soon.

As she recalls, in May 2016, something told Diana to check on Gabriel, who was a barista at the café. It must have been her motherly instinct, because Diana simply *knew* something was wrong with her son that morning. Moments later, as Diana rushed to her café, she saw the ambulance carrying away her son's body. Gabriel had just passed away from a heroin overdose. At the time of his death, Gabriel's partner, Paola, was pregnant with their baby girl.

"My people don't talk about their problems," Diana says. "That's what happened to me when I found out my son was using [drugs]."

Diana remembers that when she learned her son had an addiction problem, her family just kept it to themselves. Unfortunately, this is pretty common among many Latinx families across the country: sometimes it's hard for us to confront our own biases. According to the National Center for Biotechnology Information, fewer than one in eleven Latinos will contact a mental health-care specialist. We're scared to ask for help, especially when we need it most.

"If I would have shared it, maybe I would have gotten help," Diana tells me with tears running down her cheeks. Yet although she didn't ask for help then, Diana did become one of the first people in her Chicago community to go public about the meaning of her Latino son's death. "I decided that I cannot just sit back and mourn and do nothing and say nothing and just sink in my sorrow. . . . Because there is a problem, and the more noise we make and the more we talk about it, the more people will come out and ask for help."

Unlike the earlier places I visited, here you find that food produces a different type of refuge, one that evokes a vulnerability that's less scared to face reality. There's something freeing about that. In the middle of my conversation with Diana, a young Latina woman walks into the café with her kids.

"Hey, Diana, how are you?" she said.

From afar, I could tell the exchange between them went deeper than the realms of this room.

"Who was that?" I ask Diana when she comes back.

"She has a brother who passed away from opioids. We have that connection."

These types of exchanges aren't rare for Diana. After Gabriel passed, Paola and Diana had a lot of people reach out to them. People who want to find peace in their grief but, more than anything, who want to share their own stories of pain and addiction.

People are finally talking.

Since Gabriel's passing, Diana hosts Narcotics Anonymous every Thursday in her café. She also started holding free naloxone trainings. Naloxone is a medication that can help to temporarily reverse the effects of an opioid overdose. It can help a person keep breathing. Diana mentions that the majority of attendees at the last workshop she held were Latino. "I call it How to Save a Life," she tells me.

According to a study performed by the Centers for Disease Control and Prevention in 2017, every single day 128 Americans die from an opioid overdose. It's an epidemic that has long been painted as a "white" issue here in the Midwest, but the endless Catrinas hanging around the café—these vibrant Mexican skulls—remind us that death knows no color. Forever immortalizing Gabriel's presence over us, forcing us to break with any silence that once kept us in the dark.

"My son was a little artist. He left a box full of sketches and art. I'm just holding on to all of that for his daughter," Diana tells me as I'm getting ready to leave. And just as I walk outside La Catrina Café, I stumble upon a massive mural that

Paola, Gabriel's widow, standing in front of the mural of Gabriel. The mural was created by graffiti artist Sentrock.

covers the café's exterior. The mural was created by a local artist who used Gabriel's sketches to memorialize an image of Gabriel and his family. In it, you see Gabriel, his partner, Paola, and their daughter, Olivia, glaring at you from above.

Even after every meal I've had today—the *tacos sabinas* in the morning, the *pan dulce* this afternoon, and the *mollete* at the café this evening—the sense of fullness eventually dissipates. But here on this wall you find immortalized faces, history, and stories that could never perish the same way food can.

In art, you can find permanence.

I follow its colors and drive to the Twin Cities: De'Ara's town.

A couple of months ago, I was informed that Diana closed La Catrina Café. Diana and her husband have now moved to Mexico.

FOLLOWING COLORS: TWIN CITIES

For years, De'Ara exuded color, and this midwestern city is starting to show me why.

Looking back at my relationship with my partner, De'Ara, I think one of the reasons I ended up falling in love with her was the color she added to my life. And I mean that in every sense of the word. Not only did she add immeasurable love but she also, *literally,* has added color. Blues, yellows, greens, oranges, peaches, and reds. When we moved in together, her first request was to paint some of the white walls. She also started to slowly chip away at the sterile minimalist look my Brooklyn apartment carried by adding paintings, posters, and images in corners throughout the place. Now, when I open a kitchen cabinet, closet, bathroom door, or even the fridge, there's more color than my eyes were used to seeing.

But there's more to De'Ara's love of colors. It's her way of holding on to her family's Mexican legacy.

De'Ara comes from a black and Mexican family from Minnesota. But when you meet her, it's easy to forget that she's Mexican. When we worked on the Clinton campaign, where we met, I remember she was never invited to our "Latino staff meetings." In fact, when Latinos find out that De'Ara is Mexican, many pause and say, "No way, seriously? I thought you were black!" I've seen the reaction time and time again, and I myself was guilty of that bias when I first met her, unconsciously questioning her heritage because her accent, family, and skin color didn't match mine. The reality is that De'Ara's great-grandparents were born in Mexico, and after crossing the border, they met in Minnesota, had children, and adapted as best they could to life in the Midwest. Many of their children married into black families, much of the Spanish was lost among generations, and the "Avaloz" last name eventually subsumed into "Bauer," "Balenger," and "Long."

Yet all along the years, the colors that followed this family never let go. I remember walking up the stairs and into her brownstone apartment on Madison Avenue for the first time. The *one* front door that stood out in that entire Brooklyn block—the *one* that was different from everyone else's: a beautifully painted light blue door. Painted with the same resilient blue Diego Rivera made dreams of, the one Mayans made rain with in the Riviera and the one painters use to blend big Mexican skies over vast, deep oceans. The decision to paint that tiny front door, like many other ordinary decisions De'Ara makes throughout her day, was her subtle way of never letting go of where she comes from. And it's exactly the same way young Latinx in Minnesota, De'Ara's place of birth, are using colors: to make sure their torch never dims.

One of the first things I notice in Minnesota is one of its biggest clichés. Everyone is so nice around here, I think to myself. But soon, young local Latino activists start to point out a different reality.

"That's what they call 'Minnesota nice': they'll be nice to you, but they call the cops on you," says Anaïs Deal-Márquez, a local poet.

"Racism here is real. Because it's so white, it's very passive, but it's very consistent," says Arianna Gennis, an organizer.

Rebekah, an artist, points out, "I experienced this particular kind of midwest racism . . . an exotification of the other."

But while their ancestors—just like De'Ara's grandparents—may have been prey to these devious smiles, a new generation of Latinos is resisting. And this form of resistance can look very different depending on which corner of the Twin Cities you're standing in. It can take the shape of clothes, murals, street art, and even pottery. It may be invisible if you keep looking straight forward, but it's overwhelming if you take a look around.

Lift up your head:

In one corner of Minneapolis, I walk into Bris Carbajal's art studio, where she's working on her clothing label, "Yessenya." On the racks, I see striking orange pants that look like giant girasoles; I see green winter coats with small blood orange buttons; I see countless yellow, green, and blue flowing blouses, evoking the colors of Mexico and the warm air there. As I walk around her studio, I find it hard to believe that Minnesotans would want to swap their flannel for Bris's eccentric work. It almost seems out of place. But the reason these creations live in the Midwest—amid long, gray winters—is the very reason they were birthed in the first place: to stand out. To make people pause. To make a pedestrian look at their wearers as they pass on the sidewalk.

"I feel like I grew up very invisible and secondary, and I think through my work I stand out through quality and the color. . . . It commands eyes," she says.

It does command eyes.

Bris is a Latina in her twenties who grew up in a migrant farm just forty minutes away from where we're standing. Her family, who's from Chihuahua, Mexico, came here to work in the fields, where they grew corn, cucumbers, cabbage, strawberries, and watermelons. The same yellows, greens, pinks, and reds I saw in her designs. Bris tells me that just to get by, her family had to endure injustices similar to the harsh realities faced in California's Central Valley farms.

"That's how I grew up, thinking, You're here to do that shit work," she says. (To be clear, Bris clarifies that she uses the word "shit" to define the way her family has been treated, *not* the actual task of farming.) Bris also recalls how her teachers would tell her she wasn't allowed to speak Spanish in school.

"The assimilation is real," she stresses.

"So, what inspires you?" I ask.

"I think I'm different from my parents because they don't disturb the peace. They go with it. *Yo no me dejo.*"

The answer is a direct response to the injustices her family has undergone in the fields every day. Her work, Bris reinforces time and time again during our conversation, is inspired by the sacrifice her parents have made for her. So, here's what *Yo no me dejo,* which means "I don't let myself," really translates into:

"Yo no me dejo" = Bris doesn't let herself succumb to fear.

"Yo no me dejo" = Bris doesn't let herself become invisible.

"Yo no me dejo" = Bris doesn't let herself bury her accent.

"Yo no me dejo" = Bris doesn't let herself be silenced.

That's what color means in the Midwest: to not give in.

From where I stand in Minneapolis, I also notice a city that is currently undergoing a serious affordable housing crisis. Left to right, the local government is in the midst of implementing new zoning policies to address the crisis, families of color are being forced out of their homes, segregation is becoming increasingly defined, and stability is now an even more expensive, unattainable dream. So if you're being pushed out, how do you even see yourself in the picture?

If you continue to the southwest corner of 42nd Street

and Cedar Avenue, you'll drive past one of the biggest murals in the city. It's called *Oleadas de cambio,* or *Waves of Change.* The mural was created by a young Puerto Rican artist named Olivia Levins Holden.

"People have told me that it's their favorite mural in the Twin Cities," Olivia tells me. It's impossible to miss. From afar, you see a brown hand gripping the source of the Mississippi River as the water makes its way to a grandiose cedar tree that awaits on the other side of the giant mural. Through the waves of the blue river—it swirls in ups and downs—you see the faces of people who have made this stream of history flow for centuries: Native Americans and migrants, LGBTQ leaders and Muslims, the elderly and black children, protesters and tenants.

Part of *Oleadas de cambio* mural by Olivia Levins Holden in Minneapolis.

Any other day, I'd drive past this corner and give it a quick glance. But today I notice that Olivia is creating a home for the displaced with her art. A portrait for the invisible, a mark for the forgotten, and a page that was never written in the history books about the Midwest.

On July 7, 2016, a day after Philando Castile was murdered by police officer Jeronimo Yanez at a traffic stop in the Twin Cities, Olivia and several other artists did an impromptu public mural to honor Castile. "That will always stick with me," Olivia tells me.

The artists gathered in a predominantly Latinx neighborhood in the south side of Minneapolis, right on East Lake Street. With wooden panels and a couple of buckets of paint, they did what no one else could do in that moment: they found some form of justice. A life was taken, but a soul was erected through colors. In a matter of hours, as the group kept working on the mural, crowds of people started forming around them—cheering on the artists, mourning with each brushstroke, and protesting through grief. After twenty-four hours, the mural read:

> **What do we tell our children when . . .**
> **Education didn't matter.**
> **Compliance didn't matter.**
> **Age didn't matter.**
> **Your guilt/innocence didn't matter.**
> **Our outrage didn't matter.**
> **Straight up, evidence didn't matter.**
> **The truth is our lives do matter.**

A couple of weeks after Castile's death, the mural had to come down because the building it was painted on was in the process of being demolished. But Olivia tells me that even after the art disappeared, local neighbors created an altar near the mural. For days and weeks to come, pedestrians—most of whom were people of color—continued to stop by the corner. The canvas was gone, but candles were lit in its place.

Do you *see* the effect color had in this small midwestern intersection? Everything Officer Yanez rejected in Castile, this corner gave life to; everything he loathed in this thirty-two-year-old black man, this corner embraced; and everything he targeted with deep implicit bias, this corner shielded with deep unabashed pride. It became a home for the broken. And in those quiet, unexpected broken corners filled with color and grief, there's *a lot* to learn about the Latinx community. That's where we can learn about our solidarity with black people, our own intersectional identities, our own internal biases, and the way this country sees *us* from the outside.

That mural may be long gone, and the altar may have vanished, but Castile's legacy was once again honored by the thousands of protesters who took to the streets of Minneapolis in response to the murder of George Floyd on May 25, 2020, in response to the killing of another black man. There was something different about this uprising, though. This time, many Latinos weren't just standing in solidarity with their black neighbors to demand the end of police brutality and reinforce that #BlackLivesMatter. They were also confronting their *own* role in perpetuating racism and antiblackness. Let's remember that the officer who shot Philando Castile was a white-passing Latino. Let's also remember that George Zimmerman, the man who shot seventeen-year-old

Trayvon Martin on February 26, 2012, was a white-passing Latino. Instead of brushing aside these details, we are finally realizing just how ingrained racial bias is among us. And that painful yet necessary awakening is part of the Latinx movement: accountability.

As I'm leaving Olivia's art studio, I ask her: "In your eyes, what *is* the purpose behind these murals you make?"

"It's a big, loud declaration of truth that feels like it can be healing," she responds in her calm voice.

There's one more corner of this city I want to go to. The one that is perhaps the brightest but the easiest to miss— and that's because it's very likely that memories have erased these colors.

Before coming to the Midwest, I didn't really have a good understanding of our people's indigenous presence in this part of the country. And my ignorance, I'm confirming, is emblematic of a larger problem that continues to be pointed out to me: it's easy for us to forget where we come from. We can't see what's no longer in front of us.

"I think one of the worries that I have for Latinos in the future is a foreshortened view of history. People are not remembering their roots far enough back," Rebekah tells me. As I mentioned earlier, Rebekah is a young member of the indigenous Lencas, the first ancestral nation of Central America and one that has laid roots across the Americas for centuries. Her family, who is part Salvadoran and part Norwegian, moved to the Midwest decades ago.

Rebekah shows me her Maya Lenca Nation ID, a form of identification that was officially recognized by the United Nations. A form that legitimizes her indigenous roots and her place in the United States. I had never seen one of these IDs before. "By having this, I use it as a way to prove myself to the naysayers. 'Here's the proof. You wanna see my papers? Here they are!' This is my right as a First American," Rebekah tells me.

That's exactly how Rebekah uses the power of art in Minnesota, not only to uplift indigenous people but to push us all to understand where we come from and *whose* land we're actually standing on. She uses different ways to shift consciousness through theater, music, visuals, handmade pottery, and curated events. But what strikes me the most is the simplicity behind the colors in Rebekah's paintings—the geometry, the coordinates, the dots, the lines, and the petroglyphs. It all feels so abstract at first. But these colors are grounding, because they tell the story of our own history.

One of Rebekah's paintings is called *Reframing Turtle Island as Crocodile.* In it, you see a white canvas divided

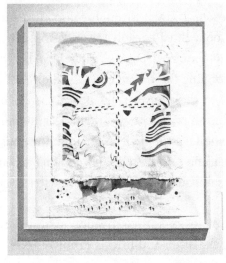

Reframing Turtle Island as Crocodile
by Rebekah Crisanta de Ybarra.

into four coordinates. There are small footprints covered throughout the canvas, motioning toward the north, south, east, and west. But when you look closer, entire footsteps transform into the frame of a crocodile whose body stretches all the way from the top of North America to the bottom of South America.

"We call her Las Americas," Rebekah writes in her description.

When you start looking at colors in a different way, you start seeing history through a different frame. Rebekah's ancestors tell the tale of one land, divided by nothing. Seeing the world through Rebekah's colors is designed to display how people belong no matter what others say.

"I encourage people to look into their own family roots. All of a sudden, home literally comes. It opens up in a different type of way," Rebekah tells me.

Home *does* find its way to you.

In Minnesota, I saw it through colors. In Chicago, I saw it through food. But Rebekah reminds me that it can also come through musical beats. That's how her dad started finding belonging in this country. When Rebekah's dad first arrived in the Midwest, he was often the only Latino around. Rebekah recalls how her dad became fond of native drums. As she tells me, her father found friends and community by joining drum circles. He couldn't explain *why*, but those drums felt oddly familiar in a place that was otherwise foreign.

"Humanity looks for connection and belonging, and people hear the *drum* and it feels familiar and they want to connect," she says.

I take the car and start driving from Minnesota to Wisconsin. Around me are strawberry farms, fields of greens, and lots and lots of "Cheese!" signs. After all, I'm entering the land of dairy.

FOLLOWING MUSIC: WISCONSIN

For miles and miles on this road, the warm scents and scenes I leave behind start fading into a landscape that feels increasingly remote. Its people, its land, its hills, the occasional "TRUMP" signs I see on bumper stickers—it all feels slightly far and divided right now.

But then, as I enter the city of Madison and drive down the street and to its capitol, I unexpectedly find hundreds of Latinos lined up for a May Day protest. Old and young, workers and students—there's now a thumping beat among the mundane. I hear the expected protest chants, but more than anything, I hear Latinos finding their voice in songs. To my right, high school students blast Marc Anthony's "Vivir Mi Vida," and to my left, a group sings "Mexico Lindo" at the top of their lungs as it plays on the megaphone.

Who knew? Well, it actually all makes more sense than I thought.

Wisconsin is home to one of the country's largest Latino music festivals: Los Dells. For the past three years, Los Dells has been taking place in the state's farm country, hosting artists like Daddy Yankee, Bad Bunny, Cuco, Maná, and Flor de Toloache. You'll find reggaetón, but you'll also find bachata, indie, mariachi, and electronic music. Again, this happens *not* in Florida, Nevada, California, or New York: it happens in *Wisconsin*.

Music is one of the ways the Latinx community has held

Stumbling upon a May Day protest in downtown Madison.

on to its soul since the early twentieth century, especially in a place like Milwaukee, the most segregated city in the United States. If you're brown in Milwaukee, your chances of being unemployed, incarcerated, and racially targeted are through the roof.

And even though reports indicate that the Latino population in Milwaukee's metro area has more than tripled in the past thirty years, it's still hard to hold your head up high in this city.

That's one of the many reasons music holds the Latino people up around here: it's hard to keep your head down with a beat that's forcing you to look up. It's even harder to hold still—to blend in with the masses—when music forces your body to move to its notes. For years, the Latino community here has found its pride in rhythms, lyrics, and sounds that have reassured their belonging. All you have to do is close your eyes and follow the hymn of violins, guitars, and cellos coming from Dinorah Marquez's classroom in Milwaukee's south side.

The most beautiful mariachi symphony transports Madisonites from the middle of these cold American streets to the middle of those warm, bustling Mexican *calles*. I find myself surrounded by students from the Latino Arts String Program, an effort Dinorah started in 2002 to offer precollege musical training to low-income Latino students. It started with twenty-six kids, and now more than two hundred are enrolled.

The students—first- and second-generation Latinos—are all seated in a circle around Dinorah, rehearsing for a big event they have next week. They may be young students, but in this room, with their instruments in hand, they command a huge presence. That speaks to their power: musicians *can*

Latino Arts String Program students in class practicing with their instruments.

stir emotions. With a simple chord, they can shift the balance of power. This is something Dinorah knows.

"The idea, from the very beginning, was for the students to take home songs that their parents recognized," Dinorah tells me about her program. She wanted the students to bring back memories but also to play symphonies that would be appreciated by white audiences. The purpose wasn't to necessarily gain acceptance by the mainstream but to have the students feel proud of themselves and of the joy they were able to give to people. "No matter the color of your skin, people are saying, 'Whoa, you guys are great; this music is awesome,'" Dinorah says.

In many cases, these instruments are a shield of the reality that exists outside these walls. One student tells me that he was always the "only Latino in the classroom" and that his teachers gave him a hard time for speaking *"en español."* Another student says he always feels he has to "switch" his personality between his brown friends and his white friends and attempt to be "less political around Caucasian students."

Then Dinorah, with teary eyes, tells me about Claudia. Claudia is one of the first students she ever had, and she is doing her final college senior recital that day—a milestone that was once hard to imagine for her. Dinorah explains that years before, Claudia was abducted by *coyotes* as she was crossing the U.S.-Mexican border with her family. After months of extortion and abuse, Claudia was eventually hospitalized and reunited with her loved ones in Milwaukee.

"It was a miracle she survived," Dinorah says. Yet one of Claudia's first requests after she was released from the hospital was to play the guitar. She told her mom, *"Quiero tocar la guitarrita chiquita."* I want to play the small guitar. And

Dinorah and her students onstage, practicing for an upcoming performance.

so she did. Seventeen years since and multiple classes after, Claudia has beaten the odds.

No matter what the verdict is outside these walls, inside Dinorah's room music helps these students transform. I saw how their confidence rose when they picked up those instruments and struck that first chord. I saw how their voices found oxygen the louder they sang. How their feet stomped the ground without holding back. And I saw how there was *no* other place they'd rather have been than right there, feeling they were home.

But just a couple of blocks away from Dinorah's classroom, home has a different ring to it. From afar, I notice how the mariachi songs and guitar strings are slowly being replaced with hip-hop beats and rap. Following this new melody, I walk into St. Augustine Preparatory Academy's gym, which is packed with third graders sitting on bleachers. It can be so hard to get the attention of middle school students, but they're all completely captivated by what lies in front of them: it's Browns Crew, known around here as "Milwaukee's Latin hip-hop duo."

Sebastián Daniel and Chris Piszczek, two locals from the city's Latino south side, started Browns Crew in 2011. Standing with their jeans, hoodies, and baseball caps in front of the young school audience, Sebas and Chris begin to rap. The crowd goes *absolutely* wild. A crowd that consists mostly of low-income Latino students who are too young to see the fragility of their dreams right now. Sebas and Chris first sing a song in Spanish titled "Autonomia" and then another song in English that talks about "reaching up for a star."

When they're done performing, Sebas and Chris pause.

They look up to the kids and say, "To know where you're going to go, you gotta know where you're coming from."

Again, the crowd goes absolutely wild. I wonder why, because the kids are still too young to really understand the meaning behind all these lyrics and beats. Upon hearing one of their lyrics—*"No me parará un pinche muro o un güero"* ("No wall or white person will stop me")—these kids respond with claps, laughs, roars, and giant smiles.

"People don't even know what we're saying sometimes, but they rock with us because they know it's coming from a place of love and that it's sincere," Sebas and Chris tell me. The students seem captivated by the image of these two hip-hop artists who suddenly resemble a future that could look like them fifteen years from today: unapologetically proud of who they are. A future where they're no longer sitting down but standing tall, with the confidence that's necessary to be on a stage.

"So, what's the meaning behind the Browns Crew name?" I ask.

"We wanted to represent brown pride. When we say we want to put culture at the forefront of what we do, that's *in* the name," they say. "Culture shapes who we are and how you see yourself, too."

To be a young Latino in the United States today is to see yourself wearing many different hats and living many different realities. Yet traditionally, music genres have tried to put Latinos in a box, under the labels of "Mexican music" or "Latin music." And while there's so much beauty in preserving the traditions of those chords, Browns Crew shows us that today's stories can be cut short through those conventional notes. One's whole self no longer fits in that beat. And that's why Sebas and Chris play Latin American sounds, but they also fuse it with hip-hop and cumbia. In their songs, they rap about immigration, but they also talk about identity in the Midwest and segregation in Milwaukee. They sing in English but also in Spanish and Spanglish. They make those schoolkids feel they can break out of *any* box they want.

From coast to coast, young Latinos are trying to navigate their identity, but I'd never think that Wisconsin would be a place where we could all find answers to our questions. Sometimes it's not verbal answers that people are searching for—it's rhythms and melodies that put them at ease and give them the assurance they need. I met countless other young artists in Milwaukee like Browns Crew who are breaking down stereotypes left and right: DJ Loop, who is one of the few Latina DJs in Milwaukee. Her goal? "To blur the lines of what Latina women can do," she tells me.

Vianca Fuster is a Puerto Rican journalist and documentarian. Her purpose? To be in charge of our stories. "There's a lot of white people that are in charge of our narratives, and what inspires me is to say 'no,'" she says.

Enrique "Mag" Rodriguez is the director of a local accelerator program for musicians, including hip-hop and R&B artists. His struggle? When other Latinos tell him he's not "Mexican enough." In the music industry, there's this expectation that if you're Latinx, you're probably managing Latino artists or, at least, music genres that are more traditionally in line with "Latino culture." As he told the *Wisconsin Gazette* in an interview in 2016, "Being raised on the South Side, nobody really rapped; that wasn't a thing over here." The fact that Enrique is known around town as a manager who is representing the "hottest up-and-coming hip-hop artists" hasn't always been met with acceptance from some members of his own Latino community. "We're attacked in the media for being Mexican," he says, "but we also forget how racist our people are to other communities."

Together, all these young artists are changing the image of what being "Latino enough" looks like.

Before I leave St. Augustine Preparatory Academy, I ask Sebas and Chris: "Are you able to see the impact you're having on these kids? What does that look like from your eyes?"

They pause. Not too long ago, Sebas and Chris were two of those brown Latino students sitting in the school bleachers. And today they are the ones performing.

Finally, they respond, "When the kids are looking at us and saying, 'Damn . . . they are from right here. Look at them!'"

As I cross Wisconsin's border and drive into Iowa, the music on the radio starts to sound slightly different. I can't find any of the Latin beats I heard before, but if I open the windows, it *is* possible to hear the choir that's singing in the St. Alphonsus Catholic Church located in the small town of Mount Pleasant. No more than eighty-five hundred people live there—in a county that voted for Trump in 2016 and a town where about 7 percent of the population is Latino. I could have gone to some of Iowa's more popular destinations on the political map, like Des Moines, Iowa City, or Cedar Rapids. But there's *something* about this choir that catches my attention. First of all, it's a bilingual symphony. Second, as I'll soon find out, this sound has a unique capacity to unite a town that has been deeply divided along party, racial, and immigration lines.

FOLLOWING RELIGION AND LANGUAGE: IOWA

When I step inside St. Alphonsus Catholic Church in Mount Pleasant, I realize that the church is commemorating the one-year anniversary of the ICE raids that took place in this eastern Iowa town.

On May 9, 2018, ICE raided a concrete plant in Mount Pleasant, detaining thirty-two undocumented workers, most of whom were from Guatemala. Since then, some of the workers have been released, some are still awaiting hearings, and some have been deported. But all thirty-two families remain torn and traumatized.

As some of them told me, many of the men have not been able to find jobs again, their kids (the majority of whom are first-generation U.S. citizens) have faced bullying in school,

The wife and daughters of one of the thirty-two undocumented workers who were detained on May 9, 2018, standing outside St. Alphonsus Catholic Church in Mount Pleasant, Iowa.

and crippling fear is a feeling they wake up to and fall asleep to every day. Sadly, we hear these types of stories all over the national media—but Mount Pleasant is a town that barely makes it into the spotlight.

Amid the crisis, Mount Pleasant came together in a way that I haven't seen in many places across the nation. And that was thanks to the power of religion, which created a place that many people from all walks of life were able to call "home."

Inside the church, I sit in one of the last pews. From that seat, I have a perfect view of the audience. Some of the thirty-two families sit next to white families. The pastors lead a bilingual service—visibly struggling with their Spanish but nevertheless articulating every single word as best they can. *"Hermanos y hermanas,"* they say with joy. The choir, com-

St. Alphonsus Catholic Church in Mount Pleasant, Iowa.

posed of mostly elderly white people, sings the chorus in English *and* Spanish. Left and right, brown or white, wealthy or poor, *everyone* in this room belongs. This is a scene that's truly hard to find in other corners of this country.

Before stepping out of the church, I see a small donation sign for individuals to contribute to the affected immigrant families. IowaWINS, a community commission of the First Presbyterian Church of Mount Pleasant, and other local groups have been helping the families with rent, legal fees, food, and utilities as the men get back on their feet again. The wife of a man who was deported a few weeks ago tells me that the church has *never* left her side throughout these painful months. "*No nos han dejado solos.* It's been almost a year since it happened, and they keep helping and helping us," she says with surprise. Sometimes it's the ones you least expect who show up for you.

I ask Trey Hegar, one of the pastors who led the service

Trey Hegar with a young parishioner.
(Courtesy of Claudia Montaner)

and one of the key allies Mount Pleasant immigrant and Latino families have here, "Why is it that religion is working to unite people here?"

His response is simple. "The golden rule is in Mark twelve: 'Love your neighbor as yourself.' That comes first and foremost, and that message to me is what promotes the change of the world."

In this remote town, I found how words and Bible verses could be so powerful, containing an ability to heal a country that is jaded by hate. Embracing immigrants is not something laws alone can do: "It has to come from the heart and the mind, and *this* is where pastors and religion have to step in. To start changing people. To start reclaiming some of that language that has been taken by politics," Trey tells me.

Sometimes, something as simple as language is *all* you need to make someone feel they're at home. As Pastor Hegar tells me, making their Sunday service in both English and Spanish was a strategic decision the church made to send a welcoming signal to Mount Pleasant's Latino community. It's true: familiar accents can assuage fear. Nostalgic words can help people let their guards down, to show the face that lies behind that guarded veil of ours. And to my deep surprise, the preservation of the Spanish language is something that is actually very valued in this midwestern region. Not just in Mount Pleasant but in other parts of the state, too. In fact, if you drive two hours north of Mount Pleasant, you'll stumble upon West Liberty, Iowa, where Spanish is almost as common as English (if not more so).

I head over there.

So far, throughout this entire road trip across the Midwest, I've seen Latinos—young and old—perform a dance with the Spanish language. Some embrace it, others reject it; some hold on to it, others let go of it; some are told to be proud of it, others to be ashamed of it; some remember, others forget. It's a complicated tango. But West Liberty, a town of approximately four thousand people, has somehow figured it all out—whether they're brown or white, Spanish is part of who they are. It's how this town was built in the first place.

West Liberty is Iowa's first majority-Latino town. You heard that right: there are *more* Latinos there than there are white people. And that's because, like many other midwestern cities, the town has a long history with migrants who settled there in the early twentieth century to work on the railroads.

I talk to Cara McFerren, a descendant of one of the very first Latino families to lay roots in West Liberty. Her grandfather John Edward Ponce was *the* first Latino to graduate from high school in the city, in 1933. As Cara tells me, her grandfather had to learn English through the school system, eventually becoming fully bilingual and instilling in his loved ones the importance of becoming fluent in English. As the story goes, integration through assimilation became the norm for many Latino and immigrant families, but the flow of migration to West Liberty never really stopped through the years, which means it was hard to fully let go of Spanish. Like Cara's grandmother, countless Latinos found jobs at West Liberty Foods, a turkey-processing plant that was the town's largest employer, up until it became a COVID-19 outbreak site. (If you have ever had a turkey sandwich from Subway, chances are the turkey you ate came from this plant.) Latinos built the backbone of this town, and almost a century later, they continue to drive its growth.

When a home is built speaking Spanish, its infrastructure can never really be erased. From the original layout to the finished product, it lingers in every corner of the house. Why not embrace it?

In the fall of 1998, the West Liberty Community School District implemented Iowa's first dual-language program. It was originally offered only to pre-K and kindergarten students, but it's now available through the twelfth grade. The effects it's having in West Liberty are pretty incredible. More than half of the district's students are enrolled in the initiative, the school system's graduation rate is 97 per-

Cara McFerren and her mother, descendants of one of the first Latino families to lay roots in West Liberty, Iowa.

cent, and there's currently a waiting period to enroll in the program.

And guess what? Most of the students on that list are white kids who are eager to learn Spanish.

I spent a couple of hours in the school, and the level of integration they have accomplished is truly remarkable. In the elementary school, I see tables of brown and white kids, playing together with an innocence that hasn't learned to discriminate against color yet. During Mr. Ortiz's fourth-grade period, there are students learning about Don Quixote, and right across the hall, there's a science class being taught in Spanish. Salvadoran, Guatemalan, Mexican, and white students work together as they all figure out how to power a lightbulb. In the middle school, there's a class discussion about Gabriel García Márquez's *One Hundred Years of Solitude*.

"What's the impact you notice?" I ask one of the kindergarten teachers.

"They don't have to be afraid to speak Spanish," she tells me.

In many ways, that answer carries the legacy of Cara's grandfather, a man who built the foundation for the younger generation of Latinos to stand on. Today, Cara's son, Mr. Ponce's great-grandchild, is enrolled in West Liberty's dual-language program.

I ask Cara: "What do you think your grandpa would think of all of this?"

"I think he would be very proud."

The bell rings. It's the end of the school day.

13

America's Queen

Oddly enough, the Midwest is also the place where I most learned about the power of drag.

Drag queens have an ability to completely transform themselves into an alter ego that is limitless. They don't just push beauty standards and gender norms; more than anything—if even for only a couple of minutes—they have a capacity to attain a power that would otherwise be unreachable in the "real world." Through drag, a queen can do anything. She can be anyone, say anything, and inspire everything.

Dorian Corey, the infamous New York City drag queen and black trans woman who starred in Jennie Livingston's 1991 documentary *Paris Is Burning*, described it best:

"In real life, you can't get a job as an executive unless you have the educational background and the opportunity. Now the fact that you are not an executive is merely because of the social standing of life. . . . Black people have a hard time getting anywhere. And those that do, are usually straight. In a ballroom, you can be anything you want," she said.

In a ballroom, you can be *anything* you want. There's a small caveat to that, though: Unless you're undocumented.

RuPaul's Drag Race, the hit VH1 reality TV show where queens compete to win the title of "America's Next Drag Superstar," has gone viral. It's a show many have attributed to "mainstreaming" the LGBTQ community and giving visibility to trans women of color, offering an unprecedented sense of liberation. Yet undocumented immigrants allegedly cannot compete in the show. Being a queen, it turns out, is not a right everyone has.

My friend Ado Arevalo sent me a text one morning that read:

> With drag culture growing so much through RuPaul, many of us cannot audition for RuPaul due to our status . . . so, I'm on my way to the national title for "Miss Gay America" as an undocumented queen. . . .

As I would later find out, Miss Gay America was pretty much the only option Ado, who's undocumented, had if he wanted to compete in a national beauty pageant for drag queens. Evidently, the Miss Gay America platform has been around since 1972 and has become the oldest, largest, and most prestigious pageant system for female impersonators in the nation. If, for whatever reason, you cannot wrap your head around what this looks like, think of the Miss America or Miss USA pageant. Now, imagine that the contestants are men impersonating women. Each year, contestants from all across the country, representing various states, compete for the Miss Gay America crown.

The thing is, Miss Gay America has never seen a contestant like Ado.

Ado is a twenty-eight-year-old man from El Salvador who fled his country as a teenager after his father was murdered. He was held in a detention center and separated from his family, but against all odds he built a life of his own in the United States—and now he is determined not only to win the Miss Gay America crown but also to become the *first* undocumented queen in the pageant's history.

At a time when the country wanted Ado silenced, he was choosing to live as loudly as possible, in every possible space he walked in. People like Ado were once meant to live in shadows and closets—a shadow that kept many from revealing their undocumented status and a closet that hid their sexual orientation from their more conservative Latino community. But Ado chose to abide by none of those rules, and in drag, he saw not just a shiny crown but an opportunity to make a political statement. An opportunity to disrupt.

Disrupt your definition of what it means to be undocumented, your understanding of what a gay man should look like, your assumptions of what Latinos stand for, and your notions of what drag is meant to achieve. Drag shows are there not just to entertain but mostly to challenge all biases—whether you're drunk at #DragBrunch or not.

Out of all the strategies Ado could use as an activist and an organizer, why was drag an effective tool to open people's eyes toward compassion?

"Sometimes it's easier for people to take you more seriously when you have a wig on," he responded.

In his response, Ado remembered the first time he protested in drag in the streets of Phoenix, Arizona, where he lives, and he said it suddenly, immediately, opened doors to more conversations and interactions with strangers. In a way, he felt more seen. He must have felt something similar to what Marsha P. Johnson experienced in the 1960s—trailblazing her way through stages, the Stonewall riots, and marches. As Johnson looked back at her life in a 1992 interview, she said: "I was no one, nobody from Nowheresville, until I became a drag queen."

Because think about it: What would catch your attention more? Someone holding an "Abolish ICE" sign in normal civilian clothes or in a panther leotard? Someone who's wearing sneakers as they talk about the inhumanity happening at the border or someone who's wearing four-inch stilettos asking you to pay attention to those same atrocities? Who's capable of diverting your attention from your phone screen? Who makes you look twice? And when you *do* prolong your stare that second time, what's being inculcated in you?

As Ado reminded me, that was the original intention of drag culture, as much a transformation of self as of those around us. Through drag, people's perception of Ado started changing—with curious spectators intrigued not just by his appearance but also by his message. What was DACA, anyway? What's actually happening at the border? Why are they militarizing our communities? How does all this affect *me*? And, it turns out, it was Sicarya Jr., Ado's drag persona, who could best answer those questions to the public.

Ado was selected to represent Miss Gay Arizona as the first alternate for the 2020 national Miss Gay America pageant, which was taking place in St. Louis, Missouri. His journey to that stage was way too important to not document. It was so much more than a story about drag; it was a story that could set policy conversations and the politicization of immigrants to one side and, instead, drive people to genuinely fall in love with a community. The type of love that goes against conventional wisdom but then ends up winning over the masses. Ado could have that effect on people.

So I asked my dear friend Luisa Conlon, an amazing filmmaker I had worked with in the past, if she'd be game to do a small documentary about Ado. I already knew what her response was going to be.

A JOURNEY TO MISS GAY AMERICA IN ST. LOUIS, MISSOURI

We soon find ourselves in St. Louis, alongside Ado and his partner, Jerssay, who was traveling with him.

When I first see Ado, I immediately remember the very first time I met him more than two years before during an organizing event for Dreamers. A humble, handsome man with a boyish face. Always present and attentive. His partner, Jerssay, is also an undocumented drag queen, who goes by the name Anitta Greencard in shows. Jerssay has come to support Ado and watch him win the crown here in Missouri.

The truth is, Ado is not someone you're likely to bump into in Missouri, though.

Less than 0.4 percent of all Latinos in the nation reside there, a state that overwhelmingly voted for Donald Trump in 2016. In St. Louis, the city's crisp wind, blowing its way through old warehouses, cutting its way past humans who now live on the streets, and piercing its way through segregated neighborhoods, is a stark contrast to Arizona's dry

Ado (right) and his partner, Jerssay, standing outside the shop where they buy the fabrics for their drag dresses.

warmth and desert winds. There is a different feel in the air; things feel slightly off around here.

It's the first official day of the 2020 Miss Gay America beauty pageant. The Hampton Inn, situated directly across from the pageant venue, is full of eager contestants who've just arrived from all over the country. From Ohio to Arkansas, Oklahoma to New York, America's best drag queens are in the house. We have Espressa Grande, Kali Coutour, Ivy Dripp, and L'Oreal, among many others. Everyone is anxiously going up and down the elevators as they're getting ready for the evening—some men already dressed in drag, others rocking their tight tank tops, many halfway in between those two looks. But none of these contestants look like Ado. Almost everyone is white. Out of thirty-seven contestants, there are maybe six men of color participating in the pageant. And it's not just the color of their overwhelmingly white skin that strikes me at first but the way in which

Sicarya crossing the street, walking from the hotel to the Miss Gay America beauty pageant while Luisa films.

they walk with such ease and certainty. Undeterred. Almost as if the crisp air outside could never stand in their way. Ado carries that in him, too, but unlike the others, he can lose everything in the blink of an eye due to his undocumented status.

"If you benefit from being masculine, white, and documented, and now you have gay marriage, it's almost like you're set," Jerssay tells me. He says that when we typically think of the queer community, we think of them as very progressive. We think of them as a group of people who understand the true meaning of human rights and equal rights. "But a lot of the times it doesn't go beyond marriage equality or working rights," Jerssay reflects. "We are out of the closet, but we are still in the shadows because we are not recognized nationally as undocumented."

But this evening, Ado is about to take the stage and expose himself as an undocumented immigrant.

How will the crowd react? What will the other drag queens think about Ado? What about the judges? Will they think it's honorable, or will they judge him for that? Ado had received support from his fellow community in Arizona, but how many residents of this midwestern city have ever met an openly undocumented immigrant before? Being more than one thousand miles away from the U.S.-Mexican border, few have ever been challenged to think about family separation, kids in cages, or ongoing racial abuse.

This night is perhaps the most special evening of the entire three-day Miss Gay America contest, because it's when many participants get to perform their "talent" pieces. As the rules indicate, the talent portion is the highest point category in the pageant, where the drag queens are "judged on their quality of lip-sync, live vocal or other entertainment." In other words, this is when you get to put on your own show. You get to say what you want, dance how you want, and act how you want. Meanwhile, Jerssay is sitting in the front row of this extremely packed room, twirling his thumbs, moving his feet, and, with his eyes dead set on the stage, anxiously anticipating Ado's entrance.

Jerssay, once again, puts things into perspective for me: "By saying you're undocumented, you're already putting [forth] a narrative of what people assume you are. So, you're walking into a room full of people doubting you or people having a perspective. To change that is double the work because it's not just a queen, it's an undocumented queen. It's like you're playing to win, literally their hearts and minds, all day."

Ado is contestant number thirty-five. He'll be one of the last ones to go out onstage. At this point, there've been over two hours' worth of performances. So far, there was that one drag queen who sang like Cruella de Vil; then there was the other one who did a skit à la Lady Gaga and that incredible one who used a clip from *The First Wives Club*. So far, we've danced. We've clapped. We've laughed. We've cheered. Contestants have played by the rules, and we've been properly entertained.

Between performances, there are glass *click-clacks* in the background, more rounds of vodka sodas have been ordered, and pickup lines are being thrown around left and right. The crowd is buzzing.

"Contestant number thirty-five: Sicarya!" is announced.

Ado walks onto the stage as Sicarya.

Sicarya's hair is long and puffed. Her eyebrows artfully sculpted. Her lashes curled as can be. Her diamond earrings are glowing. And her eyes are now piercing blue. Beautiful Sicarya, always holding on tightly to Ado's soul. While everyone before her has walked onstage to a song, Sicarya picks up her mic and starts lip-synching the words to a poem. It's titled "Borders" by Denice Frohman, a queer Puerto Rican Latina. Then the first words come out of Sicarya's mouth:

> It starts before she gets here
> before the stairs tell her she's alien to a country that
>   knows her great-grandfather's Mexican hands all
>   too well

Everyone around us has suddenly stopped fidgeting, and all eyes are set on Sicarya. Not just on her beauty but on her words, on what she's trying to tell us.

Sicarya keeps going, reciting:

She walks with her two uncles in a desert for one week,
*   with nothing more than a few gallons of water and a*
*   prayer tucked into their pockets hoping both will last*
*   them long enough . . .*
Another step, she is too young to know what border
*   means . . .*
after her family arrives she will learn there are some
*   borders you can't cross by foot*

The room is still dead silent.
Sicarya ends the poem:

So when they ask you for your papers, Ana, show them
*   your skin,*
wear your tongue like a cape,
throw up your fist like a secret you can't keep any longer,
they can't keep you any longer
Afraid, you can't ever afford to drop a dream, so when
*   they come for you, tell them, in the language that*
*   you know best*
That you are not scared anymore.

And when you think Sicarya is done with her performance, she surprises you with more. She makes it clear that her time is not done. Sicarya heads toward the back of the stage and sits down by the piano she's built with her very own hands. Andra Day's "Rise Up" is now playing, but that's not what the audience is fixated on at the moment. It's the images Sicarya has chosen to screen in the background of her performance that they're watching. Images of refugees migrating from Central America; of mothers reading the Bible to

Sicarya onstage, moments before she received a standing ovation for her performance in the Miss Gay America pageant.

their sons in a cold detention center; of boys and girls who are currently waiting to seek asylum; of makeshift shelters; of desperate families attempting to cross the border; and of Border Patrol agents using force against migrants. And so many images of the sky and the sun we all share above the fence and barbed wire that separate us.

In the crowd, there are the gazes of people who have once again been reminded of these painful truths. But mostly there are the gazes of people who have avoided this type of eye contact for far too long. Avoided seeing these images, avoided looking beyond themselves, avoided looking around them and beneath them. For the first time, they are *really* looking at Sicarya. Not just as a queen or as an entertainer but as an undocumented immigrant queen with a message. Perhaps Sicarya is someone they have demonized in the past or simply neglected and disregarded most of their lives. But in this moment, Sicarya is seen.

When Sicarya finishes her performance, she receives a standing ovation. The first and only standing ovation of the *entire* night. When we told Sicarya what happened once she left the stage, she could barely believe it.

"They gave you a standing ovation!" we tell Ado.

"No way!" he responds in shock.

But, unfortunately, you know how this story ends.

Despite how well received Sicarya's performance was, by the end of the competition, she didn't even make it to the top ten finalists. Sicarya lost the 2020 Miss Gay America beauty pageant. What's worse, according to Ado, some of his fellow contestants allegedly ended up questioning his eligibility to participate because of his status as a Dreamer. Some were even making jokes about "CBP being in the building" to deport him. They were mocking him. Even though the approximately eight hundred thousand Dreamers in this country have grown up in the United States, pay taxes, fuel the economy, and abide by the laws, their lives are in constant limbo. As I'm typing these words, their fate is in the hands of the Supreme Court, as they decide whether the Trump administration can effectively terminate the Obama-era program that has protected Dreamers from deportation since 2012. Ado can't even get through a beauty pageant without a reminder of how uncertain his future is.

Yet as uncertain as it is, that's not stopping Ado from sharing his message: America's queens look more like him than you think. Queens are meant to be fearless, kind leaders. They are meant to do good and lead by example. Their beauty is meant to glow inside and out—through their appearance but, most importantly, through their soul. And all you have to do is see it right before your eyes, to believe they are entitled to that crown.

Maybe just walk into a ballroom and see it for yourself.

Between the Shadows and the Sun

Finding Latinx

As I make my way home again from the Midwest, I think about what has been illuminated for me on this journey.

From the fields in Fresno to Miami's Little Havana to South Carolina's southern corners, I witnessed realities about my community I hadn't noticed before. For decades, millions of us were in some way, shape, or form living under our own shadows. Latinas abided by gender norms, queer people loved in shame, indigenous folks coexisted in silence, farmworkers normalized pain, Afro-Latinos felt erased, undocumented parents resisted fear, and youths carried the burdens of generational trauma. Members of the Latinx community abided by a story that compressed our differences and painted us all as *one—as one bloc, one voice, one monolith.* Yet the sun that has been following me for months on the road, over highways and across the sky, has shed a new light on my surroundings, showing me the portrait of a country that abruptly looks different from what I imagined. The sun hasn't just brought the Latinx community to light, all around us, living with multiple identities; it's also uncovered new regions of the United States that aren't traditionally thought of as homelands for these demographics.

That's the thing about the Latinx movement: it *forces* you to look at sixty million people in a different way, but it also forces you to reframe the country's own geography. Lands that once felt foreign now feel ours. Borders become the heartland; the Midwest becomes home; Florida becomes less familiar; and the Deep South becomes sacred. The history, people, institutions, and places we all thought we knew start to take on a different meaning through this movement. And COVID-19 demonstrated that we have learned how to navigate systems that weren't built for us by filling in the gaps ourselves.

This journey has inspired me to walk around clear-eyed, always searching for what the eye cannot see. But before I fully finish this trip, there's someone I've been meaning to meet in person. In my eyes, she defines the Latinx movement, but I have to see for myself.

On social media, she goes by the name "AfroDominicanxthings." Her (real) name is Danyeli Rodriguez del Orbe (pronounced Dan-Jelly), and she's an Afro-Dominican from the Bronx. As I learned from Instagram stalking, Danyeli is an activist and an artist, and she was also formerly undocumented. And the more I scroll down her page, the more confidence her profile exudes. Confidence in her identity as an Afro-Dominican, confidence in the way she talks about blackness and Latinidad. Her photos, her poses, her art, her writing, her videos—Danyeli seems like someone who is clearly, unapologetically *her*.

On the phone, Danyeli and I talk for a while.

She first takes me back to her childhood in the Dominican Republic. Because of her dark skin tone, Danyeli recalls how some of her family members would comment on her "big and black nose" and how others would call her "Haitian." "As a kid, I didn't like that because basically what I connected the term Haitian to was ugly. It was ugly, poor, dirty," she says. That's because "anti-Haitianismo" has brewed on the island for centuries. Not just through the authoritarian and racist Rafael Trujillo regime of the 1930s but dating back to a colonial era that glorified the Spanish, whiter side of Hispaniola against its darker, poorer neighbor.

As Danyeli tells me, it wasn't until she left the island and migrated to the Bronx with her *mami* that she started feeling comfortable in her own skin. Surrounded by thousands of other Dominicans who had also made New York City their home, Danyeli rediscovered the island she'd left, eventually finding normalcy in her dark skin, her beauty, and her mixed background.

"New York provided me that foundation to kind of grow as a Dominican American," she states.

Undoing years of biases that taught her to fear blackness, Danyeli found pride in an identity that didn't run away from her inner self but instead strove to embrace every aspect of her being. As an undocumented person. As a Latina. As a black woman. As a Dominicana. And when she talks about New York City, specifically about Washington Heights, I can sense the excitement in Danyeli's voice. It's where she fell in love for the first time, where she found her community, and where she found her voice as a spoken word artist.

I want to see Danyeli perform. I want to meet her in

person, in these streets that took her in. But Danyeli had moved to Los Angeles. And here's where things start to shift a little: the story of Danyeli on the East Coast is slightly different from the story of Danyeli on the West Coast. It's not because Danyeli herself has changed. In fact, she carries that same confidence more strongly than ever. Rather, the story is changing because the way Danyeli is now *perceived* by others has changed. Including the way she's suddenly seen by other Latinos.

Understanding the essence of Latinx means recognizing that color can look very different depending on where you're standing—not just in Latin America but across the United States as well. Our country is covered not just by mountains, rivers, and lakes but also by shades of colors that dictate regional power dynamics and the story lines ingrained in narratives. All of this can change depending on what part of the country you are in. Under the Latinx premise, it's a given that who you are in New York can be different from who you are in Los Angeles.

I decided to fly to Los Angeles to meet Danyeli in person. Danyeli tells me to meet her at UCLA, so I take the car and start heading that way. At this point, I don't know exactly what to expect or what I'm walking into, as Danyeli simply tells me that what I'm about to see is part of her work.

As I enter campus and go inside Boelter Hall, I open a door that takes me to a classroom. It's absolutely crammed. I take a seat on the floor, look around me, and realize that I'm surrounded by dozens of teenage summer camp students. As I learn, the students are all undocumented—and every single one of them is completely fixated on Danyeli and her colleague Ernesto, who are both giving a presentation about their experiences as undocumented activists. The students are somewhat accustomed to hearing Ernesto's uplifting words. In many ways, Ernesto's story is one they've lived—or *are* living—in some shape or form: migrated from Mexico, came to California, turned his undocumented status into resilience. All part of the "California Dreamin'" story.

But every time it's Danyeli's turn to talk, I notice something in the students' expressions: an innocent awe. Most of these young students have never seen, heard, or talked to an undocumented person who *looks* like Danyeli: a black Latina. Someone who doesn't come from Mexico, who doesn't have a relationship with the border, and who isn't brown. Someone who doesn't fit perfectly into California's dominant narrative.

The more Danyeli talks, the bigger their eyes get.

Danyeli is talking about life on the island. She's talking about how she used to deny her blackness, how she then learned to love it, how she transitioned into it, and how she eventually found a home in New York City. She's teaching the students that immigrants don't have to look like *them*. They can look darker, migrate in different ways, and hold different stories, told in different accents, even in different languages.

The students are still listening. No one's fidgeting, staring at their iPhones, or texting their summer crushes.

At the end of the presentation, many of the students raise their hands to ask questions. But there's one comment that sticks with me:

"I like how you didn't wait for answers throughout your journey. You figured it out on your own," someone tells

Through the window, I watch students eagerly gathering to take a photo with Danyeli after she's done with her presentation.

Danyeli, and I notice that it's one of the few darker-skinned students in the room.

The truth is that throughout her life, had Danyeli waited for answers, chances are she wouldn't be where she is in that moment. Not in this UCLA classroom; not on this Pacific Coast—transforming spaces, deconstructing colorism, and eliciting confidence in those who need it most. She closes the night with: "I want all the little Danyelis to see themselves."

"When black immigrants see themselves during your talks and presentations, what do they tell you?" I ask Danyeli.

"The first thing they say is, 'Thank you,' always," she says. "It usually comes to me in the face of gratefulness because they don't see their stories anywhere. Because not only do we share this black experience, but then when we share that immigrant experience, it changes the view of what migration looks like. They don't feel alone anymore."

But not feeling alone doesn't mean that you don't feel out of place.

The following day, Danyeli and I meet up in one of her favorite restaurants in Los Angeles.

"So, what made you leave New York?" I ask her immediately with curiosity.

"I wanted to navigate what it was like being Afro-Latina in a space where Afro-Latinas were not common, where we didn't have such a big community," she tells me. She continues: "I wanted to do work in spaces where it was needed, where people needed to be educated about black immigrants."

What exactly does she mean by "needed"?

As Danyeli explains to me, the immigration narrative tends to be dominated by brown voices, and in California those voices overwhelmingly showcase the Mexican angle. Danyeli questions that power dynamic not only because of the singular lens from which stories are told but also because of the *messengers* who are often narrating those stories. In her eyes, far too many light-skinned Latinos are co-opting the term "brown," speaking from a perspective that actually does not *truly* belong to them. A color they do not own. A pain that is not theirs.

She comments: "When I came to the West Coast and saw lighter Mexicans calling themselves 'brown,' I was like: 'How?!' But I'm learning a lot about how language is being interpreted where you are." Danyeli continues, "The West Coast has created a community of themselves, based on their own terms. I think it's challenging for people to let go of that. For anyone to come in and challenge that, to say, 'Actually, on the East Coast, you are white passing. Actually, on the East Coast you are *not* brown.'"

Just as skin color changes depending on where you stand in the country, so does language have an ability to become distorted under the different coordinates of the map. What may be white to you is brown to them; what may be Latina to her is black to him; who may be considered an immigrant there is unaccounted for here.

Time and time again, through all these travels, this question keeps coming up: "*How* do we identify?" It's the same conversation I had with my high school friends in Florida, who didn't really realize they were "Latinas" until they left Miami. It's the same conversation I had with members of the Mayan community, who wanted to be labeled not as "Latinos" but as indigenous peoples. It's the same conversation I had with Ado, who wanted to be seen not just as an undocumented activist but also as a drag queen. It's the same conversation I had with Enrique, who didn't want the color of his skin to define his ideologies. And it's the same conversation I had with other Afro-Latinos who, alternatively, wanted both their skin color and their heritage to shine. From coast to coast, I met people who couldn't see eye to eye on their identity—and at the end of the day, that's one of the main points of this story: It's okay to differ. It's okay to not see eye to eye. The point is that there is not one way to be Latino in the United States. There is not one way to feel Latino in this country. Not one way to look Latino or sound Latino. And at the moment, the *only* label that can honor that collective truth and accommodate that spectrum of ambiguity is the Latinx banner.

You really feel the importance of that banner—of the Latinx movement—in California, where so many people are trying to find their place. I ask Danyeli: "So, how is blackness seen in the immigration conversation in the West Coast?"

"It becomes a footnote," Danyeli tells me.

I ask Danyeli what she feels when she walks into these West Coast spaces. "Where do you feel more comfortable? With whom do you feel more at home?"

Before she answers, I imagine her walking around New York's Washington Heights. I can perfectly picture Danyeli on West 181st Street and St. Nicholas Avenue, eating that *habichuela con dulce* she would have every Sunday with her *mami* when she was growing up. I can picture Danyeli with that unwavering confidence she radiates, reaching every corner of New York City.

Without any hesitation, she answers: "I definitely feel more comfortable in black spaces than with Latinx people. [Black] people are more supportive. People are more welcoming. And people are genuinely interested—not out of threat or malice, but just generally curious about where my blackness comes from. . . . There's more of a curiosity to understand where I come from as opposed to a pushback," she says.

After we finish lunch, I walk around Danyeli's neighborhood to get a sense of what her new life looks like here in Los Angeles. She's in Crenshaw, which is located in South Los Angeles, one of the city's historically black neighborhoods. As I'm strolling, I see the First African Presbyterian Church in America down the street and, outside Hank's Mini Market, a massive poster honoring Nipsey Hussle, which reads: "A visionary of the Slauson and Crenshaw District." Out of nowhere, an old black woman pulls up in her car and asks me:

"Honey, can you buy me two cigarettes from the dollar store and run back with them?"

"Yes, ma'am," I say automatically.

When I bring them back, she rolls down her window: "Thank you, honey!" and drives away.

You feel loved here. You feel supported. You feel welcomed. I now imagine Danyeli walking down Crenshaw Boulevard, inside the heart of a community whose pulse beats differently from that of Washington Heights but whose love wraps her in the same way. This is Danyeli's home now. And now I can perfectly picture her here: radiating that unwavering confidence.

Before I go back to the airport, I have one more stop to make. I go to Boyle Heights, where Danyeli is doing a spoken word performance. Now facing gentrification, Boyle Heights is home to Mexican culture. Every time I visit Los Angeles, this is where I stop by to drink my glass-bottled Mexican Coke and devour my *tacos al pastor*.

But from where I stand inside this Boyle Heights store, backgrounds and cultures and accents and colors and statuses don't really matter right now. That's because Danyeli's poetry is transcending any lines that may have ever been drawn between us. With words that tell stories of love, lyrics that tell stories of heartbreak, beats that praise *mami,* sounds that make us cry, and rhymes that make us remember—every single one of us in that room is Latinx, not because of the color of our skin but because of the connection we

Danyeli performing her poetry.

have to everything that she is saying, because of the way we identify with it from our own experiences. With mesmerized faces, we stare at Danyeli the same way the students did in that UCLA classroom. Only this time she's not trying to educate, she's trying to do something even bigger: to get us to *see* her.

"What is the power behind this art?" I ask her. I can see it, but I want her to tell me with her own words.

"In front of the stage, it's different because people are taking my stories. There are people connecting with what it means to be an immigrant kid, whether you're black or not. With what it means to learn English. With what it means to be behind. They get to see through that narrative."

When I say good-bye to her, I tell Danyeli that I hope to see her in our beloved New York City soon. "I now can't wait to see you perform there. This was incredible."

But as I say that, I realize that Danyeli is exactly where she's supposed to be right now. Because, after all, this city may be more hers than we all realize.

Driving through East Los Angeles, I think back to the foundation of this city. Most people don't know this, but according to Dr. William D. Estrada, the *original* founders of the city of Los Angeles included Mexicans of African descent. There were forty-four Mexican settlers who migrated from northern Mexico and established El Pueblo de Nuestra Señora la Reina de Los Ángeles Sobre el Río de Porciúncula in 1781. Among them, it is said that *more than half* were of African descent, while several others were mestizos and mixed.

Unsurprisingly, this part of L.A.'s history is barely known, as there have been numerous attempts to bury it. According to a *Los Angeles Times* piece by Cecilia Rasmussen, published in 1995: "The city seemed to regard its multiracial history as something of an embarrassment." As was reported in the 1950s, a plaque was installed in what is now known as the Los Angeles Plaza Historic District. The plaque honored the founders and made a specific note of their racial background. However, as Rasmussen states, the plaque soon disappeared from the public eye. "Rumor had it that several Recreation and Parks commissioners had been displeased by its public display of the role blacks played in [the] city's founding," she writes.

More than two decades after the plaque vanished, it was eventually replaced—this time without any mention of the founders' Afro-Mexican descent. Then, by the early 1980s, the plaque was reinstalled "with a simple bronze tablet that tells the *pobladores'* names, race, sex and age. It was installed through the trailblazing efforts of Miriam Matthews, California's first college-trained black librarian."

In other words, Afro-Latinos built this city. From its inception, they made it an interracial enclave. And the reality is that if it weren't for a simple bronze plaque—one that fought against social currents and inscribed a new identity in the history books—we would have *never* known this city belonged to them. The plaque carried surnames people had never heard of. It carried ethnicities people weren't comfortable with. More than anything, it carried an honor people weren't ready to acknowledge. But it nonetheless emblazoned a community that was once forgotten. That's why language matters. Because unless you intentionally allow it to evolve, you risk erasing someone else's existence. And in many ways, the Latinx movement is attempting to re-create

Zuri, one of the many blaxicans (black and Mexican) who live in Los Angeles.

Vero, also a proud blaxican, is the daughter of a black man and a Mexican mother.

that same effect: affixing a plaque with an "x" that includes and affirms everyone's belonging.

I realized that everyone I had met on my journey—from strangers to loved ones—was partially standing inside their own individual shadows. All of us, in our own ways, paralyzed by fear, social expectations, and pain. Although all of us traveled different paths, had different memories, and told different stories, I realized we all felt the same frustrations: that feeling of always being on the brink of glory but not fully there. So close to change, so close to feeling at home, so close to finding justice, so close to seeing our full reflection, so close to becoming visible, so close to loving ourselves, so close to letting go of the past, so close to feeling American, so close to overcoming pain. So close, but not there *yet*.

Perhaps, for our parents, *abuelos,* and great-grandparents, that's where the story ended. As the immigrant story goes, so many of our ancestors were forced to settle for mediocrity for the sake of being accepted in this country. In all their fights and accomplishments here, suffering and sacrifices were inevitable parts of their journey. Wanting *more* and asking to be valued in this country were, at times, principles that felt more like privileges than rights.

Today, that story is changing.

I believe that the labels "Hispanic" and "Latino" don't capture the full breadth of who we are, what we aspire to, and what we deserve. In many ways, they are terms that have been written and defined by others, not us. By politicians, historians, and marketing gurus who for decades have otherized us as monoliths have set expectations for us. Our story, through American history, was based on numbers and hard data. It makes sense. It's easier to win "the Latino vote" if you think all Latinos are the same. It's easier to tell our stories if you neglect the nuances of our backgrounds. And it's easier to sell us products if you believe our tastes are simple, not complex. But in all those analyses, the one thing that's always been missing has been the *full*, unleashed voice of our community—one that believes not in what's *good enough* but in what is *ours*. That warrants turning a page in the history books and creating a new label for us: Latinx.

All around us, we are stepping into new realms of unparalleled power. Every thirty seconds, a young Latino is turning eighteen and becoming eligible to vote. Latinos have become the second-largest voting bloc in this country, surpassing the African American vote. Latino millennials are breaking stereotypes, becoming the group most likely to self-identify as LGBTQ. Latinas, once constrained by social norms, are organizing and leading movements against sexual violence.

On our radios and in our dance clubs, Latin music has now officially become more popular than country and electronic dance music in the United States. On our TV screens, for the first time in history, we have an Afro-Latina anchoring a national newscast. White-passing Latinos are using their privilege to demand justice for their fellow Afro-Latinos for the first time, too. Coast-to-coast, Latinos are opening up more small businesses than any other population, becoming the fastest-growing demographic of small-business owners. And in Congress, more Latinos are serving than ever before. A new, powerful movement is happening outside our windows. For years, we haven't been able to fully articulate what this movement is about, what it represents, and what unites it, but it's undoubtedly the wave of what it means to be part of the Latinx community: millions of people coming out of their shadows and into their power.

The thing is, this is only the beginning of that wave.

That's exactly what I've seen these past months on the road. I've seen a community in the process of running toward the sun, courageously exposing the true colors of their skin, their deepest vulnerabilities, and the depths of their joy. Inside trailer parks, ballrooms, classrooms, and churches, outside in the valleys, on mountains, borders, and oceans, they were all uncovering a part of them—large or small—that had once been buried. They were all, myself included, finally coming out.

That's the story of the Latinx community: America has never seen us under the sun. We, as sixty million strong, have barely even seen *one another* under the same light. And when we do, different corners of the nation will feel

Me, on the road with my disposable camera, finding Latinx.

changed; our voices will become louder, and our power will reach unfathomable new heights.

There's no precedent for what that could look like.

That's why it's important to call us by our *full*, complete name to get there: LATINX.

Acknowledgments

I'll close the book the same way I began: I never really came out, until recently.

As I hope these pages have shown, the overarching story of *Finding Latinx* is that there is a community full of people who, after decades of suppression, are coming out. All in their own way. It's Dreamers who are stepping out of the shadows, mothers who are calling out sexual abuse, Afro-Latinos who aren't shying away from their blackness, trans-Latinas claiming their rights, Gen Zers breaking stigmas . . . the list goes on. While these pages represent only a fraction of the community, they are full of voices that didn't just challenge, educate, and inspire me—they have also encouraged me to *keep* coming out. To be my most authentic self. The Latinx story isn't static, it keeps evolving. And so I give my deepest appreciation to everyone who, through this journey, allowed me into their space and helped me write the beginning of our new chapter as one.

Looking back, I remember different moments in my life that culminated in the creation of this book. The entire premise of *Finding Latinx* is based on a very simple concept: to look beyond what lies directly in front of the eyes. I learned that from others throughout my education and career. In the classrooms at Barnard College. In the Obama White House hallways from Dr. Jill Biden, Cathy Russell, Anthony Bernal, Ashley Williams, Kirsten White, Melanie Kaye, Shira Miller, and Allison Zelman. In my lectures at the Kennedy School from Professor Tim McCarthy and Professor Steve Jarding. In the Hillary Clinton campaign headquarters from Jorge Silva and Xochitl Hinojosa. In the Telemundo studios from Leticia Herrera, Luis Fernandez, Rubi Hurtado, and Paula Gonzalez. In VICE's lounge from Adri Murguia, who trusted me with hosting the *LATIN-X* series. In the Inside Out/ Dreamers and Vote trucks with Meredith Webster, Robin Reck, and Jaime Scatena. And out in the real world from Theresa Vargas Wyatt. These are just a few of the people who have helped me, throughout different parts of my life, to always keep my eyes open.

One of the most rewarding parts of writing this book was learning about the incredible work different groups on the ground are doing. I had the honor of interacting with some of the groups—organizers, volunteers, designers, artists— that are driving change in this country. These include the Center on Race, Poverty and the Environment, ACT for Women and Girls, Justice for Migrant Women, Mariposas sin Fronteras, Familia: Trans Queer Liberation Movement, Diversidad sin Fronteras, Casa Alitas, Blake Gentry and his services for indigenous communities, Alianza Indigena sin Fronteras, Catholic Charities Center in McAllen, Texas, Freedom Network, National Latina Institute of Reproductive Health, Whole Women's Health Clinic, National Women's

Law Center, Stories Untold US, Maya Heritage Community Project at Kennesaw State University, Canton's and Greenville's Mayan communities, Florida International University's Puerto Rican Student Association, Asociación de Madres y Mujeres Venezolanas en el Exterior, the Climate Crusader, CLEO Institute, Struggle for Miami's Affordable and Sustainable Housing, New Florida Majority, Latinegras, Mijente, Huella Negra, UndocuBlack Network, Just Leadership USA, New York Latino Muslims Coalition, Dolores Huerta Foundation, Make the Road New York, Grupo Folclórico de Poughkeepsie, Latinx Project, Miss Rizos, Latina Theory, Latina Trans New York, Yessenya, Latino Arts String Program, IowaWINS, West Liberty School District, the Miss Gay America beauty pageant, United We Dream, Undocubae, and many, many more.

I would like to thank Emerson Collective for supporting my work and, particularly, this book. Stacey Rubin and Laurene Powell Jobs believed in me the moment we met years ago at the U.S.-Mexican border. Since then, they have trusted me not just with projects but also with my vision for change. I will always be grateful for that. Paola Piers-Torres, Alicia Benis, Estefania Mitre, Olivia Raisner, Dayana Morales, Joey Morales, Samantha Bloom, and my cousins Sandra Ramos and Claudia Montaner were also instrumental in helping me with background research for this book. They helped me think through different angles and story lines and provided valuable insight throughout the entire process.

Mostly, this book would not be possible if it weren't for Penguin Random House's editorial team. The concept of "Latinx" is one that is admittedly hard to sell to the public. It's controversial and hard to articulate. Yet from day one,

Cristobal Pera understood the historic importance of telling this story, stood by my vision, and gave me the tools to turn this idea into reality. Maria Goldverg didn't just edit these pages, she pushed me and constantly challenged me to be a better writer and therefore to turn in the best version of this book. Beyond the Penguin Random House crew, I want to thank my editor, Felice Laverne, for molding and shaping this book beyond my own expectations and hopes. As many edits as were made, Felice never once allowed me to lose my voice. And to Josanne Lopez, my manager, my thanks for making me believe that I can do everything I put my mind to.

Finally, I want to thank my family. My father, Jorge, taught me to use my voice. My mother, Gina, taught me to raise it. My partner, De'Ara, taught that voice to stay true to itself. My siblings, Gabriela and Nicolas, taught me to speak up for others. My *abuelo* Carlos and *abuela* Linda taught me the meaning of resilience. Chiqui, Mari, and Carlota have given new meaning to joy. My family in Mexico—my dear *abuela* Yuyu, *mis primas, tíos, y tías*—have taught me to remember, no matter the distance, the beautiful place I come from.

Together, you've all formed my voice.

Further Reading

Flores-González, Nilda. *Citizens but Not Americans: Race and Belonging Among Latino Millennials*. New York: New York University Press, 2017.

González, Sergio. *Mexicans in Wisconsin*. Madison: Wisconsin Historical Society Press, 2017.

Guidotti-Hernández, Nicole M. "Affective Communities and Millennial Desires: Latinx, or Why My Computer Won't Recognize Latina/o." *Cultural Dynamics* 29, no. 3 (2017): 141–59.

Morales, Ed. *Latinx: The New Force in American Politics and Culture*. Brooklyn, NY: Verso, 2018.

Ortiz, Paul. *An African American and Latinx History of the United States*. Boston: Beacon Press, 2018.

Zepeda-Millán, Chris. *Latino Mass Mobilization: Immigration, Racialization, and Activism*. New York: Cambridge University Press, 2017.

Notes

1. Introduction: Coming Out as Latinx

5   sixty million Latinos living in the United States: "Who Is Hispanic?," Pew Research Center, last modified November 11, 2019, pewresearch.org/fact-tank/2019/11/11/who-is-hispanic/.

13   "Latinx consumers represent one of the most sure bets": "La Oportunidad Latinx: Cultural Currency and the Consumer Journey," Nielsen, Diverse Intelligence Series, 2019, https://www.nielsen.com/wp-content/uploads/sites/3/2019/09/nielsen-2019-latinx-DIS-report.pdf.

14   Young Latinos were more likely to be Independent: "Hispanics of All Ages Tilt Democratic," Gallup, July 15, 2013, https://news.gallup.com/poll/163451/hispanics-ages-tilt-democratic.aspx.

1. The Heartland

23   There are approximately 2.5 million farmworkers across the country: "Selected Statistics on Farmworkers," Farmworker Justice, 2014, https://www.farmworkerjustice.org/sites/default/files/NAWS%20data%20factsht%201-13-15FINAL.pdf.

2. Shining Light

42 to be a transgender Latina in the United States: "Report on the Experiences of Latino/a Respondents," 2015 U.S. Transgender Survey, last modified November 2017, https://www.transequal ity.org/sites/default/files/docs/usts/USTSLatinReport-Nov17 .pdf.

4. The Other Wall

64 ICE arrested 280 employees at a technology company: "ICE Raids Texas Technology Company, Arrests 280 over Immigration Violations," National Public Radio, April 3, 2019, https://www.npr.org/2019/04/03/709680162/ice-raids-texas -technology-company-arrests-280-on-immigration-violations.

65 The *Houston Chronicle* reported: "New 'Zero Tolerance' Policy Overwhelms South Texas Courts," *Houston Chronicle,* June 9, 2018, https://www.houstonchronicle.com/news/houston-texas /texas/article/New-zero-tolerance-policy-overwhelms-South -12981190.php.

66 In June 2018, it was reported that the shelter was seeing: "Sister Norma, the Border Battle's Fiercest Fighter, Is 'Astute as a Serpent, and Gentle as a Dove,'" *Dallas News,* June 20, 2018, https://www.dallasnews.com/news/immigration/2018/06/21 /sister-norma-the-border-battle-s-fiercest-fighter-is-astute-as-a -serpent-and-gentle-as-a-dove/.

69 According to the American Civil Liberties Union: "Access Denied: Origins of the Hyde Amendment and Other Restrictions on Public Funding for Abortions," American Civil Liberties Union, accessed March 13, 2020, https://www.aclu.org /other/access-denied-origins-hyde-amendment-and-other -restrictions-public-funding-abortion.

70 there are almost forty anti-abortion bills in session: "Texas Has Its Own Bad Abortion Legislation. And It's About to Become

Law," American Civil Liberties Union of Texas, last modified May 21, 2019, https://www.aclutx.org/en/news/texas-has-its -own-bad-abortion-legislation-and-its-about-become-law.

70 bill would assign an attorney to an unborn fetus: "Texas 'Unborn Child Due Process Act' (HB 1901)," Rewire.News, last modified October 24, 2017, https://www.aclutx.org/en/news /texas-has-its-own-bad-abortion-legislation-and-its-about-be come-law.

70 another would ban abortion after a fetal heartbeat: "Bill HB 1500, Legislative Session 86 (R), Council Document 86R 9861 SCL-F," Texas Legislature Online, last accessed March 13, 2020, https://capitol.texas.gov/BillLookup/History.aspx?LegSess =86R&Bill=HB1500.

70 barring local governments from partnering with abortion pro- viders: "SB 22: Interfering with Reproductive Freedom," Amer- ican Civil Liberties Union of Texas, last accessed March 13, 2020, https://www.aclutx.org/en/legislation/sb-22-interfering -reproductive-freedom.

77 in 2016 they increased among adolescent and adult Latino men: "HIV Incidence: Estimated Annual Infections in the U.S., 2010–2016," Centers for Disease Control and Prevention, last modified February 2019, https://www.cdc.gov/nchhstp/news room/docs/factsheets/HIV-Incidence-Fact-Sheet_508.pdf.

5. Unbroken

82 "Latinos experience a type of discrimination": "Racial/Ethnic Discrimination Associated with Lower Well-Being Among Adolescents," American Psychological Association, Septem- ber 18, 2018, https://www.apa.org/news/press/releases/2018 /09/racial-ethnic-discrimination.

92 more than twenty-five hundred educators were able to point: "The Trump Effect: The Impact of the 2016 Presidential Elec- tion on Our Nation's Schools," Southern Poverty Law Cen-

ter, November 28, 2016, https://www.splcenter.org/20161128
/trump-effect-impact-2016-presidential-election-our-nations
-schools.

6. K'exel

104 the South saw the fastest Latino population growth: "U.S.
Hispanic Population Reached New High in 2018, but Growth
Has Slowed," Pew Research Center, July 8, 2019, https://www
.pewresearch.org/fact-tank/2019/07/08/u-s-hispanic-popu
lation-reached-new-high-in-2018-but-growth-has-slowed/.

104 at least 25 percent of Latino adults in the United States consider themselves: "Chapter 7: The Many Dimensions of Hispanic Racial Identity," Pew Research Center, June 11, 2015,
https://www.pewsocialtrends.org/2015/06/11/chapter-7-the
-many-dimensions-of-hispanic-racial-identity/.

7. Ground Zero

131 nearly 50 percent of Americans do not even know Puerto
Ricans: "National Tracking Poll 170916," Morning Consult,
September 22–24, 2017, https://morningconsult.com/wp-con
tent/uploads/2017/10/170916_crosstabs_pr_v1_KD.pdf.

132 roughly one thousand Puerto Rican college students transitioned: "Puerto Rico Sees Hundreds of College Students Leave
in Hurricane's Aftermath," *Wall Street Journal*, last updated
November 8, 2017, https://www.wsj.com/articles/puerto-rico
-sees-scores-of-college-students-leave-in-hurricanes-aftermath
-1510146001.

145 approximately 114,000 Cubans with Chinese ancestors: "Bar-
rio Chino: Meet the Chinese-Cubans Fighting to Keep Their
Culture Alive," *Document Journal*, July 15, 2019, https://www
.documentjournal.com/2019/07/barrio-chino-chinese-cubans
-keep-culture-alive-in-havana/.

156 Almost 80 percent of Latinos say they are worried: "Climate

Change in the Latino Mind," Yale Program on Climate Change Communication, last modified September 27, 2017, https://climatecommunication.yale.edu/publications/climate-change-latino-mind-may-2017/2/.

8. Erased

163 During the colonial period of 1502 to 1866: "What It Means to Be 'Black in Latin America,' " National Public Radio, July 27, 2011, https://www.npr.org/2011/07/27/138601410/what-it-means-to-be-black-in-latin-america.

163 To increase their white population, governments encouraged: Ibid.

163 governments across Latin America started adding racial data: "Afro-Latin America by the Numbers: The Politics of the Census," *ReVista: Harvard Review of Latin America* (Winter 2018), https://revista.drclas.harvard.edu/book/afro-latin-america-numbers-politics-census.

163 when the government included Afro-Mexicans in the official national census: "Now Counted by Their Country, Afro-Mexicans Grab Unprecedented Spotlight," National Public Radio, February 6, 2016, https://www.npr.org/2016/02/06/465710473/now-counted-by-their-country-afro-mexicans-grab-unprecedented-spotlight.

9. Dark Shadows of Freedom

175 70 percent of black and mixed Cubans don't even have access: "Cuba's New Social Structure: Assessing the Re-Stratification of Cuban Society 60 Years After Revolution," German Institute of Global and Area Studies, last modified February 2019, https://www.giga-hamburg.de/en/system/files/publications/wp315_hansing-hoffmann.pdf.

176 "Tarrio, who identifies as Afro-Cuban, is president": "Why Young Men of Color Are Joining White-Supremacist Groups,"

Daily Beast, September 6, 2018, https://www.thedailybeast
.com/why-young-men-of-color-are-joining-white-supremacist
-groups.

180 Up to 15 percent of Cuban families live in poverty: "Facts on
Hispanics of Cuban Origin in the United States, 2017," Pew
Research Center, last modified September 16, 2019, https://
www.pewresearch.org/hispanic/fact-sheet/u-s-hispanics-facts
-on-cuban-origin-latinos/.

183 in 2017, the FBI reported that hate crimes increased by 17
percent: "2017 Hate Crime Statistics Released: Report Shows
More Departments Reporting Hate Crime Statistics," Federal
Bureau of Investigation, November 13, 2018, https://www.fbi
.gov/news/stories/2017-hate-crime-statistics-released-111318.

183 By 2018, the FBI found that hate crime violence and threats
had reached the highest level: "2018 Hate Crime Statistics," Federal Bureau of Investigation, https://ucr.fbi.gov/hate
-crime/2018/hate-crime.

10. The Act of Being Ordinary

192 approximately 4.2 million black immigrants in the United
States as of 2016: "Key Facts About Black Immigrants in the
U.S.," Pew Research Center, January 24, 2018, https://www
.pewresearch.org/fact-tank/2018/01/24/key-facts-about-black
-immigrants-in-the-u-s/.

192 black people in this country are incarcerated at more than five
times: "Criminal Justice Fact Sheet," National Association for
the Advancement of Colored People, https://www.naacp.org
/criminal-justice-fact-sheet/.

192 "black immigrants are much more likely than nationals": "The
State of Black Immigrants," Immigrant Rights Clinic at NYU
Law School and Black Alliance for Just Immigration, http://
www.stateofblackimmigrants.com/assets/sobi-fullreport-jan
22.pdf.

196 "In Panama, we've been denouncing the fact that poverty's

face": "Discriminación y pobreza rezagan a afropanameños," *La Prensa,* June 9, 2019, https://www.prensa.com/impresa /panorama/Discriminacion-pobreza-rezagan-afropanamenos _0_5322967699.html.

197 black people are more than twice as likely to be killed by police: "The Population of Poverty USA," Poverty USA, https://www .povertyusa.org/facts.

197 black women are twice as likely to die giving birth: "The U.S. Finally Has Better Maternal Mortality Data. Black Mothers Still Fare the Worst," NBC News, January 30, 2020, https:// www.nbcnews.com/health/womens-health/u-s-finally-has -better-maternal-mortality-data-black-mothers-n1125896.

197 black students are three times more likely than white students: "Scarred by School Shootings," *Washington Post,* March 25, 2018, https://www.washingtonpost.com/graphics /2018/local/us-school-shootings-history/.

11. Invisible

204 the NYPD stopped 581,168 people . . . were found to be innocent: "Stop-and-Frisk Data," New York Civil Liberties Union, 2019, https://www.nyclu.org/en/stop-and-frisk-data.

204 more than seventeen thousand people were added to the "gang book": "Does NYPD Gang Database Fuel Mass Incarceration?," Crime Report, last modified December 17, 2019, https://thecrimereport.org/2019/12/17/nypd-gang-database -fuels-mass-incarceration-report/.

204 whose names are inscribed in that book: "NYPD Added Nearly 2,500 New People to Its Gang Database in the Last Year," Intercept, last modified June 28, 2019, https://theintercept.com /2019/06/28/nypd-gang-database-additions/.

207 in 2017, Latinos accounted for more than 20 percent of inmates: "The Gap Between the Number of Blacks and Whites in Prison Is Shrinking," Pew Research Center, last modified April 30, 2019, https://www.pewresearch.org/fact

-tank/2019/04/30/shrinking-gap-between-number-of-blacks -and-whites-in-prison/.

217 women . . . voted at higher rates than men: "In Year of Record Midterm Turnout, Women Continued to Vote at Higher Rates Than Men," Pew Research Center, May 3, 2019, https://www .pewresearch.org/fact-tank/2019/05/03/in-year-of-record -midterm-turnout-women-continued-to-vote-at-higher-rates -than-men/.

217 Latinas drove a lot of those trends: "Key Takeaways About Latino Voters in the 2018 Midterm Elections," Pew Research Center, November 9, 2018, https://www.pewresearch.org/fact -tank/2018/11/09/how-latinos-voted-in-2018-midterms/.

217 in important battleground states like Nevada: "Exit Polls," CNN Politics, https://www.cnn.com/election/2018/exit-polls /nevada.

222 In 2018, prostitution-related loitering arrests increased: "Surge in Prostitution Related Loitering Charges Affects Undocu-mented Immigrants," *Documented,* December 19, 2018, https://documentedny.com/2018/12/19/surge-in-loitering -charges-may-affect-undocumented-immigrants/.

225 Oaxaca is . . . one of the poorest in the country: "Chiapas, Guerrero and Oaxaca, the States with the Most Poverty in Mexico," *Mazatlán Post,* last modified August 8, 2019, https:// themazatlanpost.com/2019/08/08/chiapas-guerrero-and -oaxaca-the-states-with-the-most-poverty-in-mexico/.

225 As reported by the *HuffPost*'s analysis of an Oxfam report: Rodrigo Aguilera, "On the Margins: Why Mexico's South-ern States Have Fallen Behind," *HuffPost,* August 10, 2015, https://www.huffpost.com/entry/on-the-margins-why-mex ico_b_7967874.

12. Home

251 every single day 128 Americans die from an opioid overdose: "Understanding the Epidemic," Centers for Disease Control

and Prevention, 2017, https://www.cdc.gov/drugoverdose/epi
demic/index.html.

264 Milwaukee, the most segregated city in the United States:
"Black-White Segregation Edges Downward Since 2000, Census Says," Brookings Institution, December 17, 2018, https://
www.brookings.edu/blog/the-avenue/2018/12/17/black-white
-segregation-edges-downward-since-2000-census-shows/.

264 your chances of being unemployed, incarcerated, and racially
targeted: "State of Black and Brown Wisconsin Address
Brings Attention to Racial Disparities," WUWM Milwaukee's
National Public Radio, February 13, 2018, https://www.wuwm
.com/post/state-black-and-brown-wisconsin-address-brings
-attention-racial-disparities#stream/0.

Finding Latinx

304 "seemed to regard its multiracial history as something of an
embarrassment": Cecilia Rasmussen, "Honoring L.A.'s Black
Founders," *Los Angeles Times,* February 13, 1995, https://www
.latimes.com/archives/la-xpm-1995-02-13-me-31591-story
.html.